TERRACE AT WALL · FL. ELEV. 254.5·

·ELEVATION· OF· WINDOWS· No. 16·17·&18·

NOTE: DOTTED LINES
INDICATES FORMER WINDOW
ON THIS ROOF.

FIN. 2ND FLOOR

FIN. 1ST FLOOR

TOP OF CONCRETE FOUNDATION

·AVON· CONNECTICUT·

DRAWN BY   DWG Nº 103
DATE JAN. 15, 1925
CHECKED BY
REVISED   JULY 18, 1925   (W.B.)
DORMER ADDED OCT. 15/25   W.B.

Dearest of Geniuses

From a letter by John Wallace Riddle
written in 1937
to Theodate Pope Riddle

Dearest of Geniuses

A LIFE OF THEODATE POPE RIDDLE

SANDRA L. KATZ

WINDSOR, CONNECTICUT

Also by Sandra L. Katz
Elinor Frost: A Poet's Wife

Copyright ©2003 by Sandra L. Katz
Published by Tide-mark Press, Ltd.
Windsor, Connecticut

Editor: Carolyn Wilcox
Designer: Evelyn Pelati Dombkowski

Printed and Bound in the United States of America

Library of Congress Cataloging-in-Publication Data
Katz, Sandra L.
Dearest of Geniuses: A life of Theodate Pope Riddle
cm.
Includes Index

ISBN 1-55949-828-5 Hardcover Edition

Library of Congress Control Number
2003103555

FOR
Stacey, Jim, Char, Missy, Andy,
Charlie and Max

CONTENTS

ONE

"She will probably end up in jail"
1867—1886

IN 1915, the Nugent Publishing Company asked Theodate Pope to send a photograph for use in a book that listed New York's most prominent architects and described their accomplishments. A few weeks later, Theodate received a telephone call in her New York architectural office. Not having a receptionist, she answered, "Theodate Pope. May I help you?"

A few seconds passed. Then a male voice asked, "Are you really Theodate Pope?"

"Yes," she replied.

Her caller paused again and then identified himself. He was associated with Nugent Publishing Company, and said that, unfortunately, he had bad news. Because of Theodate's name, the editors had assumed she was a man. After seeing her photograph, the Nugent editors now realized that she was a woman. That being the case, it was "impossible" to include her in their book.

Theodate did not protest. "Although art has no sex, I am discriminated against," she calmly informed her mother, Ada, adding that she did not care. "It is 'to laugh' as the Jewish people say."

As one of the country's first female architects, working in a field that was then considered a "gentleman's profession," Theodate was accustomed to prejudice. Despite acclaim for her achievements, she had difficulty obtaining commissions, receiving them mostly through social connections. Because Theo did not expect acceptance, she had been surprised and pleased about being included in the book, but in the letter to her mother, she shrugged off disappointment.

In contrast, Ada was upset, for she had been proudly telling friends and relatives to look for Theodate in the book when it was published. She also could not understand Theo's seeming unconcern. Ada always found her daughter's nature incomprehensible.

Theo's parents met in Salem, Ohio, in 1856, when Ada Lunette Brooks was twelve years old and Alfred Atmore Pope was fourteen. Dressed in Quaker clothes—Eton roundabouts with turnover collars and striped gray trousers—Alfred would walk past Ada's home, and she would run from one window to the next to catch a glimpse of him. The young lovers were handsome. Ada was petite with fine, cameo features

1

and dark hair; Alfred was tall and blond, with blue eyes, straight nose, and square chin. Despite their families' disapproval, because of differences in religion and social standing, the youngsters' devotion to each other persisted.

Alfred's family were Orthodox Friends who had moved from Maine to join a large Quaker community in Ohio. Alfred's mother, Theodate Stackpole, had given up the man she loved, who was not a Quaker, and in 1834 married Alton Pope, a devout Quaker but a poor businessman. Alton built woolen mills first in Maine and then in Baltimore and Ohio, but they all failed. Still, his wife Theodate insisted that it would have been a great mistake had she married her first love, a rich lawyer. "It would have taken me into an atmosphere of gaiety," she explained. "The religious life is best."

Young Alfred disagreed. He refused to give up Ada Brooks, even though she would not convert to his faith. When Alfred was sixteen, he gave Ada an engagement ring.

In contrast to Alfred's family, Ada Brooks's relatives were successful businessmen and politicians. Unlike the Popes, who were not college educated, most of the Brooks men were Yale graduates. In addition to being a lawyer for the western division of the Pennsylvania Railroad, Ada's father, Joseph Judson Brooks, had established one of America's first iron foundries. Concerned that Ada was serious about Alfred Pope, Brooks sent his daughter to boarding school in New Haven, Connecticut, and forbade her to write the boy for a year. Dutifully, Ada obeyed, but the following year, she and Alfred resumed their relationship.

After the deaths of Ada's parents, Alfred and Ada married on a Tuesday evening, May 3, 1866, in a Presbyterian church. Alfred's parents apparently accepted their son's marriage, and the young couple moved in with them on Wilson Avenue in Cleveland. Their house was a modest two-family structure with railroad tracks running through the backyard. The parlor of the flat displayed souvenirs of Maine, where Popes had lived since the middle of the 17th century. There was a seashell on the mantle with the Lord's Prayer carved on its surface, and on a table stood a stuffed loon under an oval glass.

Nine months after Alfred and Ada's marriage, Ada gave birth to a daughter, whom they named Effie Brooks Pope. Ada later told Effie that she had been born at midnight, on February 2, 1867. In later years, Effie, who had subsequently changed her name to Theodate, was suspicious about the true date of her birth, believing that she had been a "love child." She said that she had been born "greatly to my mother's resentment," and she was right. Her mother had not wanted Effie.

When Effie was quite young, she overheard Ada tell Alfred that she would not bear a child for him every year.

Envious of families with a house full of children, Effie blamed her lonely existence on Ada. The child did not know that Ada was terrified of pregnancy because her own mother had died during a miscarriage when she was forty-four, leaving eight children. The eldest child was twenty-one; the youngest, two; and Ada was sixteen. Effie also was unaware that Ada had suffered a miscarriage not long after Effie was born.

Ada, Alfred, and little Effie lived with Alfred's parents for several months. Then the young couple and their daughter moved nearby to a plain, small house. Effie was glad that they lived close to her grandparents' home because she loved to visit Grandmother Theodate.

Grandmother's kitchen always smelled wonderful, and Effie especially looked forward to her grandmother's specialty: light, crispy donuts. Wearing a starched, white net Quaker bonnet and a brown apron over a drab or black dress with a white, pleated front, Grandmother Theodate appeared to be a severe, austere figure, but she adored Effie and called her a special name, "Birdie."

Effie was a pretty child, short and plump with light blonde curls, blue eyes, a straight nose, small mouth, and porcelain complexion. She had an uneventful childhood until one morning when she was nine years old. She was sitting silently on the stairway, one of her favorite places. She could see through the doorway of a room across the hall, and she watched and listened to Ada instructing the family seamstress. Suddenly, Effie realized that she was staring at herself from outside her body. She heard a voice say, "Why, this body isn't me."

Effie was terribly frightened. From that day on, she refused to look into mirrors because she feared that the reflection would bring back the feeling of being detached from her body. But she did not tell anyone what had occurred. As an only child, she was accustomed to keeping her thoughts to herself, and she confided only in a diary.

Effie's relationship with Ada was distant at best. Even when Effie was very young, she sensed that Ada could barely tolerate her. Ada never held or kissed the child. Although Alfred was more affectionate, he was preoccupied with making a fortune in the business world and had little time to spend with his daughter.

During the first years of Alfred and Ada's marriage, Alfred worked with his brothers in their father's failing woolen business. Then, in 1869, using some of Ada's money and borrowing from Robert Hanna, a fellow Quaker and the uncle of the powerful political figure Mark Hanna, Alfred acquired the position of secretary and treasurer of the Cleveland

Malleable Iron Company. By 1877, he had become the president of the business, which he expanded into the National Malleable & Steel Castings Company, with sites in various parts of the country, including Chicago, Indianapolis, Toledo, Sharon, and Melrose Park.

Alfred always expressed a strong distaste for the commercial world, however. Once, after meeting with some associates, he told Effie that "they smelt of business." But he enjoyed remarkable success. With his quiet, calm Quaker manner, Alfred got along well with other business-men. He was known to be fair and honest, and he dealt effectively with the workers. He was able to settle strikes, including one that briefly closed down his factory in Chicago.

In addition, Alfred's business prospered because, after the Civil War, the country's rapid industrial growth and the expansion of railroads created a tremendous demand for malleable iron, which was ideal for fastening rails to ties. His company also manufactured a new railroad-car coupler that became standard on all trains. Before the invention of the Tower Automatic Coupler, which safely attached and disengaged railroad cars, gruesome accidents commonly occurred when railroad workers, going between cars to join or separate them manually, were crushed to death.

As the Popes became wealthier, they moved from one house to anoth-er. Finally, in 1886, Alfred built a home on Euclid Avenue, Cleveland's "Millionaires' Row," where the Hannas, Sherwins and Rockefellers lived in showy mansions behind high, cast-iron fences. The street was noted in *Baedeker's Guide to the Continental United States* as "one of the most beautiful residence-streets in America." At the same time, although the mansions stood on a hill above the city, they did not escape the soot from the factories below. The pollution in Cleveland was so severe that in the winter the snow was black.

Teenaged Effie was unhappy in the family's new home, a three-story, Queen-Anne-style brownstone with arches on the portico and a dark, richly furnished interior. She preferred their former, more modest house. As much as she appreciated beautiful things, she felt that a home should not be a showplace that proclaimed one's wealth.

In contrast, Ada was delighted. Moving to the Euclid Avenue mansion announced the arrival of the Popes to high society. Quickly becoming one of Cleveland's loveliest and most gracious hostesses, Ada became determined to make Effie a society girl and, despite heated protests, insisted that she attend social affairs.

At teas and parties, Effie felt ill at ease and bored. "I am seldom myself," she scribbled in her diary, "as I feel that to make myself agreeable to the average person I must talk 'sweet nothings.'" She called those she met "surface people." Even worse than talking was listening and responding to them. "My eyebrows are tired," she wrote. "I have raised them so many times to express polite surprise."

The only advantage to society life was that one dressed well. Effie enjoyed buying and wearing expensive clothes, especially those made of fine silk. Her stylish attire contrasted with her wholesome but plain face and figure. Instead of growing up and becoming a beauty like Ada, Effie looked like a short, female version of Alfred.

As a young adult, Effie stood at about five-feet, two-inches tall. She had light blonde hair, piercing blue eyes, and a square chin like Alfred's. On a man, a prominent chin was a positive feature, suggesting determination and strength, but it was considered unfeminine on a young woman. Effie's sturdy jaw added to the impression that she was difficult and stubborn, an opinion Ada often expressed.

At Miss Mittleberger's School for Girls, an exclusive private high school that Effie attended in Cleveland, most of the teachers agreed with Ada. Effie was a behavior problem as well as a recalcitrant student. She hated mathematics, and she would not learn a foreign language. On a spelling test, she once missed twenty-three words out of fifty.

She admitted that she felt "utterly stupid," especially in mental philosophy class where the teacher, Miss Nesmith, expounded on the great truths of the ages. Confused because these truths did not always seem conclusive, Effie envied another student—pretty, bright Belle Sherwin. "I do not see why I am not able to understand my Mental Phil. as Belle does," she lamented. "I am so slow in grasping anything."

With the exception of Miss Winters, a young teacher who was genuinely fond of Effie, most of Miss Mittleberger's faculty found the girl irritating. Her schoolmates, on the other hand, admired Effie and valued her friendship. She could hardly believe it. "How can anyone like me when one day I am laughing and the next crying or often doing both several times in one day?" she asked her diary. The answer was simple. Effie's friends knew that life was never boring when she was around.

One day Effie drew a caricature of a teacher and passed it to the other students. Miss Blake heard the giggles of the girls and intercepted the drawing. Despite being reprimanded, Effie relished the incident. "It has been a long time since I acted so bad in school as I have today," she wrote. "I could not stop laughing much as I wanted to."

While some teachers complained about Effie's lack of interest in class, others were upset when indeed she did participate. "I do get into such deep water when I attempt to argue," Effie despaired. "Half the time I don't know what I am trying to say." In mental philosophy class, she argued constantly with Miss Nesmith. "It is so odd that we have not agreed upon a single thing," Effie mused.

Effie doubted everything and enjoyed taking the unpopular, negative side of an argument. "I never agree with anyone and get quite mad at them when they do not agree with me," she observed. Realizing that her outbursts were considered inappropriate, she made a resolution that she would find almost impossible to keep: "I must control myself."

Effie even questioned religion. "Why don't I love Christ as others do?" she wondered. "Why do I doubt everything?" One day she announced in class that she did not believe in the Trinity.

"What do you think the deity is," Miss Nesmith asked, "if not a personality?"

"I don't know yet," responded the girl.

"It is wrong in people to give up one faith," the teacher explained, "unless they could supply its place with another."

"I think it is wrong to cling to an idea that one knows is wrong until we could find another," Effie countered. "I would rather believe in nothing at all rather than stay by what I firmly believe to be a false idea."

Effie's battles with Miss Nesmith continued. Finally Effie made a resolution. "Miss Nesmith is so against me when I argue," she said, "that I think I never will agree or disagree with her any more."

Six weeks later, Miss Nesmith announced, "People are born with evil tendencies."

The girls waited. They knew that Effie was trying to remain silent. "It is circumstance that makes them go wrong," Effie finally declared.

When Miss Nesmith told the class, "To be saved, we must believe *and* lead a good life," Effie again could not restrain herself.

"I think that if we lead a good life, whether we believe or not," she retorted, "we are safe."

Then the teacher denigrated the affections of schoolgirls. "They love or they hate," she asserted, "and neither in a very great degree." Effie became furious. Her relationships with classmates and with her favorite teacher, Miss Winters, were worth more than anything else in the world.

At Miss Mittleberger's School, where the students lived in an entirely female world, they developed intense attachments to each other and to teachers who were kind to them. They kissed, hugged, and shared the same bed. They expressed and received physical affection and did not consider it sexual. They saw nothing wrong with their actions, spoke openly about "crushes," and gossiped about the latest romance. Effie intensely loved both Miss Winters and Belle Sherwin, and she was not ashamed of her ardor.

More astute than most of the teachers, Effie's friend Belle knew that Effie was intelligent, clever, and a sophisticated reader, and she enjoyed discussing literature and philosophy with her. Belle's favorite author was Dickens, while Effie preferred George Eliot, whom she considered a greater genius because "delineation of character is the quality to be most aimed at by a novelist."

The friends had much in common. The Sherwins were also Euclid Avenue millionaires, and, like Effie, Belle loathed the luxurious and empty existence of the excessively rich. Both girls declared their approval of what they assumed were the worthwhile lives of the working class.

When Effie's other love, Miss Winters, announced that she was leaving Miss Mittleberger's School to take a position as the governess for the children of Reverend Moxam in Boston, Effie said, "I do not ever remember having felt so badly about anything." But she added, "I have said too much to her about my feelings."

Several weeks went by and Effie continued to grieve. "I wonder if there ever was a more perfect woman," she asked herself, "and if she truly does love me."

A few months later, Miss Mittleberger invited Miss Winters's employer, the Reverend Mr. Moxam, to give a sermon at the school. Effie approached the minister and told him how she felt about his governess. Amused at the girl's ardor, he solemnly replied that Miss Winters would live with him always. Effie retorted that she wanted her. "You will outlive me," he teased, "and then you could have her."

Effie imagined sharing her life with the woman. "I wonder if my dream of owning a country house and farm in the East and having Miss Winters spend most of her time with me if not live with me will ever come true," she wrote in her diary. "That is the brightest idea of the future that I have."

By the time she was ready to graduate from Miss Mittleberger's School, nineteen-year-old Effie had concluded, "I think it is so foolish to study....I thought that study brought with it happiness, but the more I learn the unhappier I am." Regarding religion, she asked what kind of God would be so "mean to put us here with just enough sense to appreciate that we never can solve the mystery that surrounds life?" About her behavior, she realized that even if she were a boy, "I would be pretty hard to manage."

Certainly her mother found Effie difficult to control. Time and again Ada would say, "I do wish you would listen to advice" or "I do wish I could get your attention." Mother and daughter argued about practically everything, from minor to more serious issues. When Effie returned home with material to make a dress, Ada scolded her because she had not bought a different silk. The girl burst into tears. "I had felt so happy about my costume," she despaired, "until mama took all the enthusiasm that I had for it away."

When Ada insisted that a dress jacket be made more tight-fitting, Effie walked out of the dressmaker's shop, leaving Ada alone and humiliated. Effie had felt "righteous indignation." After all, she was "plenty old enough" to know how she wanted her dresses made.

One evening, Ada came to Effie's room and said that she had been asked to take in a five-year-old orphan. At first, Effie was elated. On second thought, she doubted that her mother would allow a stranger to live in their home. "I wish we could take her," she lamented. "I can think of nothing else since Mama spoke to me about her. I am sure I would love her." But Ada had no intention of accepting a "waif" into their family. Effie made a resolution: "Sometime I mean to have my own way and adopt a child who has dark eyes."

By this time, Alfred had made his fortune and was starting to pay more attention to Effie. Sometimes he treated his daughter like a son, talking with her about his work and taking her to visit the Cleveland factory. He liked to indulge his child. "Had great fun as I always do when I shop with him," Effie wrote, in implied contrast to her mother. "He bought me two neck pins, a tortoise shell hairpin, and a pair of cuff buttons."

After dinner, father and daughter made a charming picture: the two blond heads leaning against each other, the large, tall man holding the girl on his lap, kissing her and singing old songs. Alfred listened to Effie and encouraged her ambitions. Like him, she felt a disdain for business and wanted to do something more important in life than making money. Perhaps she could become famous. Maybe she could become an artist, a musician, or a writer.

While at Miss Mittleberger's School, Effie had written a composition, "An Ideal Educational System," which she discussed with Alfred, who voiced his approval. He thought the essay could be worked over and made into a story. Elated, Effie crowed, "How I should like to send it to the *St. Nicholas*,—and have it accepted."

For a while Effie considered writing either a biography or a novel with the character of Miss Winters at the center. Alfred thought it a good idea and told his daughter that what was most important was originality, which he was positive she possessed.

Alfred believed that Effie had many talents, including promise as an artist. "Papa is anxious that I shall do well in my drawing," she told her diary, describing a charcoal sketch she had made of a little newspaper boy.

She showed the sketch to Alfred, who praised it. She then thought that she might become a portrait painter.

After he had acquired great wealth, Alfred became a serious art collector, and Effie accompanied him on viewing and buying trips. "Went to see the Morgan collection this morning," she noted. "Of course I was much interested in the pictures but cared nothing about the porcelain." Ada collected porcelain.

Alfred had learned about art on his own and taught Effie what he knew. Soon she shared his passion. "I wish I had lots of money to spend for pictures!" she exclaimed after father and daughter returned from a trip to a gallery. "I should have liked to have bought that head of a young republican by Couture and that landscape that fairly sings to one by Daubigny." Sometimes, though, she did not share Alfred's taste. "Will I ever like Millet's pictures?" she wondered.

As the bond between father and daughter developed and strengthened, Effie became disturbed by jealous feelings. After introducing a school friend to Alfred, she was "kind of knocked speechless," because "Papa seems quite fond of Maud, called her Maudie etc."

One evening while Effie and Ada were sitting at the dinner table, Alfred walked in. Effie looked up at him to say, "Good evening," but stopped. He had shaved his mustache off! First she laughed, but then she nearly cried. "I felt as if I never could look at him again," she wrote. "I felt as if he wasn't my father and could not imagine myself sitting on his lap or ever kissing him again." Without a mustache, Alfred looked much younger, an image that his daughter found disturbing.

Effie's strong feelings about Alfred surfaced dramatically when the family visited the Whittemore family in Naugatuck, Connecticut. Alfred's friendship with his business associate, John Howard Whittemore, was so close that each man had his portrait painted for the other to hang in his home. When Effie saw her father's portrait in the Whittemores' house, she was appalled. She thought that the artist had given Alfred "a very dissipated look." Her beloved father was the antithesis of dissipation and licentiousness!

Early in the morning, while everyone else slept, she sneaked out of her room and, standing on a chair, took her penknife and slashed the painting. At breakfast, she admitted what she had done. The others sat shocked. "Well," Alfred said calmly, "she will probably end up in jail."

Like many girls growing up during the Victorian period, Effie was repulsed by what she had heard about the sexual appetites of men. Hearing Ada tell Alfred that she would not bear him any more children convinced Effie that sex was dangerous and unpleasant. She thought, or hoped, that her parents' relationship was platonic. She believed that Alfred would never force himself on Ada and that he was too refined to harbor sexual desires.

Effie was also confused about her own sexuality. To maintain the innocence of the relationship with her father, which included sitting on Alfred's lap when she was a grown woman, Effie could not acknowledge the possibility that Alfred harbored what she called "dissipated" thoughts nor could she accept the more disturbing idea that sexual desire lurked in her own psyche.

In the spring of 1886, Effie made a startling decision. She demanded to be called Theodate, the name of Alfred's strong-willed, Quaker mother. She refused to answer to Effie and dropped her middle name, Brooks, Ada's maiden name. She was Theodate Pope and signed correspondence "Theo" or "TP." "Theodate," which means "gift of God," was a more dignified name than the jolly "Effie." An additional advantage of the new name was that people could mistake it for a male name, especially when she shortened it to "Theo." Being mistaken for a man would be helpful if she pursued a career.

More significantly, Theo had created a new identity based on a choice —Alfred and his Quaker family—as well as on a rejection. Theodate was disassociating herself from Ada, whom she considered weak and frivolous, and from the Brooks family. Alfred inscribed his daughter's new name and the date in the family Bible, and added "with the consent of her parents."

Ada was upset, but she wanted to please Alfred and to establish a better relationship with her child. She found it difficult to call Effie "Theodate," but she made a valiant effort.

"I seldom have to correct her," Theo told Alfred. Clearly, she felt free to express disrespect toward Ada without fear of being reprimanded. "I sometimes feel like laughing in her face when she says it [Theodate]," she confided, "but I control myself because I am so afraid she will stop."

During the summer after Theo graduated Miss Mittleberger's School, she had oral surgery, probably to reduce the prominence of her jaw and improve her appearance. Facing three months of torturous dental work as well as a tonsillectomy, Theo hoped the experience would result in "moral improvement as well as physical," and she braced herself to have "the strength of character to go through it bravely."

For most of the summer and into September, Theo stayed in Oxford, Ohio, with Mrs. Alleman, a hired companion whom she called "grim," while Dr. Keeler worked on her jaw. He used some sort of gas or ether, but without novocaine or other medication—not even aspirin was yet available—the pain was excruciating. Theo admitted that as much as she tried not to, she wept like a baby. After having several teeth extracted, she moaned, "My nerves are all unstrung. Have done nothing but cry all day. Every tooth in my head hurts me, my head aches, my eyes ache, and one side of my throat is swollen as if I had the mumps." Ada and Alfred visited their daughter only once, briefly, during her ordeal.

Lonely and miserable, Theo thought constantly about Belle Sherwin. "She is with me always. I love the girl with my whole heart, and wish, how I do wish I could give her as much as she does me. I am not so clever as she and so I wonder how she can love me." She wrote but did not send the following note: "Dear Belle, I am full of feeling tonight. Put your arms around me Belle and I will sleep in peace. Theo"

Earlier in the spring, Theo had been tempted to apply to Wellesley College because Belle planned to go there. Although most people were impressed by the ivy covered buildings, when Theo visited the campus with her mother, she thought the college looked like an asylum. Since architects who designed asylums and prisons usually were the ones who designed women's colleges, this was a rather perceptive response. The premise guiding these types of institutions was that they were fortresses that would keep their inmates safely enclosed. In addition to disliking its architecture, Theo feared that Wellesley College would be too difficult academically. She knew that she would have to study more mathematics to pass an entrance test.

Ada asked Theo to consider Miss Porter's School for Girls, an elite boarding school in Farmington, Connecticut, that Theo's favorite cousin, Elizabeth Brooks, planned to attend. Theo liked the idea of being with Betty but thought that another year of high school would be a wasted year. Besides, at nineteen, she worried that she would be "antique" in comparison to the other girls.

Alfred's opinion about educating Theo was colored by his own experience. As a child growing up in Maine, he had been taught at home and then at the Locust Grove Academy for Quaker Children, a private school established by his father and two other Quakers. In Ohio, Alfred went to high school, but his family had been too poor to send him or his brothers to college. He continued to study on his own, especially art, philosophy, and history, but despite the wealth and prestige he had achieved, he admitted that he felt ashamed that he did not have a college degree.

Alfred wanted Theo to go to college but not yet. Convinced that she was not ready to live away from home, he advised his daughter to remain in Cleveland and spend another year at Miss Mittleberger's School.

But when Theo visited Miss Porter's School with Ada, she fell in love with Farmington. The rural New England village, surrounded by rolling hills and blue mountains was "one of the prettiest places" she had ever seen. Impulsively, Theo made up her mind. She announced to her parents that she would join Betty Brooks at the Connecticut school. On October 14, 1886, Miss Sarah Porter, headmistress and founder of the school, wrote Alfred Pope a receipt for $2,012 "in advance for board & tuition of his daughter."

Betty and Theo would fit in well at Miss Porter's School, which had been established for the daughters of America's aristocracy. The cousins could trace their ancestors back to colonial days, and their families were among the richest and most prominent in America.

Theodate looked forward to arriving in the idyllic village of Farmington. With a new name and her teeth and jaw fixed, she wondered, "Am I too happy?"

Theodate in her teens. *Hill-Stead Archives (HS)*

Theodate Stackpole Pope, 1805-1887 *(HS)*.

Alfred Atmore Pope. *(HS)*.

Ada Brooks Pope. *(HS)*.

Effie at three. *(HS)*.

Effie at eight. *(HS)*.

TWO

"This, what I want...is making me miserable"
1886—1888

IN OCTOBER 1886, accompanied by Alfred and Ada, Theodate left for Miss Porter's School. From Cleveland, they traveled by train to New York City and then a few more hours to Hartford, Connecticut. When they arrived at Hartford's Union Station, Alfred hired a horse and carriage.

The day was fair, and the fall air felt crisp and cool. Theo, Ada, and Alfred settled into the carriage and began the final part of their trip, the thirteen miles from Hartford through West Hartford to the village of Farmington. As the carriage made its way along Farmington Avenue, it passed Nook Farm in Hartford, a cluster of three large houses famous for their literary residents: Charles Dudley Warner, a novelist and the editor of *The Hartford Courant;* Harriet Beecher Stowe, the author of *Uncle Tom's Cabin;* and Samuel Clemens, better known as Mark Twain. Clemens had designed his home to look like the Mississippi riverboats of his youth. From its porch, which looked like a boat's prow, the reddish stone house commanded a view of the Park River that wound its way east to the Connecticut River.

Theo's excitement grew as they passed meadows and farms in West Hartford and approached the center of Farmington village. They turned left onto Main Street, where stately elm trees shaded white, colonial houses. Instead of Cleveland's massive, pretentious stone-and-brick estates, the homes in the New England town were charming. And, in contrast to the soot always present in Cleveland, the air here was clear and fragrant. After a few blocks, the carriage stopped at the portico of the three-storied main building of Miss Porter's School for Girls.

Sarah Porter, the founder and headmistress of the school, was a descendent of Robert Porter, one of the original settlers of Farmington in 1640. In 1843, when she was almost thirty, Sarah and her friend, Mary Dow, established Miss Porter's and Mrs. Dow's School for Girls. Eventually Mrs. Dow's name was dropped, but she remained second in command. Students, alumnae, and other insiders never referred to the school by its official name; they called it "Farmington."

"I would prefer to guide the thoughts of those who would direct homes," Miss Porter asserted, "rather than those who would direct business enterprises," but she was herself a successful businesswoman. For over forty-three years, the school had attracted the daughters of wealthy, prominent families from as far away as California. In 1886, Theo joined a student body of approximately one hundred boarders and a dozen day students.

After her parents left, Theo was not lonesome because she was sharing a bedroom with her cousin Betty Brooks at one of the school's boarding houses. Slender with dark eyes and straight, dark hair, Betty was shy and serious. She admired her more outgoing cousin, and Theo adored her. Six other girls also boarded at Miss Dunning's, including another pair of cousins, Alice and Agnes Hamilton.

The first night, Theo immediately established herself as the leader of the group, inviting the other girls to her and Betty's room. Soon, they all were friends and began confiding in each other. Sue Usher wept because she was homesick. Alice Hamilton, wearing a red dressing gown, shook her black curls emphatically and announced that someday she was going to become a doctor. One reason she wanted a career, she confessed, was that she had a bitter aversion to marriage. Years later, Alice realized her ambition and became the first female physician on the faculty of Harvard Medical School.

Theo later wrote in her *Memoirs* that she also had foretold her future. She had declared a determination "to build an indestructible school for boys." That she actually said this is unlikely, however, because she did not record it in her diary at the time.

Theo began the school term enthusiastically, certain that she would do well because she was one of the oldest students and had previously studied some of the same subjects at Miss Mittleberger's School. But she soon ran into problems with the teachers. If she asked difficult questions or challenged them, they quickly put her in her place.

"The person who is fond of argument," an annoyed teacher told her, "is not fond of the truth."

"Doubt may become a habit of the mind," another teacher warned, "and the indulger is as morally accountable for it as he would be for opium eating."

One night Theo's housemother, Miss Dunning, came to Theo's room looking solemn. She had something unpleasant to say. There were several people at the school, the older woman began, who thought that at times Theo was almost impertinent.

Shocked and hurt, Theo tried to remember what she had done to displease her teachers. She implored, "What should I do?"

"Think before you speak, and try to speak even more politely than you otherwise would" was the answer.

Theo, however, knew that she could never control her impulsiveness, and, because she greatly needed to feel loved, she could not tolerate the teachers' disapproval. Loneliness for Alfred washed over her. Unable to go to him for comfort and reassurance, she became depressed and nervous, and she began doing poorly in her studies.

"Why is it I was made with a so much smaller, and more trifling mind than the average girl?" she wondered. "Am I a perfect blockhead. I am so ashamed of my stupidity."

A young teacher, Miss Mary Hillard, noticed Theo's melancholic state and became concerned. She feared that the girl was dangerously depressed and was heading toward a complete breakdown. One late afternoon, Mary saw Theo outside the classroom building and called to her. Theo waited and the two walked together to Miss Dunning's house.

Tall and athletic, Mary Hillard was an attractive woman with dark hair, fair skin, dark eyes, and large, regular features. Usually dressed in a modest hat and gloves, a shirtwaist with a collar and bow tie, and a long skirt, she carried herself with a dignity that made her seem older than her twenty-three years.

Unlike the wealthy girls that she taught, Mary had grown up in genteel poverty. The large Hillard family lived on the meager salary her father earned as the pastor of a Congregational Church in Plymouth, Connecticut. The older children took care of the younger ones, while Mary's mother found solace for a difficult life in mysticism, an interest that Mary shared.

In contrast to Miss Porter, Mary Hillard expressed progressive ideas. She urged her students to become "not only wives and mothers, but teachers, doctors of medicine, professors, ministers, statisticians, hygienists, psychologists, and Socialists." She told them that the duty of women was "to educate and elevate the human race."

Theo began to consider transferring her affection from the perfect but absent Miss Winters whom she had worshiped at Miss Mittleberger's School to this radical and compassionate new teacher. "I wonder if I can get to like Miss Hillard very well?" she mused. "Seems very possible."

Theo did get to like Mary, and her feeling quickly changed to love, a love that the young teacher returned. As in Miss Mittleberger's all-female world, there were many such relationships among students and teachers at Miss Porter's. When Mary came to Theo's room and stayed a long time, another girl who also loved the teacher camped in the hall next to the bedroom door and writhed in jealousy.

Every Saturday, Theo attended a dance at the school, where she danced with the other girls. The activity helped lift her spirits. "So depressed all afternoon," Theo reported in her diary, "but at Study Hall tea I completely recovered and danced my feet nearly off."

Ecstasy, however, was not the opposite of depression but another sign of it. Mary Hillard warned about such extremes, and Theo promised that she would attempt to avoid dramatic mood changes. But in church on Sunday morning, she laughed out loud, and that evening she threw a tantrum.

Only during art class did she feel contentment. "Yesterday I enjoyed one of the best drawing lessons I have ever had," she noted. But the next day, when the teacher corrected a drawing, Theo fought to hold back tears. That night, she angrily scribbled, "Hate to have a drawing on which a teacher has put even one line."

Too tired to study, she had a nervous collapse and spent several days in bed. "I felt for the past week as if I were going mad," she lamented.

One way to avoid depression, she heard, was to concentrate on others rather than on oneself. She became determined to "work for the comfort of others even if the motive for doing so is not of the highest." She tried to be kind and altruistic, but she could not always restrain herself. "Poor Miss Gribble the seamstress always gets it when I feel cross," she admitted. On the other hand, she felt calmed after releasing anger. Poor Miss Gribble, she added, "is such a fool that she always deserves all she gets."

Lethargic and plagued by headaches, she could not control fits of crying. She now knew that her father had been right when he said she was not ready to live away from home. She wanted to leave Farmington but despaired because she would miss Betty, Alice and Agnes Hamilton, the other girls, and especially Mary Hillard.

Why, she kept asking herself, was she so unhappy and dissatisfied when she was blessed with a most privileged and pleasant life? She came to a startling conclusion: wealth was causing her distress. "I have too many things," she realized, "so that, this, what I want, though I know not what it is, is making me miserable because I lack it." She envied the poor, who did not worry about society's expectations and who, she supposed, had greater freedom to do what they wanted.

She wished that she were not a woman. Having had almost no interaction with young men and being ignorant about sex, she dreaded becoming a wife, mother, and society hostess like her mother. She expressed the fantasy of disguising herself as a man and going out West to seek her fortune. She felt a strong need to accomplish something. Any ordinary male was applauded for his ambition, but a woman would have to be extraordinary to pursue a career. Theo liked to discuss ideas, but she had not proved to be a scholar. Though she loved to draw, she doubted that she had enough talent to become an artist. She sometimes wondered whether she might become a writer.

Christmas brought a welcome relief from Farmington. Back in Cleveland, Theo spent the first day home in bed, with Alfred sitting by her bedside. Throughout the school vacation, father and daughter kept each other company. In January, Theo returned to school in good spirits. "The snow is very deep and the trees look clumsy fingered with their covering of ice," she rhapsodized upon seeing Farmington village.

Almost immediately, Theo met with Miss Porter, who warned that she must not break down again. She was to hold herself back and not get too excited. She was not to enter into things so vigorously as she had the previous term, and, the elderly woman concluded, she also was not to resume French lessons.

Within the first week that Theo was back at school, however, depression returned. When friends tried to comfort her, as much as she cared for them, she realized that they could never understand how she felt. She now considered them boring. "Their talk does not satisfy me," she told her diary.

Theo could not concentrate on schoolwork, and, instead of being the feisty young woman who challenged teachers, she sat in class with a vacant look. At the same time, Theo read constantly, and on her own was trying to understand the theories of Spinoza. She became attracted to progressive ideas and thought about the unfairness, inequality, and poverty in the world. "Almost repent having bought my gray and pink wrapper," she confessed, "when I think how much I might have helped some poor person with the money I spent for it."

In May 1887, after several hours of crying and feeling ill and angry, Theo concluded that she could no longer remain in Farmington. She sent a telegram to Alfred asking him and Ada to come immediately, but they did not obey the summons. Convinced that she could stand no more, she decided to run away from school. She would leave her privileged, miserable life and find a job on a farm in the nearby rural community of West Hartford.

On Saturday morning, she left a note where Betty could easily find it, telling her cousin and the other girls not to worry. She then quietly slipped out of Miss Dunning's house. It was going to be a long walk, so first she found a piece of wood to use for a staff. She felt exhilarated—it was a fine, sunny day.

When she finally reached the center of West Hartford, about eight miles from Miss Porter's school, it was late afternoon. Exhausted and hungry, she sat down on the front steps of a church. After a few minutes, she stopped a woman walking past. Theo told the stranger that she had run away from Miss Porter's School and asked if she might sleep in her home that night.

"Are you in trouble?" the woman asked, her eyes sweeping Theo's figure.

Not comprehending the woman's meaning but aware that there was an implication of something peculiar in the question, Theo answered, "No." It was many years before she realized what a girl's being "in trouble" meant.

The woman shook her head. "I cannot take the responsibility," she explained. She left and entered a nearby house.

Theo continued walking. Suddenly, the woman reappeared and called out that she had changed her mind. Theo could spend the night, but they would have to share a bed. Once inside the house, Theo decided that she didn't want to sleep with a stranger. She thanked the woman and left.

It was getting late, the sun was setting, and Theo began to worry. Betty surely had discovered the note by now. What if she told Miss Porter? And what if Miss Porter sent the groundsman Rufus to look for her? How embarrassing it would be to return in Rufus's cart. She could not abide such a disgrace. Theo decided that she should return to school.

She started the long walk back, using the staff as she trudged up the steep hills. Suddenly, a carriage appeared on the road. It stopped and two of Miss Porter's students called to Theo. In excited voices, they said that they had just passed some rough-looking men. These men would probably speak to Theo! She should get into the phaeton, they warned, and ride back to Farmington with them.

When Theo arrived at Miss Dunning's house, she discovered that no one knew that she had left. Assuming that Theo was depressed and wanted to be alone, Miss Dunning had told the girls not to bother her, and Betty had never discovered the note.

The next day, while the others were in church, Theo remained in her room. Always willing to give advice, Miss Dunning told the unhappy girl that she was in danger of becoming a crank if she kept giving in to impulses.

Not answering Miss Dunning, Theo ran out and raced to Miss Porter's house. Miss Porter invited the distraught girl into the parlor. The elderly woman sat across from Theo, held her hand, and now and then gently patted her cheek. "Theodate," she asked softly, "do you do queer things simply to be considered odd?"

Receiving no reply, Miss Porter spoke about school and, finally, about Theo's depression. After a while, she leaned over, kissed the girl, and said, "Cheer up. Always be happy."

Theo left in better spirits, thinking, "Was there ever another such a woman as Miss Porter, her equal in cleverness and goodness?"

Miss Porter's equal was Mary Hillard, who became even more loving to Theo after the infamous runaway attempt. The young teacher made Theo promise that whenever she felt depressed she would come to see her.

A few days later, Theo felt nervous. "Tears come without any provocation," she recorded in her diary. "Headache all day." By the end of the week, she was "wild...and cross and blue."

She decided to forget about studying. Instead, she and Mary went on walks together. The weather was mild, flowers were blooming, Main Street's majestic elms were in tiny leaf, and the birds had returned. "Really glad I was born," Theo rejoiced.

By the time Alfred and Ada arrived to take Theo home at the end of the spring term, they found her comparatively happy but still disturbed about the future. "When will I find my vocation?" she despaired. "Have I one? Will I ever find something on which I can expend all my energy?"

In October 1887, Theo returned to Farmington, eager to start another term—not to study but to develop as a musician. Her goal was to become a pianist, and she began practicing every day for at least three hours. In January a finger became arthritic and her wrist started to hurt. She broke down, unable to stop crying.

A few weeks later, Theo received an invitation from Harris Whittemore, the son of Alfred's business associate, to come to Yale for a gala weekend that included a concert, a prom, and a play. Three years older than Theo, Harris was boyishly handsome with clean-cut features, light brown hair, and a fair complexion. It was no secret that the Popes and the Whittemores hoped that their children would someday marry.

Theo accepted and seemed to have a good time in New Haven, but when she returned to Farmington, she did not respond to a letter from Harris. On February 2, he sent roses for her twenty-first birthday

Theo later told Betty that she was afraid to become involved with Harris because she dreaded a sexual relationship with a man. Several years later, after Betty had married, she tried to convince Theo "how natural how simple and how great a pleasure it all is." But like Alice Hamilton, Theo harbored an aversion to marriage. Her dream was to live with a female companion (Miss Winters, Belle Sherwin, and, of late, Mary Hillard) and adopt children.

Theo might also have confessed the intensity of the love Mary and she shared. The students and teachers, as well as Miss Dunning, gossiped that the bond between the two had put a strain on the girl, and they blamed Theo's erratic behavior on the relationship.

Theo's headaches and depression worsened, and at the beginning of March, she wrote a desperate letter home. After reading it, Alfred became frightened and insisted that Ada accompany him to Farmington and take care of their daughter.

Wanting to surprise Theo, the Popes did not tell her their plans. They arrived on Saturday, March 10, 1888, took rooms at the local inn, and then went to Miss Dunning's house. Theo was not there—she was out on a drive with Mary Hillard. Alfred and Ada waited impatiently. Finally Theo returned, and when she saw her parents, started crying.

The next day a heavy snow started to fall, and it soon became apparent that a major storm was coming. At Miss Dunning's house, as the wind howled, Mary helped Theo with a homework assignment. Then the house began to shake. Mary tried to calm the terrified girls who had run to her from their rooms.

The Great Blizzard of 1888 was the worst storm of the century on the Atlantic seaboard. Many who were caught in it perished. Some died of exhaustion when they tried to walk through the snow after other means of transportation became impossible. In New York City, which became cut off from the rest of the country for two days, the storm killed 400 people. The snow came down in blinding sheets, and the wind blew with such fury that great drifts paralyzed the railroad. The trains did not run for over a week, until plows finally cut through forty-foot drifts.

Snowed in at Miss Dunning's house, a few girls ventured outside, but they did not get far. They fainted on their return and were given wine. The cold drafts caused the girls to become ill, and Theo developed a sore throat. On the fourth day, Theo looked out the window. The sky was a clear blue, and the sun shone brightly on the glistening, quiet, snow-covered landscape. In the distance a snowplow was approaching. As it came closer, Theo saw that a board had been placed across the plow. On the board sat the elderly Sarah Porter, who had come to see if her girls were all right.

By Wednesday evening, the roads were passable, and the Popes entertained twenty-three of Theo's friends at the Elm Tree Inn. Eagerly they consumed oyster stew, chicken salad, ice cream, chocolate, and the inn's famous waffles. The girls enjoyed talking with Alfred and Ada, but they were upset that Ada was determined to take Theo to New York City the following day. "I think Mrs. Pope ought to have waited until Monday instead of exposing her to the sharp air," one friend bristled. "Mrs. P. is a bright woman, but she doesn't entirely understand Theo yet."

What Ada did understand was that she must separate her daughter from Mary Hillard. Ada was convinced that, at twenty-one, Theo should be thinking about marriage. Ada spoke candidly to Mary and bluntly demanded that she see less of Theo. The young woman was indignant and insulted, so much so that she told a student what Ada had said.

Horrified, the girl defended her teacher: "As if she [Miss Hillard] had run after Theo!"

Pale and tired, Theo was too ill to travel, but she left with her mother. Now that Ada had her alone, she made Theo feel worse by talking about and praising Harris Whittemore.

Theo returned to Farmington at the end of March but only to say good-bye. Deciding that she needed a rest cure, the Popes planned to send their daughter to Philadelphia to be under the care of Dr. Weir Mitchell, famous for treating female patients suffering from hysteria and neurasthenia. He usually prescribed prolonged inactivity and sometimes "electric treatments," a primitive kind of shock therapy.

Although Theo realized, "I am always happy when I keep so busy that I cannot stop to think of the sadness of life," she did not protest. Meekly she accompanied Ada and Alfred to Philadelphia and put herself under Dr. Mitchell's care.

"I am very very glad to hear that you will be safely in bed for some weeks to come and *really* excited when you come back to us," wrote Mrs. Dow, Miss Porter's second-in-command. "Only last night I was telling Alice Hamilton about the Rest Cure—and she said Oh how I wish Theo could try it!"

A rest cure, however, did not help Theo nor did it cure a worsening sore throat. In April, she had to have yet another tonsil removed. Several years earlier she had undergone two tonsillectomies, but the doctor had discovered a third infected tonsil.

In June, accompanied by a nurse, Theo returned to Farmington and took rooms at the inn. She had withdrawn from Miss Porter's School, but she was not ready to go home to Cleveland. Although the day she arrived was unusually warm, she was glad to be back. "I'd rather be hot in Farmington," she declared, "than cool in any other place on the face of the earth."

Bringing flowers and other gifts, Miss Porter's girls and teachers visited Theo at the inn. Some asked questions about the siege she had undergone, but she was too tired to talk. She had difficulty sleeping and needed to take the sedative, valerian. The term ended on July 10, 1888, and the students left Farmington. Theo wanted to remain. She wrote in her diary, "If I could only live here always!"

Miss Sarah Porter.
Miss Porter's School Archives (MPS).

Harris Whittemore.
Courtesy Robert N. Whittemore. *(HS).*

Mary Hillard.
Westover School Archives. (WS).

Betty Brooks, Agnes Hamilton, Theo, Alice Hamilton, unknown friend. *(MPS).*

THREE

*"Of all the unlovely things in the world,
an unwomanly woman is the worst"*
1888—1890

HARRIS WHITTEMORE now worked for Alfred in Cleveland. A bond had developed between Alfred and Harris, which had grown so strong that, despite a generation's difference, each considered the other his best friend. Harris and Alfred shared a passionate interest in art and spent a great deal of time together visiting galleries and museums.

When Theo took the rest cure in Philadelphia, Harris showered her with letters and gifts, but she did not respond to his overtures. Throughout the summer he continued to court Theo at the Popes' Euclid Avenue mansion. At first, he met with some success. "Harris has told me that he loves me," Theo confided to her diary. "I shall pray that I may return it, for I do like him so much." She believed the doctor who said that she would not suffer from depression if, like most other girls, she had a husband and a home of her own. "How happy I will be," she declared, "if the day ever comes when I can without fear put on the gold collar."

The image, a gold collar, indicates how she viewed marriage: a husband owned a wife as if she were a dog. Being a rich man's possession, a woman traded independence for status and security. She became a pampered pet who could go no farther than the master's leash allowed.

On the other hand, believing that Harris's nature was similar to Alfred's, Theo assumed that he would support her ambitions. It was not so much a loss of freedom that she feared. Rather, it was the sexual duties he would expect her to fulfill. She was fond of Harris, but she worried, "Perhaps I am not capable of loving a man."

Although Theo thought him a gentleman, several times Harris made indelicate remarks that distressed her. On one occasion, she described a dress she was having made, and, to her dismay, he suggested a more revealing design. How dare he think she would "wear a dress that would be criticized in a certain way?" she demanded. The abashed young man apologized.

Another time, Harris remarked with a smile that looked more like a smirk, that there was something suspicious about Miss Winters' living in the same house with the widower, the Reverend Mr. Moxam.

"Miss Winters could not do wrong in a way like that!" Theo hotly retorted.

Harris laughed and teased that she was naïve.

When Harris proposed, she demurred, and he promised that he would never press for an answer if she would allow him to continue his visits. He was using the wrong strategy, Theo confided to Betty. She was too sure of him. If he flirted with other girls, she might be "brought around quickly."

In early August, Harris took Theo to a minstrel show. On returning home, they discovered that Alfred and Ada were out and that the servants had retired for the evening. Sitting next to Harris on the stairway, Theo confessed that she did not love him and did not know if she ever could. Harris responded that she would never have to tell him if she felt any love for him. He took out a gold piece from his pocket and pressed it into her hand. "Just wear it," he said, "when you feel one inch of love." Then he added with a grin, "I expect you to wear it soon." Suddenly the front door opened. Holding the gold dollar, Theo rushed up the stairs, leaving her blushing suitor to face Alfred and Ada with as much dignity as he could muster.

Theo did not wear the gold piece. The days passed, and Harris became impatient. Alfred and Ada had invited him to join them and Theo on a trip abroad in November, but Harris warned Theo that, unless she professed her love, he would not go. Unable to decide what to do, Theo took to her bed.

Ada was losing patience. Theo had admitted that no one could please, understand, or love her better than Harris did, but she still held back. "You never act as other girls do," Ada complained.

Theo did not argue. She answered that if she ever fell in love, it would "not be quite the usual way," and refused to comment further.

Coming home one evening, Theo saw Ada and Harris having a tête à tête in the parlor. Assuming that they were discussing her, she greeted them icily and went up to her room. After Harris left, Theo threw a violent temper tantrum and accused Ada of conspiring with him. The next day, just as Theo was about to go to lunch with some friends, Harris arrived at the house. He started to walk over to the carriage to speak to Theo, but she ignored him and drove away.

Later, ashamed of being rude, Theo apologized and explained to Harris why she had been angry. He acted dumbfounded. The truth was, he said earnestly, his conversation with Ada was not about Theo. Furthermore, it had been so boring that he had kept hoping Theo would interrupt. His sincerity was convincing. By the end of August, Theo decided that she did love Harris "a little." "I do not know," she worried, "but perhaps I have gone too far." She had let him hold her hands.

Besides providing their daughter with a grand tour of Europe, the Popes had several other objectives for going abroad that fall. Alfred planned to purchase paintings for his collection and to meet with European business associates. Ada looked forward to buying gowns for herself and Theo in Paris and to sightseeing with her sister Nora, who also was coming along. Most important, since Harris had accepted their invitation, Ada and Alfred hoped that the young people would return home engaged.

Just before they left, Theo asked Ada if she could invite a school chum, Fanny.

No, Ada curtly replied. Fanny was an outsider.

But the girl was a "good traveler" and "sweet-tempered," Theo insisted. "I do not know of any girl who I would rather go abroad with."

When Theo told Harris that she wanted Fanny to join them, she could tell that he was "just sick about it." Although he guessed that she wanted a friend to act as a buffer between them, he agreed that she should invite the girl if that would make her happy. Fanny, however, did not go. Perhaps Ada prevailed, Theo changed her mind, or Fanny refused the invitation.

The Popes left right after the November election of 1888. Alfred had earlier supported Cleveland's William McKinley, but Benjamin Harrison won the Republican party's nomination on the eighth ballot. Harrison lost the popular vote but won the electoral vote, becoming the country's twenty-third President.

At least during the first weeks of their vacation, Ada seemed to be right about proximity and romance. "I am certainly slipping, sliding, falling in love," Theo realized. "I want to be near Harris and never grow tired of his telling me of his love for me."

In Paris, the entire group went to see a play. The Parisian theatre was infamous for its loose morality, and when actors appeared on stage and began a risqué dance, Theo immediately stood up, turned to Harris, and asked him to take her back to the hotel. He nodded his assent, and the young couple left. Alfred, Ada, and Aunt Nora remained at the play. Since no one would ever accuse Ada or her sister of having a liberal attitude toward sex, the dancers were probably not so lewd as Theo's reaction suggests.

Theo appreciated that Harris respected her fastidious sensibility, and back at the hotel, they talked comfortably. Then the conversation turned to Theo's future. She announced that she now wanted to become a professional writer and that she had submitted several stories for publication in a magazine. She expected Harris to be impressed, but instead he responded that he would not allow her to pursue a career if they were to marry.

Seeing the stunned look on Theo's face, Harris realized that he had made a serious mistake. He quickly retracted his words and stuttered that he was proud that she was ambitious.

Theo's misgivings returned. The gold collar of marriage would choke her aspirations. She decided that she must show Harris that if she did marry him, she would not be a passive wife whom he could control. She would marry him only if he accepted her strong will and intention to do whatever she desired.

A short time later, Theo found an opportunity to prove her mettle. She and Ada were talking in a church in Luxembourg, when a gendarme approached. He warned Theo that, if she weren't quiet, he would put her out. Insulted by the man's rude tone, Theo calmly replied that she would neither stop talking nor leave. The gendarme grabbed her arm, jostled her to a standing position, and pushed her toward the door of the church. Theo went along with the officer but then began forcing him to circle back. Breaking free of his grip, she sat down next to Ada and glared at him. Intimidated by the short, blonde American girl, the gendarme left.

Theo hoped that the incident would show Harris that she had strength and determination, but he seemed unaware of what had occurred. "My spunky fit was all for nothing," she complained. Theo was perplexed. She liked Harris, but she much preferred the company of Alfred. She began avoiding her suitor. Instead, she visited galleries and museums with her father.

Alfred was one of the first major buyers of Impressionist paintings. Self-educated about art, he had developed keen aesthetic tastes and appreciated the genius of modern artists, some of whom he knew personally. Mary Cassatt was a close friend as was James Whistler, and recently he had met Claude Monet.

At first Theo was skeptical about Impressionism. She suspected that some men were using "this coming craze to make inexcusable pictures," and were selling them to "the uninstructed (or fools)." After Alfred explained to Theo why he valued the movement, she saw the paintings differently, though with some reservations. "Now the impressionists are interesting," she admitted, "but I doubt if any of the work they are now doing will last."

As Theo's informal art education continued, she became enthusiastic about Monet. She admired the artist's pictures of haycocks, especially one painted in the early morning with the sun shining on the frost.

Alfred bought two of Monet's *Haystacks*: the picture Theo liked and another in which the light had changed to later in the day. Theo entreated him to buy a third. Alfred refused because he did not like that particular painting. "Too bad," Theo sighed. She now believed that someday anything by Monet would cost a small fortune.

After meeting the art critic, Sheridan Ford, Theo read his book, *Art: A Commodity,* about the business of collecting art. The following day, when she and her father visited another dealer who specialized in the work of young artists, Theo did not say much about the paintings' artistic merit. Influenced by Ford's book, she urged Alfred to buy seven pictures. "They are very cheap and the day will come, and it's not far away," she was certain, "when they will be worth two or three times the present price." She was pleased when Alfred purchased a large picture of a young girl at her toilette by Tournier. It was not only "a *very* fine picture," but "*very* cheap."

As Theo and Alfred made the rounds of galleries and private collections, she concluded, "*Now* I like Corot and think him one of the greatest of landscape painters. Such poetry in art I never saw before, wonderful!" She had become convinced that the Impressionists "have something new to say and I also think it well worth paying attention to. Did men of any other school ever paint sunlight as the Impressionists do? No!"

She spent most of her time with Alfred and ignored Harris until she learned that he had attended a Parisian students' ball, which, she said, "was not a nice place to go." She hated lack of refinement. "All men lack it a little," she knew, and there was "depravity in everyone," but "it must be fought against and not encouraged by going to places where none but evil thoughts come to the mind." She seemed not to care that Alfred had also attended the entertainment.

Theo fumed, "I have taken such a dislike to Harris. I hate to see him or hear him talk." At the same time, she did not have the courage to tell him how she felt.

That evening, she went to her father's hotel room. Sitting in his chair, Alfred looked like a bank president. His straight blond hair was combed neatly back, and he wore wire-framed spectacles. He motioned to Theo to come over and sit on his lap. With his arm around her, Alfred asked what was the matter. Theo sobbed. She didn't want to marry Harris.

"You must not feel you are bound to love Harris," Alfred responded.

"I never want to become engaged to a man unless I am so much in love that I cannot do otherwise," Theo declared.

Alfred nodded. As much as he wanted the marriage, he knew that Theo was not ready. He told her not to worry. He would speak with Harris.

Theo's spirits lifted. When she returned to Cleveland, she would not be an engaged woman. She promised Alfred that she would go along with Ada's plan for a debutante party. She would buy beautiful dresses in Paris and be a society girl.

About to leave France and go on to Spain, Theo hoped that, after Alfred spoke with Harris, he would leave their party. She was disappointed, however. Harris boarded the train to Madrid and shared a compartment with Alfred.

From the train's window, Theo gazed at the landscape and felt soothed by the picturesque Spanish countryside: the olive and orange groves, the hedges of century plant that bloomed only once every decade, and the cacti. The small stone houses, she noted, looked as if "they had grown up from the soil." She hated buildings that stood out like sore thumbs in nature. They should seem to be a natural part of the surrounding terrain.

Leaving the train, she saw that outside influences were spoiling the native Spanish culture. "What makes me groan," she complained, "is to see intensely American gimcracks and underwear for sale in their shops."

She resumed a friendly comradeship with Harris, and the two went sightseeing to the royal palace and the Prado. Delighted that he was "behaving so beautifully," she began to wonder if she might yet grow to love him.

From Cadiz, the group sailed to Tangiers. The sea was rough, and when they went on to Gibraltar, the waters were so turbulent that, to escape their small cabins, the party sat on the deck, where the spray soaked them. Despite the danger and discomfort, Theo enjoyed looking at the mountainous shores of Spain and Africa, which were especially beautiful with the shadows of storm clouds on them.

In Pisa, Theo caught a cold and stayed in the hotel room. Deciding to work on her ambition of becoming a writer, she composed a story but was "afraid no one would like it."

In Rome, the Popes attended a gathering at an ancient palace. Theo sat admiring the ornate loveliness of the surroundings, when, suddenly, a riot occurred outside. Unemployed workers were smashing store windows and calling for bread for their starving families. Theo felt sorry for them even though the guide explained the uprising as being encouraged by priests: "The Catholics cannot get over their loss of power, so if they can find a chance to make the king uncomfortable, they do it."

By mid-February, Harris evidently realized that Theo was not going to marry him. Without telling her, he left and went alone to Florence. Soon after, Theo and Alfred had another father-daughter talk. This time, she informed him that she did not want to assume the role of society girl that she had agreed to after rejecting Harris. She wanted a career, though she did not know what it should be. She had given up the idea of being a writer.

As always, Alfred tried to help. "Would she like to become a bookkeeper?" he asked. She would not. She wanted to do something important and aesthetic. Believing that his daughter had artistic ability and appreciating her desire to create something beautiful and permanent, Alfred came up with a startling suggestion. Why not consider architecture?

Alfred's idea was not so radical as it might seem. He thought Theo might like to design her very own house. That is, she would draw a picture of a house, which he would then have built on a vacant lot he owned near his Cleveland plant. But Theo did not want to live in an industrialized city. She always had dreamed of being in the country. Alfred replied that this was fine. He would buy land outside of Cleveland for a farmhouse. She would live in the farmhouse, manage the farm, and sell dairy products and canned fruits to their Cleveland friends.

Theo liked the idea. Now that the future was settled, that she would be an unmarried, independent woman, she mentioned Harris's departure. She felt guilty that she had consented to Harris's accompanying the Popes on their trip and then had hurt him. "Nonsense," Alfred replied. She should not blame herself. If there were any censure about what had occurred, he would shoulder it.

After Naples and Pompeii, the family returned to Paris, where Ada and Theo went to Pingot's and Redfern's to buy dresses. Their butler, Earnest Bohlen, happened to be out walking when, by chance, he encountered Harris. Theo thought that the meeting was "a trifle embarrassing for all of us," but Alfred contacted Harris, and the two went to the theatre that evening. Theo spent the next day in bed.

Learning from Alfred that Harris was not completely discouraged, Theo decided to reconsider his proposal. "The time may come when I will be sorry I refused him," she speculated, "because I really believe I would like to get married and this will be certainly my only chance." She knew that no other man would want to marry a woman who was "perfectly able to take care of and think for [her]self." Harris, however, did not contact her, and in April, the Popes left for England.

On their way to London, passing fields dotted with sheep and farmhouses of brick and stone, Theo felt moved by the delicate loveliness of the scene. Rural England reminded her of Farmington's peaceful, idyllic countryside. From London, the family made excursions to Hyde Park, Kensington Gardens, and the homes of Carlyle and George Eliot. Inspired by the houses and the grounds, Theo began drawing a plan for a farmhouse. She had doubts, though. Was Alfred letting her follow a "will-o-the wisp" with his encouragement to become a sort of architect? She confronted him and received the reassurance, "No...but keep the design [of the farmhouse] plain and inexpensive."

A few days later, Alfred told Theo that Harris had arrived in London and wanted to speak to her. She went to the hotel lobby, where he was waiting. His straight brown hair was neatly combed, his boyish face was clean-shaven, and he wore a spotless three-piece suit.

Theo saw that Harris was on the verge of tears. Without any preliminary conversation, he blurted out that he would do anything to make Theo love him.

She shook her head and replied that the situation was hopeless.

"Is there anyone else?" he asked earnestly.

"No," she answered. She liked and respected him, but, unfortunately, she did not love him.

Harris wanted to know why not. Did she think him too young? "You cannot prevent me from trying to improve myself," he countered, "and grow more manly!"

Theo repeated there was no hope.

Did she think him unsophisticated? "Would it make any difference in your feelings toward me," he demanded to know, "if I were to study?"

Theo shook her head again. "If a girl loves a man, such things are of no account....You cannot force true love into being," she explained.

Suddenly she thought of a perfect solution. Perhaps Harris could learn to fancy her cousin Betty and she, him. They were "so suited to one another."

Disheartened, Harris left and immediately booked passage to sail home.

"I feel like my old dreadful self, am blue and *nothing seems worth while,* not even the farm," Theo wrote the following day. Perhaps she should have accepted Harris even if she did not love him. "He would try to make me happy and I think any woman, no matter how independent she thinks herself, is happier if married."

Then, bitterness followed regret. Theo hated all men. "They are wicked, more wicked than any other living thing," she sputtered. "They have the cream of everything on earth and they don't even appreciate the fact." How could she possibly marry? "The idea of my *wanting* to cherish a fondness for anything of that kind....I had better be keeping my mind on my farm and try to lead a good useful single life."

A few days after Harris's departure, the Popes returned to Paris and arranged for a doctor to examine Theo. He said that she had a certain condition that had begun long ago and most likely would last for several more years. Blaming Ada for not having taken her to a doctor years earlier, Theo wrote that she would forgive her mother "if she only loved me."

Theo's depression became so severe that she underwent electricity treatments, a remedy often used on neurasthenic women. The patient sat in a tub of water through which an electric current was run. Though the current was mild, it was a fairly dangerous practice, and sometimes a death from electrocution occurred.

The treatments made Theo feel worse. Unable to stop crying, she told Alfred that the source of her suffering was the terrible relationship she had with Ada. Alfred was sympathetic. He did not contradict Theo nor defend his wife. Instead, he advised Theo to be philosophical. That Ada was not a loving mother was difficult to bear, he agreed, but Theo should consider "how many more ills other people have to contend with."

By May, Theo's spirits lifted. At Versailles, using a new camera that Alfred had purchased, she photographed the little dairy farm and mills that Louis XVI had built so that he and Marie Antoinette could dress and play at being peasants. The pastoral scene was charming. It did not occur to Theo that her own romantic dream of living on a farm was similar to the affectations of the jaded royal couple.

The Fontainebleau palace gave Theo ideas for the interior of the farmhouse she had resumed designing. A beautiful room in brown was an inspiration. "How fine a living room would be done in that color; dark oak, brown carpet and paper with ecru colors in it," and "then have tulips in the window ledges."

In mid-May, the Popes were back in London, where Theo visited art galleries. She found little to praise at the Royal Academy. At Hampton Palace, there was "scarcely a picture worth looking at." She concluded that England was "certainly not a nation of artists."

The true art of England was its gardens and the landscape. Theo thought the Kew Gardens "inexpressibly lovely. The tree forms are superb and I never saw flowers more thoughtfully arranged in regard to their colors." Their beauty made her "long all the more for a country home." A few days later, she bought a bolt of blue gingham for a simple dress. Like Marie Antoinette, she could pretend to be a peasant.

Theo enjoyed drawing her farmhouse, but she decided that she wanted to become a true architect. Wouldn't it be grand to spend one's life creating buildings that would make the world more beautiful! She was uneasy about pursuing this ambition, however. Architects were men. If she were to become an architect, "I would be rather mannish," she despaired. "And of all the unlovely things in the world an unwomanly woman is the worst." At the same time, she worried, "If I do not act, I shall wake some morning to find myself middle aged and sorrowing because I have not tried to make the world I touch a little better."

Altruism really was not the only reason why Theo wanted a career. She dreaded life back in Cleveland "reading every morning from nine until twelve and then having the afternoon to drive, see my friends etc. and the evening for anything that should happen to turn up." Without a husband, children or a career, she imagined, "what a lonely life I have before me."

Concerned that people would consider her unwomanly and afraid that she might not be able to understand the technical aspects of architecture, Theo briefly returned to her previous ambition to become a writer, but she wondered, "Do I have enough brains to become a writer? I could perhaps learn to express myself well but have I anything to say?"

That evening, Theo asked Alfred what he thought about her writing a novel. "What do you plan to write about?" he inquired.

"Quakers," she responded.

Alfred knew that Theo had admired his Quaker mother Theodate to such an extent that she had taken her name, but he believed that to write about Quakers, it would be necessary for Theo not only to study the subject but to live in a Quaker community. He doubted that his daughter had the understanding or strength for the undertaking. Theo was disappointed, but she agreed with him.

"It's a shame I was born with a desire to *do* and *be* something in *particular*," she observed, "if I am not also born with the ability to accomplish it."

During an unusually hot June in London, the Popes attended Ibsen's *A Doll's House*, which Theo thought was one of the best plays she had ever seen. Inspired by the courage of the character of Nora, who asserted that she could live independent of men, Theo continued to work on the design of the farmhouse.

The Popes arrived in Brussels on July 4, Alfred's forty-eighth birthday. During the next month they journeyed through Holland, Germany, and Switzerland. When Theo reached Dresden, she received a "short but particularly sweet" letter from Mary Hillard.

In September, the Popes boarded the steamer, the S.S. *City of New York*, and headed home. Theo was too shy to join a group of young people who were singing college songs on deck. She wrote that she did not have "the faculty of getting acquainted with strangers." Instead, she stayed in the stateroom and read Henry James's novel, *Portrait of a Lady*.

After the Popes arrived home, Theo returned to Philadelphia for another rest cure. The treatment did not help, and, back in Cleveland, she remained mostly in her room. Meanwhile, Ada made elaborate preparations for Theo's debut. On the evening of the party, Theo wore a gown she had bought in Paris, an Algerian dress of thin cream silk with a full skirt and full sleeves. Over it, she wore a gold embroidered zouave jacket with a rolling Medici collar. Theo did not fit the Victorian ideal of the delicate beauty with a wasp waist, but the cream and gold outfit complemented her blonde hair, flawless complexion, and blue eyes.

"Papa, Mama and my Aunts seem to think I have grown so pretty," she remarked afterwards. "I am so pleased as I have spent so much time in being homely."

Feeling better, Theo began to go out in society, where the main topic of conversation concerned the forthcoming weddings of recently engaged couples. Theo had agreed to be a bridesmaid at the marriage of a cousin, George Brooks, in May, but she was nervous about meeting Harris there. She had not seen Harris since he had left England and sailed home alone. In order to avoid her, Harris told George he would not attend the wedding, but Theo feared he might change his mind.

As the date approached, Theo became more apprehensive. "After having been so intimate with him," she explained, "I should feel so constrained if I had to talk to him." As much as she protested that she did not want to see him, however, she told her diary the opposite. "Lately— that is during the last two or three months," she admitted, "I have taken it into my head to fancy myself in love with him."

Harris kept his word and stayed away from the wedding. Now that he was ignoring her, Theo became obsessed with him. "I have had Harris on my mind almost constantly," she confessed. "I love to hear anyone say his name and I speak of the Whittemores every time I get a chance simply because I love to say the name myself." But then she read the book, *Romantic Love and Personal Beauty*, which convinced her that she did not really love Harris.

The truth was that she did not want to marry any man. She accepted an eligible bachelor's invitation to a cotillion, and on the afternoon of the ball, she became agitated and nervous, complained of a violent headache, and vomited. When her escort appeared at the Popes' home, she forced herself to go with him. She felt better when she saw the guests dancing on the lawn under an immense tent made of gaily colored cheesecloth, and she enjoyed an amusing dance in which everyone had to change partners and one man was left to dance with a stuffed tiger. She also liked the favors the guests received: silver-backed hat brushes for the men and silver, heart-shaped scent bottles for the women. But later she professed that she had no interest in attending any more balls and that she was weary of teas, luncheons, and society life in general.

Lethargy and depression descended once more. Then Theo received a letter from a former French teacher at Miss Porter's School who wrote that, after moving to Tallapoosa, she and her daughter were unwell and in dire financial straits. Mme. Charpentier asked whether Theo knew anyone who would pay Pauline for embroidering or crocheting because "there is nothing else for a young lady to do here."

Wanting to help the unfortunate women, Theo asked Alfred for advice. He suggested that she send a check for $50 and then outline a plan by which Miss Porter's alumnae could contribute a monthly sum to support Madame and Pauline.

Sarah Porter disapproved of Mme. Charpentier's asking former students for financial help, but she supported Theo's plan and suggested "$50 or $75 a month for 5 or 6 months" as sufficient. She warned Theo not to be too generous and hasty, fearing that Theo's "heart and hands are so ready" that the Charpentiers would take advantage of her.

With zest, Theo collected $1,000, more than enough for the two women to live on. Helping the mother and daughter had another benefit: it lifted Theo from depression.

During these months, Theo still held onto the dream of living on a farm, but not near Cleveland. She wanted to return to Farmington to be near Sarah Porter and Mary Hillard. She realized that the idea was radical. What would people think of a young, unmarried woman living alone so far from her family? She doubted that Alfred and Ada would ever allow it, but, as she approached her twenty-third birthday, she became determined to try to create a new life. Theo asked Alfred if she could rent a cottage in Farmington and was not surprised when he refused. Surprisingly, Ada approved, assuring Theo that Alfred "will consent if I talk to him."

The reason for Ada's agreeing was that Harris had given up working for Alfred in Cleveland and was now living with his parents in Naugatuck, a town close to Farmington. Ada hoped that proximity would again sway Theo. After Ada spoke with Alfred, he agreed.

"Think what supreme fun it would be to have a simple little house with a rag carpet, make my own butter, and have a pig and chickens," Theo told her friends. She saw nothing absurd about a society girl's running a farm. Most everyone else, however, thought the plan outlandish.

"How would I do for a 'hired man'? I'm right at home with a plow or scythe, and milking is second nature to me," cousin George teased. "Rainy days I could churn and do chores around the house. I've had experience with hens, their training and education; calves look on me as a brother, and no one can feed pigs with a surer or gentler touch than mine, for I've devoted considerable attention to the decanting and serving of swill....Four dollars a week, and board, buys me."

Theo ignored humorous comments and raised eyebrows, but she was not really confident. "To stay away from Papa and Mama just as if I were married only without the sustaining love—it makes my heart feel just a little bit heavy," she admitted. Then, suspecting that, by giving permission, Alfred and Ada might simply be testing her spunk, Theo made a resolution: "Now I'll show them."

Page from Theo's diary. *(HS)*.

Earnest Bohlen, the Popes' butler. *(HS)*.

FOUR

"It will be a Pope house"
1890—1901

IN JUNE 1890, Theo arrived in Farmington and immediately ran to Sarah Porter's house. When she began to explain why she had returned, the elderly woman interrupted. She disapproved of a young lady's living alone and refused to listen further. Theo began to cry and left "in despair and dreadfully depressed." Later Miss Porter relented. "Well, you know, Theodate," she sighed, "I wouldn't approve of it for anyone but you."

Accompanied by Mary Hillard, Theo searched the village for a house to rent. Spotting an old, brown saltbox house on High Street, about two blocks from the school, they stepped from their carriage and walked up to it. No one was home. They peered through the windows. Then Jimmie O'Rourke, the old man that owned the cottage, came into the yard and asked what they wanted. O'Rourke lived in the cottage but was willing to rent it.

Even though Theo realized that she would have to do a great deal of cleaning, painting, and papering, she told O'Rourke she wanted the house. She then contacted a local lawyer and banker and negotiated a ten-months' lease.

Theo took charge of repairing and remodeling. She directed the painters to tear off old wallpaper, whitewash the ceilings, and apply the first coat of paint on the walls. She ordered a new furnace from New York and told the workmen where to place the furnace registers. Discovering that O'Rourke's house was filled with vermin, she bought sulfur to fumigate it and had the workers wash the walls and floors with lye.

Theo had agreed to let O'Rourke sleep in the house until September 1, but the workers threw his bed out the window along with the other infested furniture. Theo offered to pay for his lodgings, but, if he preferred sleeping in the house, she would put the bed back and refumigate the room after he left.

Theo also informed O'Rourke that the roof was rotten, and he replied that he would patch it. She countered that it was his duty to put on a new roof. If he didn't, she would do it and deduct the cost from the rent she had promised to pay.

Furious, the old man retorted, "I'm going to have the law on you!"

"Why?" Theo asked in surprise.

O'Rourke could hardly contain himself. The night before, the workmen who had thrown his bed out the window had told the whole town about the vermin. Because of this society girl, he was a laughingstock in Farmington.

Theo apologized but then added that his humiliation did not excuse him from paying for a new roof. Unable to contain his rage, the old man ranted on. Theo remained calm. Finally, she turned her back and abruptly left.

Later that evening, O'Rourke quieted down and visited Theo at the inn where she was staying. He blamed his temper on drinking and agreed to have the roof replaced at his expense.

Theo ordered tin for the roof, but, preferring shingles, O'Rourke refused to pay for it. Tired of arguing, Theo directed her banker to threaten that if he didn't put on a new roof and pay for it, Miss Pope would consult a lawyer. O'Rourke still refused to pay for the tin, but he did shingle the roof.

Theo oversaw every part of the renovation of the house. Watching the carpenter put in a sink and table, she stopped him and told him how to do it. "The table would have been wrong if I had not been there," she asserted. She warned the carpenter's young son not to run around barefoot in the yard because of the broken glass, and she wiped mercuric chloride from the child's face.

For the cottage's interior, Theo bought furniture, a rubber bathtub, an icebox, and lots of dimity for curtains. Green was the prevailing color. In an upstairs room, she used wallpaper that had green vines with delicate yellow-and-pink flowers on a very light green background, and she tinted the woodwork the same color. For her bedroom, she chose blue-and-gray paper. First the woodwork was white, but, because it looked too cold, she had it and the floor repainted yellow.

During this time, women engaged in restoring old houses, so Theo's efforts were not unusual. But no one expected the young woman to take such complete charge of the project and supervise every detail of the restoration. Theo's goal was to make the cottage look as it might have almost a century earlier, and she succeeded. Miss Porter exclaimed, "It is an exact duplication of the farmhouse of eighty years ago."

Theo named the cottage "The O'Rourkery" after her landlord. She took photographs of it and sent them to friends. Alice Hamilton had heard from other Farmington girls that Theo's cottage was adorable, but "I had never imagined it half as pretty." She especially admired Theo's bedroom. "Your room looks exactly like you, much more than your rooms in Cleveland did. I know it is all white and dainty and clean and fresh-airy." Theo had that same look—"as if you had just come from a bath all the time."

While staying at the inn until she moved into the cottage, Theo met several young women who were rest cure patients of a local doctor. "He is the kind of man that most women think entrancingly handsome," she observed. "So you may imagine how his women patients bow down and worship him as a god."

One evening, a patient was missing. Searchers found her hat and coat on the banks of the dangerous, fast-running Farmington River, and discovered footprints going down to the water. For three days, townsmen dragged the river bottom with hooks until they found the body. Theo heard that the girl had felt guilty about the expense of her illness and had committed suicide after her mother had dismissed a private nurse.

Upset about the incident but thinking it could provide "a fine theme for a story," Theo scribbled some notes, describing the villainous mother as "a little or rather very careful of expense and impressing it all the time on a nervous daughter."

On September 28, 1890, Theo moved into the O'Rourkery. "I look around once in a while to be sure it is reality. I am in my house and living here!" she wrote in her diary. The first night two Miss Porter's girls kept her company, and she cooked them breakfast in the morning: "uneatable potatoes, eggs with cream, steak, and coffee."

Although Theo lived with a maid in the rented house, she made every meal herself. At night, she woke frequently to light a candle to see what time it was so that she could arise at 6:00 a.m. to build the kitchen fire. "The experience was all so deliciously new to me," she later recalled, "that I felt I had stepped over a frame into a picture."

Theo spent part of every day with Mary Hillard, whom she considered her "very dearest friend, my Mary." They went on drives and walks, and, in the evenings, inspired by the critical study of the Bible currently popular in Germany and Victorian England, the two young women read the Bible aloud and analyzed it. Theo also organized a club that met in the O'Rourkery sitting room on Saturdays. The members included old Mr. Norton, a man over seventy who had written a book about flies; several teachers; and Mary. At the meetings, each person would stand up and talk about a subject of current interest.

At Christmas, Theo returned to Cleveland. Almost as soon as she arrived, she became ill with a cold and nervousness. She wrote that she "danced, played whist in the day time, had a surfeit of music, played twenty questions, told weird stories around the dining room table with the lights turned low, etc. etc." but "was by no means sorry when I got on the train to start for my beloved O'Rourkery."

In the spring, Theo planted a garden, which chickens belonging to a neighboring family, the McCahills, soon discovered. Knowing that the neighbors were poor, Theo sent over posts and wire so that they could enclose their fowl in a chicken yard. But the McCahills neither acknowledged nor used the materials. Theo gave a last warning, which was ignored. Then she bought an air gun.

Seeing several chickens in the garden, Theo went to the doorway of the O'Rourkery, raised the gun, and pulled the trigger. A chicken keeled over. Unable to believe her marksmanship, she aimed and shot again. Another chicken sank to the ground.

Theo directed her maid to carry the carcasses to the neighbors' house. Instead of capitulating, however, the McCahills retaliated. They took the two dead birds, tied their legs together, and slung them over a branch of a tree near Theo's garden. In a few days, the odor was so strong that she could not open the cottage's north windows.

Money rather than confrontation won the chicken war. After the lease expired, Theo bought both O'Rourke's cottage and the small house owned by, as she later wrote, "unfortunate neighbors for me"—presumably, the McCahills. She had the house moved and attached to the O'Rourkery, added to its width and length, and put on a gambrel roof. She called the addition the "Gundy," a reference to Miss Porter's School's student newspaper, *The Sal Magundy*. She also bought forty-two acres behind the two houses for farmland.

During the summer of 1892, Theo left Farmington to go with Alfred and Ada and some relatives on a train trip west across the country and on to Alaska. When their train reached St. Paul, Theo and Alfred viewed the art collection of a railway capitalist. They were disappointed. "Mr. Hill hasn't advanced yet to impressionism," Theo observed.

As much as she delighted in the landscape and was awed by such sights as the Badlands and the Grand Canyon, Theo was disgusted by the architecture of the buildings she saw on the trip. "The hotels are blots on the face of the earth, their style of architecture is so inexcusable," she noted. She also could not understand why materials were used that were foreign to the area. "If they had only built them of the pine logs which are so abundant," she observed, "they would have saved a great deal of expense besides having buildings in keeping with the surroundings. They could have made them just as large and had broad porches with rough pine pillars simply barked and the small branches cut off." She drew sketches of what she meant.

In Butte, which Theo called "certainly the most God forsaken place I ever saw," she noticed a large, pretentious, stone house amid the dreary brick and wooden one-story houses. It made her "sick to even think of the way it must be furnished." From Portland, Oregon, the group took a steamer to Alaska, where Theo was mesmerized by the sunsets and the incessant noise of the Taku and Muir glaciers.

Upon returning to Farmington in the fall, Theo learned that Mary had left Miss Porter's School for a position at St. Margaret's School in nearby Waterbury. Theo was disappointed that she would not be seeing Mary every day, but she still enjoyed living in the cottage. She loved Farmington to the extent that she felt protective of the village. Learning that Miss Porter had ordered the ancient wooden gates at the Old Cemetery to be taken down and carried away, Theo informed her that she lacked an appreciation for the landmark, and Miss Porter had the gates restored.

Theo begged Miss Porter to allow a photographer to take her portrait, but she refused. A few days later, he arrived with all his paraphernalia. Miss Porter just shook her gray head at Theo. "Well, you do run around town doing just as you choose," she sighed, and sat for the photograph.

Although Theo saw Harris now and then, and they considered themselves good friends, his living nearby in Naugatuck did not result in a resumption of the young couple's romance. Theo finally told Alfred and Ada what, most likely, she had earlier confessed to Betty: "The truth of the matter is the idea of marriage is really repellent to me."

In the mid-1890s, Theo adopted the Quaker forms of address, *thee*, *thy*, and *thou*, when she wrote to her parents, but even though she admired Alfred's heritage, she had no desire to become a Quaker. She also had left the Presbyterian and Episcopal churches, which Ada attended, because she had not found them satisfying.

Partly because Mary Hillard was a believer and because of Theo's out-of-body experience as a child, Theo was attracted to spiritualism, the controversial new "religion" of 19th-century America. Spiritualism had become widespread in America after the Civil War, when almost every family lost loved ones and yearned to communicate with them. When mediums entered the trance state, they reunited the living with the dead by automatic writing or "channeling" (speaking) the spirits' words. The famous Fox sisters convinced thousands of followers that mysterious rapping sounds spelled out messages from the spiritual world—until the girls confessed to a talent for cracking their toes. By the end of the 19th century, exposés of frauds had discredited spiritualism, but it continued to attract a large following.

To combat the mockery of their faith, spiritualists in England established the Society for Psychical Research. The society's mission was to investigate allegations of psychical phenomena in order to expose the fraudulent and to verify authentic supernatural occurrences. The famous American philosopher, psychologist, and spiritualist, William James, explained the purpose of such investigations through the metaphor of a "white crow." "If you wish to upset the law that all crows are black, you mustn't seek to show that no crows are; it is enough if you prove one single crow to be white." Just *one* unexplainable occult incident or *one* sane and honest medium would validate the existence of psychical phenomena.

The trance medium, Leonora Piper, whom William James had discovered, was the extraordinary "white crow" of spiritualism. For twenty-five years, the American branch of the Society for Psychical Research, which James and others had founded, paid Mrs. Piper a salary and oversaw her activities so that its researchers could study the trances of the medium in a controlled, scientific environment. By engaging a detective to spy on Piper, the society made certain that she was not getting information from earthly sources. Although the medium occasionally made errors, she continued to astound society investigators with the information she transmitted. Professor James wrote, "I cannot resist the conviction that knowledge appears which she has never gained by the ordinary waking use of her eyes and ears and wits."

In addition to the highly respected William James, other distinguished people supported the Society for Psychical Research. Its founders were the English university academics, Edmund Gurney and Frederic Myers, along with other prestigious figures, such as Prime Minister Arthur Balfour. Its members included two bishops and several famous authors, including John Ruskin; Alfred, Lord Tennyson; and Sir Arthur Conan Doyle. Among the corresponding members who contributed articles and letters to its *Proceedings* were Sigmund Freud and Carl Jung.

Spiritualists also included the gullible who were entranced by a medium's ghostly intonations, the lifting of tables, and other supposedly psychical phenomena. Some regarded spiritualism as compatible with traditional Christianity. The Christian heaven and the spiritualists' Summerland seemed similar, although spiritualists had the advantage of not believing in hell.

Quakers, in particular, were drawn to spiritualism. Like the Friends, spiritualists employed no ministers. Every person had access to the beyond. The souls of the dead spoke to children, men, and women, because all human beings, no matter what race, religion or sex, were simply containers of souls.

Women were especially blessed with having "light," the ability to contact the spiritual world. Female spiritualists confidently spoke on public platforms during an era when women and children were expected to be seen but rarely heard. Spiritualism supported the effort to win woman suffrage, and in the 1890s, leading suffragists Susan B. Anthony, Charlotte Perkins Gilman, and Margaret Sanger attended a special Woman Suffrage Day at Lily Dale, a spiritualist resort.

Spiritualists blamed society for many illnesses suffered by women. They believed that depression, or neurasthenia, resulted from loveless marriages and repeated, unwanted pregnancies. They also warned that restrictive clothes, an unhealthy diet, and lack of exercise made women weak and sick. In contrast to Protestant clergy who usually portrayed the body, especially the female body, as inherently prone to disease, spiritualists insisted that women were naturally healthy. Instead of seeking rest cures that involved the subjugation of a female patient's will to that of a male doctor, spiritualists advised depressed women to go out into the fresh air, exercise, and wear loose clothing.

As she became more familiar with spiritualism, Theo followed its doctrines and felt better than she had in years. She bicycled two to three miles every day and kept to a special regimen that included eating plenty of bread, cheese, parsley, and lettuce. She also tried to show no anger. Now that she felt strong, healthy, and confident, she decided she was ready to pursue a career as an architect.

Alice Hamilton, who already had become a physician, encouraged Theo but warned about trying to learn architecture on her own. Alice mentioned that Agnes also hoped to become an architect. She had drawn a plan of a house and purchased architect's implements: compasses, needles, tracing paper, and rulers. But without the support and direction of mentors, Agnes had not made much progress and had given up.

In the progressive 1890s, women had begun to enter professions that previously were exclusively male, such as medicine, but a female architect was almost unheard of. Almost all architects were white, middle-class males. Cornell University's architectural program did admit Margaret Hicks, who in 1878 published a student's project for a cottage, but she was not heard from after that. In 1893, Sophia Hayden, a graduate of MIT, designed the Women's Building at the World's Columbian Exposition, but then she had a nervous breakdown and no longer practiced architecture.

Because of Theo's mediocre academic record and difficulty with mathematics, she did not consider applying to either Cornell or MIT. Again she turned to Alfred for advice. Believing that Theo had the ability to become an architect and always willing to do whatever he could to make her happy, Alfred decided on a course of action. First he told her that what she needed to learn was architectural history. Alfred then contacted art history professors at Princeton University and asked whether they would teach his daughter privately through the mail.

In the fall of 1893, Theo received a letter from Professor Allan Marquand. He was willing to help but discouraged learning through correspondence. "We could be of much more service to you in Princeton, if you were here," he responded. "But this is a question for you and your parents to decide. If your Father and Mother would come with you to Princeton—say on Wednesday—I should be very happy to see them."

After the visit, Theo moved to the university town and met privately with professors during the winter and spring of 1894 and for several months in 1895 and 1896. She studied art history and filled notebooks with pictures of pyramids, Greek statues, and Renaissance paintings. She did not receive training as an architect, but she had started along that path. What she needed was experience, and Alfred provided an opportunity to acquire it.

Alfred arranged for Theo to work with the prestigious firm of McKim, Mead, and White on a retirement home for the Popes in Farmington. They would keep their Euclid Avenue mansion so that Alfred could stay there when he needed to conduct business in Cleveland, but he and Ada would reside mainly in the new house.

Although there were prominent people living in Farmington and in the next town of Avon, Ada was unhappy about the idea of leaving Cleveland high society. But she always deferred to Alfred. "I am pleased that he should have what he wishes," she told Theo, "when he is so good to us."

Theo took charge of the project. She would use the forty-two acres behind the cottage and buy more land to accommodate both a farm and the house. She asked Harris for help, and, even though he was now married, he readily agreed. "Your judgment and Harris's will be mine without question," Alfred telegraphed from abroad, where he was adding more paintings to his collection.

On August 27, 1896, the local Farmington newspaper announced that she had bought over 250 acres. "At the earnest solicitation of Miss Theodate Pope who has a home on High Street," the article explained, "her father, who lives in Cleveland, Ohio, has consented to come to Farmington, purchase some real estate and settle in town."

William Rutherford Mead, of McKim, Mead, and White, went along with the unorthodox arrangement of working with a client's daughter and accepting only a partial commission. From Austria, Alfred advised Theo, whom he addressed as his "little Rascal," to present her ideas to the architect and to have him assist in choosing the location for the house. Without asking anyone's opinion, however, Theo decided that the house was to sit on the top of a hill in the middle of the property, far back from the street, and face the back of the O'Rourkery.

Theo wanted to create what was loosely called a Colonial Revival house, that is, the kind of house that had been built before the Civil War. During the last part of the 19th century and the early 20th century, in a nostalgic longing for a simpler, more gracious time, architects recreated the houses of pre-industrialized America. Theo intended that her family's home look like a farmhouse—a rambling, white, wooden clapboard with shutters. She also knew that to satisfy Ada, the house would have to be elegant and suitable for entertaining.

She requested that the architect draw a preliminary plan based on her description, but asked him not to try to impress her with fancy lead coloring. Then, instead of using the architectural firm's sketches, Theo sent Mr. Mead the plans that she had been working on for the past few years: a three-story, twenty-eight room farmhouse with an open portico. The family would live in the front part of the house, and the servants' quarters would be in back. "In other words," she announced, "it will be a Pope house instead of a McKim, Mead and White."

At the same time that she felt it necessary to be honest and blunt, she was aware that Mead might resent a woman's asserting herself so strongly. "In conclusion, I will say that I am not nearly as difficult to deal with as this would seem," she added, "for I am very tolerant of advice and always open to suggestions and good reasoning."

"Thee was pretty plain in writing Mr. Mead," Alfred wrote, amused when he read a copy of her letter but advising more discretion in the future. "Such definiteness must be made very subtle and sugared in writing."

"Go ahead with road making, wall building, and tree planting this autumn," Alfred encouraged. He urged her to "lick it into shape" but not to *"plunge"* and spend more than necessary, and he cautioned about hiring workmen. "Don't make too hard and fast and long contract with a party until experience shows he works to advantage to our interest—all the time keep advising with Mr. Whittemore and Harris."

Ready to begin construction, Theo informed Mr. Mead that he was to deal only with her, not Alfred. "I expect to decide on all the details as well as all the more important questions that may arise," she wrote. "That must be clearly understood at the outset, so as to save unnecessary friction in the future."

Theo hired a local man, Richard Jones, as the builder, and she directed the construction of the house to the smallest detail. For example, she ordered the workmen to space the clapboards unequally in the carriage house for a less formal look. "Put cellar windows in front of house for draft. Have coal bin under all sitting rooms. Place cupboards on either side of windows. Wrap pipe surrounding stove pipe of Franklin stove in asbestos. Make upper back hall 46" by cutting it off the two bedrooms," she directed.

She penned impatient notes. *"I must have the blinds the same width!* Can you not get two windows in roof *higher up* in attic?" Next to a sketch, she wrote, "The pitch looks queer but it is just the way I want it." As in most New England farms, the barn was attached to the house by an ell. She positioned the front and back barn doors opposite each other so that when they were both open, one could see the rolling hills and purple mountains behind the house.

Theo designed the house to fit Alfred. She wanted the windows placed at a particular height. "It must be right for father and he is 5'11" tall," she explained. She also planned the rooms with Alfred's art collection in mind, making the archway of a door parallel the curve of a painting's door and raising the mantel of the dining room fireplace to accommodate Degas's *Jockeys*, a long, narrow painting.

While his daughter dealt with building his new home, Alfred enjoyed Italy and, in France, visited an old family friend, Mary Cassatt, at her country home. In past years he had acquired several of the artist's pictures. An American from an affluent family, Cassatt had the courage to live and paint abroad, where she had found acceptance in the otherwise all-male circle of Impressionist painters.

When Alfred arrived in London, he visited James McNeil Whistler. After dinner, they talked until midnight. Alfred told the painter that, although there was "a public booming of interest in art," most of his fellow Americans were ignorant and unsophisticated Philistines. Even in old age, Whistler was "full of ginger," Alfred reported to Theo.

In Whistler's correspondence to the Popes, he sent a menu from a French restaurant on which he had drawn a sketch of a seated woman with "Theodate" written next to it and the symbol, JIL. This was a logo that Theo had created in 1894, which she used on all her stationery. Theo never explained publicly what JIL meant, but she told a trance medium that it represented herself, Mary Hillard, and Mary's youngest brother John.

When Alfred and Ada returned from Europe, they stayed at their apartment at the Windsor Hotel in the heart of New York City. In March 1899, Theo joined them. One morning, promising Ada that she would return at 3:00 p.m. to go on social calls, Theo met Mary, who was in New York for a doctor's appointment.

Arriving back at the hotel, Theo was surprised to see Ada putting on a bonnet. "Why, Mama, I never knew you so near ready on time!" she teased. Suffering from a headache, Theo mentioned that she would like to take a nap first and then go visiting. Ada urged her to rest. "No," Theo decided. "You are all ready. Let's have it over with."

It was a chilly, sunny March afternoon. Theo and Ada's carriage went first to the fabulous mansion of Mrs. Louisine Havemeyer, who was not at home. As they drove along Madison Avenue, Theo suddenly saw flames in the sky. "Oh, Mama," she exclaimed, "there is a dreadful fire and I believe it is the Windsor."

Theo wanted to get out and run to the hotel, but Ada convinced her that it would be faster to go by carriage. As they approached the hotel, they saw a chaotic scene. Flames and smoke were billowing from the windows of the top floors, and policemen were trying to contain the large crowd that had gathered.

Broken glass and bricks were flying. To Ada's horror, Theo jumped from the carriage. Ada tried to grab her, but to no avail, and, because of the smoke and crowds, she lost sight of her. Ada cautiously stepped out and tried to go through the spectators to find Theo, but feeling faint, she returned to the carriage.

Mary Hillard also appeared at the scene. She had been on a streetcar when she saw the flames. Realizing that the fire was in the vicinity of the Windsor Hotel and worried about Theo and the Popes, she got off and ran to the site.

At the same time, Alfred and Harris had left Delmonico's Restaurant and were walking up Fifth Avenue to Durand Ruel's New York gallery when Harris noticed the fire in the distance. Alarmed, he urged the older man to hurry, but Alfred calmly replied, "Now, Harris, we cannot run and get all out of breath." Alfred tried to hail a cab, but there was none in sight. As the sky filled with flames and smoke, he turned and said, "We will walk fast."

When they reached the hotel, Alfred and Harris were able to approach the building. Although flames were visible in upper windows, the Popes' second floor parlor looked peaceful. There were no signs of fire or smoke behind the white lace curtains in the half-opened windows. Alfred approached a man standing with a ladder and asked him if he would retrieve some paintings from the Popes' apartment. The man agreed, climbed the ladder, went through the window and, a few minutes later, reappeared carrying Monet's *Haystacks*. After several trips, he rescued all the paintings.

Meanwhile, fighting through the crowd that had gathered in the street, Theo was lifted and carried by strangers' hands. Struggling, she got back on her feet and finally came close to the hotel. But a policeman stopped her.

"Do you have friends inside?" he asked.

"No, they are all out," she answered, almost out of breath.

"Then thank God that you are out and stand where you are."

Theo didn't argue. Forgetting about Ada back in the carriage, she stood mesmerized by the burning building. Suddenly, next to the Popes' parlor window, she saw a man on a ladder carrying a painting. She recognized Harris standing by the ladder, and she rushed across the street to him and Alfred.

That evening Ada, Alfred, Theo, and Mary checked into the Manhattan Hotel. As the hours went by, the Popes learned how fortunate they had been. The fire had taken the lives of those trapped above the third floor, and Theo had almost taken a nap in a room on the fourth floor. Ada's friend, Mrs. Upham, who had visited the Popes a few days earlier, looking, as Ada recalled, "so well in a handsome new black silk," had probably perished. At 3:00 p.m. she had been in her apartment on the sixth floor.

Others were missing as well. Many were known to be dead from fire, smoke inhalation, or injuries when they jumped to the pavement. Ada's maid had badly torn her hands coming down a rope. As Alfred listened to the reports, he felt chagrined. He said that if he had been aware of the severity of the fire, he never would have tried to rescue the paintings. The following day, the front pages of the newspapers were filled with reports and photographs of the fire, including a picture of a man on a ladder handing a painting down to another man.

During the fall of 1899, Theo took a brief vacation from building the Popes' country house. With a group of young people, including Betty, Mary, Mary's brother John, and Belle, she went on a camping trip to Squam Lake in New Hampshire.

Theo traveled with John by canoe to the campsite. Suddenly, the young man lost his balance, fell out, and disappeared under the water, taking Theo's satchel with him. She sat dumbfounded and terrified, but John quickly reappeared. "I'm afraid that the satchel is at the bottom of the lake," he said woefully. The bag contained jewelry worth about $170, but Theo laughed, relieved that he was all right.

One night, Theo and John paddled into Bear Cove to watch the sun set and the moon rise. While they waited, the Yale law student expressed his exasperation with Theo and his sister's spiritualist beliefs.

"We are so much older than you," Theo patiently reminded him. John was ten years younger than Theo. Because he was immature, John was attached to the material world, and Theo could not pull him, as she later wrote, into the spiritual world of beauty and ideals. After a few minutes, John got over his grouchiness at Theo's condescending attitude, and the two declared themselves brother and sister. They went back to the campsite, joined the others for an omelet supper, and listened to the black servants, who had accompanied the campers, sing "Sinking Down" and "Ezekial Saw a Wheel."

Upon returning to Farmington, what Theo called her "sickness" descended once again. She suddenly felt that "all power of decision was forever dead in me." She felt fatigued from working on the house, and nothing pleased her, not even Alfred's pictures. "They are paint and nothing more; to use a vulgar expression they are 'sucked lemons'," she muttered.

She also despised the bad architecture she saw everywhere, the "fluted flimsy highly colored hen houses going up"—the poorly built, cluttered, ornate, and ostentatious Victorian mansions.

She thought about death and imagined escaping "this work-a-day world which we see with our eyes" to enter the spiritual world, "the world that I can be gatekeeper of and admit what I choose." She read the *Proceedings of the Society for Psychical Research,* the British spiritualist organization's journals, "every spare minute…from morning to night."

A new century was about to begin, but she did not look forward to anything. The Popes' house would soon be completed, and that would be the end of Theo's career as almost an architect. In 1900, Sarah Porter died at age 86, and the world became an even emptier place. Theo's depression worsened, and she finally sought treatment from a prominent New York City neurologist, Dr. Charles Loomis Dana, a handsome widower in his mid-forties.

Not long after she began seeing Dr. Dana, Theo's melancholy lifted. A gentle man, who was somewhat absent-minded, he understood and charmed her. Like the women whom she earlier had derided because they fell in love with their doctors, Theo became obsessed with Charles Dana.

Theo did not reveal her feelings to Alfred and Ada or to Mary. "The best part of my life," she realized, "I must close away from them—the deepest." She vowed to "lie all my life if necessary to keep this a secret."

Theo sensed that Dr. Dana reciprocated, but "he has not tried to make l— to me," she inscribed in her diary. At first she had talked easily with him, but lately, "I think of quite clever things I would like to say to him, but my tongue feels curled."

Then, impulsively, Theo sent Charles what she almost immediately realized was "the most foolish inexcusable letter." The letter was short, written in calligraphy, and contained the Quaker "thee" and "thy" as well as purple prose. The closing line, "Thou art to me a delicious torment," was especially humiliating. "I have cut my throat," she concluded. "It is all over."

Charles did not respond to the letter. "To think of his making me well—better than I had ever been since I was a child," she observed, "and then that he should be the cause of a return of depression such as I never have known." For relief, she turned to her diary. "I must write or thinking will drive me wild," she declared. "Nothing diverts me—not the *Society for Psychical Research Proceedings* or my fencing lessons or people or shopping."

"I hate to live for there is nothing in life for me now," she despaired. "If it were not for father & mother & Mary I would ask nothing better than to die tomorrow."

Six weeks went by, and anger replaced dejection. Theo knew that Charles had taken a fancy to her, but he must be shallow and fickle if his interest could not survive a silly letter.

Finally, on her thirty-fourth birthday, February 2, 1901, Theo telephoned Charles. After a few minutes of talking about trivial matters, she told him how much she regretted having sent such an "imbecile" letter. Her agitation was so great that she forgot his response. But, she wrote, "it was something very nice."

The next day Ada found Theo cheerful. They chatted about ordering stationery engraved with the Popes' new Farmington address. The house was completed, the farm established, and the Popes had moved in. Ada agreed with Theo's suggestion to name the estate "Hill-Stead."

In March, Theo went to New York ostensibly to be treated for a sore throat, but the true reason was that Charles had written. He said that he had been ill but had tried "1200 times to call." Despite a resolution never again to act impulsively, Theo dashed off several romantic notes. Afterwards, she confessed, "Would any one ever have predicted that I could write such letters to any man as I have to him. I am distressed about it—but I cannot seem to help it. I wonder if any woman ever encouraged a man as I have him. It mortifies me to think of it."

Charles did not appear at the Hotel Buckingham, explaining that he had a busy schedule. "I see him on the street quite often but he never sees me, he is always looking abstracted," Theo remarked. "One day he dashes under our horse's nose, when father & I were in a cab, & then in front of a trolley and so across Broadway. I had to lean forward to see him safe on the other side and it fairly makes my heart skip a beat when I think of his doing things like that every day."

While Theo waited for Charles to call, Mary arrived in the city to be operated on for a small growth, possibly a cancerous tumor, under her arm. At the same time that Mary was scheduled to undergo surgery, Alfred and Ada left the city to be at the bedside of Ada's dying brother, Joshua Twing Brooks, in Ohio. Theo was incensed that they did not write to inquire about Mary. "Mary is to me what Uncle Twing is to them and they either do not see it or ignore it," she fumed, adding, "She is, of course, more to me than that." Alfred and Ada could never understand the bond Theo had with Mary: "that would be utterly beyond their comprehension."

Fearful for Mary, Theo called Charles, who told her not to worry, that Mary's physician, Dr. Bull, was an excellent surgeon. During this conversation, Charles hinted that, at a more appropriate time, he would like to talk about their relationship. "There are things serious and gay I want to say to you," he said, "and the opportunity will come."

Windsor Hotel fire. Alfred's paintings are being lowered to man on ladder. *(HS)*.

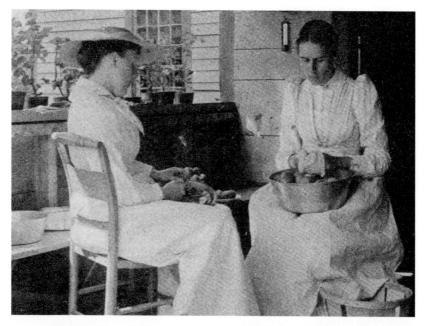

Theo and Mary shelling peas on the porch of the O'Rourkery. *(HS)*.

Theo and friends on a camping trip. *(HS)*.

FIVE

"Split the canopy and peep through"
1901—1907

ON A TRIP through New England, the novelist Henry James stopped to see Hill-Stead. Dazzled by its beauty, he compared his delight to "the momentary effect of a large slippery sweet inserted, without a warning, between the compressed lips."

Hill-Stead reflects Theo's eclectic style and complex personality. Architectural historian Mark Hewitt has called it "perhaps the finest Colonial Revival house in the United States." It looks somewhat like Mount Vernon, with two-story columns across the open portico. Inside, the wide halls and large rooms that open into each other follow the more modern example of Frank Lloyd Wright. The house's numerous working fireplaces indicate the influence of the British Arts and Crafts' movement of the 1890s, which stressed the importance of the hearth as a symbol of the home. At the time, most homes had fancy mantels over grates rather than real fireplaces.

The mansion is furnished simply, but magnificent paintings by Monet, Degas, Manet, Whistler, and Cassatt grace the walls. The library is also impressive. Books line shelves from floor to ceiling, with one wall devoted entirely to spiritualism. In the drawing room is a rosewood grand piano that Mr. Steinway built especially for the Popes, and displayed throughout the house are ornate clocks, Ada's collection of Italian and Chinese porcelain, and exotic souvenirs from the family's travels.

Theo moved from the O'Rourkery into Hill-Stead on May 30, 1901. Throughout the summer, Mary Hillard was a guest. Their bedrooms connected through a common bathroom. "We are very apt to sleep together in my room," Theo confided, "and I can slip off to her bed if she goes to sleep."

Being with Mary at Hill-Stead made Theo "radiantly happy," but she could not stop thinking about Charles Dana. She kept hearing his words—that he had something "serious and gay" to tell her. As the weeks went by, however, she lost hope. "He could not possibly act as reticent as he does," she observed, "if he has any interest in me at all."

In July, Theo accompanied Ada and Alfred to their new apartment at the Buckingham Hotel in New York. She told them that she wanted Dr. Dana's opinion on medication that another doctor had prescribed for rheumatism. In her diary, she admitted, "I went for I simply had to see him," even though she was afraid that she would suffer afterwards. She was right. Charles acted distant and professional. "Well, it is all too disappointing," she sighed. "I am frankly tired of not understanding C.L.D. and I am now putting him right out of my mind."

It was time to change direction. "I think I feel as Belle does," she decided. "There is nothing to do now but be 'clean and good.'" Belle Sherwin was busy working for worthy causes. After graduating from Wellesley College in 1890, she became a teacher, the director of Cleveland's Public Health Nursing Association, and president of the Consumer's League. In addition, Belle worked for unions and for woman suffrage, and she became the president of the League of Women Voters.

Theo decided to help Farmington's poor. She established a girls' sewing school and cooking school as well as a boys' club, and then she hired a visiting nurse for the town. In order to support these projects, she conceived of the idea of operating a little shop in the Gundy, the cottage she had attached to the O'Rourkery. A few months later, she opened the store and had a sign painted:

Odd & End Shop
Hot Peanuts Saturdays
Afternoon Tea
Notions
Apples
Bath rugs
Strictly fair prices
But profits devoted to charity.

Because of Theo's connection to Miss Porter's School, the girls were permitted to frequent the shop, which became a popular place since they were not allowed to go anywhere else in town.

Deciding to be kinder to Ada, Theo accompanied her mother to social activities and helped entertain visitors at Hill-Stead. Ada was thrilled when a Farmington socialite sponsored her and Theo for membership in the exclusive Colonial Dames Society.

By late August, Theo felt that she had to take a respite from being good. She attended a spiritualist meeting in Boston, and then, accompanied by Lucy Pratt, a cheerful young woman who worked with Mary at St. Margaret's School, she vacationed at Great Duck Island off the coast of Portland, Maine. Mary did not join them because she was taking a rest cure in New Hampshire.

At sunset, with sea gulls circling overhead, Theo and Lucy arrived at the desolate island. The two women stayed with the lighthouse keeper and his mother. Theo helped with the housework, ate simple meals, washed dishes, read, and climbed the rocks. But in a diary entry, she wrote, "The sea is so lonesome," and, in very small letters, "I dreamed of him again."

Returning to Farmington, she declared, "I have given up absolutely all hope now. A man does not act like this—that is, neither call nor write if he loves one."

On September 6, news from the outside world distracted Theo. As he was shaking hands with the crowd at the Pan-American Exposition in Buffalo, President McKinley had been shot. Theo was upset about "this democratic and useless custom of handshaking" and thought that a "President should consider having body guards." At first, the public was optimistic about McKinley's condition. On September 9, Theo wrote, "He seems to be recovering," but five days later, the church bells in Farmington tolled. The president had died during the night.

Although they mourned McKinley's death, the villagers were excited because Vice President Theodore Roosevelt, the brother of Farmington's most popular hostess, Anna Roosevelt Cowles, was now their new president. Anna, her husband Admiral William Cowles, and their young son Sheffield lived at Oldgate, Will Cowles's ancestral home on Main Street only a few blocks from Hill-Stead.

Anna's nieces and nephews affectionately called her Aunt Bamie or Auntie Bye. Both the Hyde Park and the Oyster Bay Roosevelts, as well as others who knew her well, said that she had the best mind in the family, and if she had been a man, she would have been president. Before marrying at age forty, Anna had acted as hostess for her cousin, Ambassador to England, James Roosevelt. Anna's Washington, D.C., apartment was a meeting place for Teddy and his associates, and she was her brother's most trusted advisor.

Anna's favorite niece, Eleanor Roosevelt, often visited the Cowles's Farmington home. Eleanor followed the example of Anna, who had been educated in Paris at Les Ruches, Europe's most prestigious school for aristocratic girls. Taking Anna's advice, Eleanor attended Allenswood, the school that Les Ruches's headmistress, Mme. Souvestre, had founded in England.

In recent years, Anna had lived mostly in Farmington, where she received important and famous visitors from all over the world. Despite severe arthritis, which acerbated a degenerative spinal disease that had crippled her as a child, Anna never gave any indication of being in pain.

Sitting in a wheelchair, she orchestrated delightful, sophisticated conversations with a circle of distinguished guests.

After being sworn in as president, Teddy Roosevelt arrived in Farmington to see his sister, and Anna invited the Popes to a reception. When Theo met the new president, she remarked, "One seldom sees a finer man."

To Theo's delight, Belle also came for a visit at this time. Belle shared Theo's interest in spiritualism, and the friends spent several days reading *The Riddle of the Universe at the Close of the Nineteenth Century* by Ernst Haeckel. Theo told Belle about another, more profound spiritualist book, *Human Immortality* by William James, and solemnly told her diary, "I am deep in Cosmic Consciousness and Walt Whitman."

During Belle's visit, the two young women discussed their fathers. Like Alfred, who had made a fortune in the steel industry, Henry Alden Sherwin was equally successful as a founder of the Sherwin-Williams Paint Company. Their daughters bemoaned a shared dilemma—"how much we need our fathers' minds and how little they seem to need ours."

Although Ada had always approved of Belle, she still did not accept Mary. Lately, Ada had been upset because she suspected that Mary was encouraging a romance between her brother and Theo. Not only was John ten years younger than Theo, but the Hillards were not in the Popes' social class. Neither Theo or John, however, had romantic intentions. After John graduated from Yale Law School and began work at the office of White, Daggett and Tilson in New Haven, he wrote Theo "to tell you what a trump I think you are. You are certainly a fine sister to me."

Theo confided to Belle that she had found it necessary to lead a "double kind of life" because of Ada's hostility toward Mary. Fearing that Ada would overhear, Theo could not speak frankly to Mary on that remarkable new invention, the telephone, which had been installed at Hill-Stead. She was limited to "dropping a line to Mary to tell her how I love her."

In November, William Mead, the architect who had worked with Theo on Hill-Stead, came to dinner. When he mentioned that he had seen Charles Dana and his wife at the theatre, Ada informed him that Dr. Dana was a widower. Mead replied, "Well, who was he with?" That was precisely what Theo wanted to know.

A week later, Theo wrote Charles that she would be at the Popes' apartment at the Buckingham Hotel and that she expected him to meet her there. When Charles arrived, he explained that the woman he had taken to the theatre was a casual acquaintance. Then he said that he was sincerely interested in making a commitment to Theo, but when they married, they would have to live in New York City.

That night, worried that she had encouraged Charles too much, Theo had trouble sleeping. She resented his assumption that she would move to the city to be with him rather than that he would move to Farmington. "I don't know him at all!" she realized. "I don't know what he is like or what he likes or where he was born or what college he went to or if his parents are living or how many brothers and sisters he has (if any) or how old he is or anything."

Now certain that she had his love, she could not accept it. She told Charles that she needed time away from him to think. Evidently he agreed to a separation. "I stand it just so long without seeing him and then the time comes when I do not wish to wait another minute, and I dream of him so often," Theo scribbled in her diary two months later. "And he is at the back of my thoughts all day long."

She also was thinking about another love. "Dear Mary is so in ignorance of it all," she sighed, "and that makes me feel dishonorable to her." Mary was still headmistress at St. Margaret's School in Waterbury, but she looked forward to returning to Farmington. Three years earlier, after the death of Sarah Porter in 1900, Mrs. Mary E. Dow, the woman who had helped Miss Porter establish the school, had become the logical choice for headmistress, and Mrs. Dow had promised that Mary would become her assistant.

The appointment of a headmistress also involved the inheritance of property, however, and a battle ensued between two major factions. In her will, Miss Porter had designated Mrs. Robert Keep, a former student, "as one whom she wished to be associated with her trustees in the management of the school." On the basis of this statement, Mrs. Keep claimed that legally she was the new headmistress.

The townspeople and the alumnae supported Mrs. Dow, and, in reply to the chief objection that she was too old to remain headmistress for very long, they pointed out that Mary would be her assistant and eventual successor. After a legal battle, Mrs. Keep won control of the school. "Things culminated yesterday in a way, which brings grief to every true 'old girl,'" an alumna complained.

Witnessing the bitter politics of the situation, Theo appealed to Alfred to help Mary. Alfred met with Ruth Hanna McCormick, and they decided to try to buy off Mrs. Keep. Alfred pledged $15,000, and he and Mrs. McCormick raised a total of $150,000.

Then Mary's father became gravely ill. She went to his bedside and refused to become further involved in the fray. Mrs. Dow was also under a great deal of pressure, having received an offer from Briarcliff College, which wanted an immediate response. She accepted the offer, and the

Dow-Hillard faction abandoned their cause. The battle, which became known in Farmington as the "Dow Row," was over.

Deeply depressed about her father's death and about losing the chance to return to Miss Porter's School, Mary told Theo that she planned to seek psychiatric help from Dr. Dana. A sobering thought occurred to Theo. What if, in Mary's sessions with Charles, she revealed her hope that Theo would marry John? Theo realized that she must tell Mary about the romantic relationship she had with the doctor.

Theo still dreamed about Charles, but she doubted that she would marry him. She always felt safer and more comfortable with women. She had another secret that she did not reveal to Mary. Theo had recently fallen in love with "one of the most fascinating women I have ever seen." In her diary, she referred to the woman only as "Laura S." When Theo asked Laura to go to England, she refused and told Theo to keep busy by finding occupations for the women at the Hospital for Tuberculosis in Hartford. Theo was pleased with the suggestion but wondered, "Will she ever love me?"

A month later, Theo was ecstatic. "Laura spent last night with me in Mary's room!!" she rejoiced, adding, "I only slept about an hour and a half." She blacked out the next four words. "I am just so happy today," she concluded, "it has changed the whole tenor of my mind."

Theo carried on "the briskest kind of a flirtation" with Laura S. "We are both frightfully self-conscious," she acknowledged, "and it is impossible for us to talk when others are around." The romance, however, ended as mysteriously as it began.

Instead of a trip to England, Theo went to a resort in Poland Springs, Maine, where she visited the Knights, a prominent family with important political connections. There she also met George McLean, the dashing bachelor governor of Connecticut, whom she found "very amusing." In his mid-forties, McLean was slim, with large brown eyes, patrician features, and a full mustache.

"The Governor is trying his best to be devoted. Leaves flowers…attends to my slightest wants—is afraid I am cold or hot or tired or will not sleep well," Theo observed, flattered by McLean's attentions. At thirty-six, Theo had no difficulty attracting men. When she returned to Farmington, she received a letter from McLean that shocked her. She gave it a "chilling answer."

"He is a sick man—that is why he wrote that way. I told him he would regret it when he was well and that I would be kind enough to put it out of my thoughts." She imagined that Alfred and Ada "would faint with surprise" if she told them what the Governor had written.

McLean had made another error as well. While in Maine, Theo had given him a note on which was imprinted the logo ⅢL. "This symbol of mine is a letter in itself if you only knew the meaning," she hinted. McLean responded wryly that he had shown the note to "a wise man from the East," who had been hired to perform occult manifestations to entertain the guests at the resort. McLean then relayed the interpretation: "This is the handwriting of a woman full of subtle vows and missions etc. etc. No man will ever interest her who is not a mental and moral giant."

"I am afraid the cuss was telling the truth," McLean remarked, not knowing that he had doubly insulted Theo. First, he had agreed with the mystic that the only man Theo could love had to have impossible characteristics, and, second, he had mocked psychics. Theo took both insults seriously. Her anger surprised McLean, and he returned the ⅢL note, wryly adding "Were I to keep it, I should seek its interpretation night and day until successful."

While Theo was in Poland Springs, she revealed an idea to Mrs. Knight that she had been mulling over since the Dow-Row episode. She wanted to build a school that would have Mary as its headmistress. Mrs. Knight suggested that Theo use Governor McLean as a resource. McLean would be able to help with the political ramifications of founding a new school. The older woman knew that McLean was "ready to turn hand springs" for Theo.

A few months later, Mrs. Knight arranged a luncheon for Mary and Governor McLean in New York to discuss Theo's plan. After the meeting, Mary asked Theo to thank McLean for his interest. Since Theo's reply to the "sick" letter, she had lost contact with him, but she wrote the governor. A few weeks later, Theo accepted his invitation to go coasting on a snow-covered hill in Connecticut.

Alfred also wanted to help Mary, but he was interested even more in the project because, by designing the school, Theo would have another opportunity as an architect. Encouraged by the governor and Alfred, Theo and Mary worked on plans for the school over the summer while they vacationed in Europe. They shared their ideas with Mary Cassatt at the artist's country home outside Paris.

In September 1903, Mary's brother John came down with typhoid fever. Theo and Mary rushed to Hartford Hospital, where they stayed by his bedside for almost a week. At first, the doctors were not worried, but then they said there was no way to save him. John died at the age of 26.

John's funeral service was held at Hill-Stead. Few attended; Alfred and Ada were away on a winter vacation. The burial took place at a small cemetery in Plymouth, Connecticut, where John and Mary's father had been a minister. Theo and Mary stood in the cold wind as John's coffin was lowered. On his tombstone appeared the words, "He being dead yet speaketh," and underneath was carved Theo's symbol, ⫞⫞, with an H on either side.

From France, Mary Cassatt wrote Theo, expressing shock and sympathy. "You and your dear Miss Hillard have not been out of my mind," she began. "I little thought what sorrow you were going through. I pictured you, on the contrary, full of plans and working happily and was with you in hopes for the success of the new building [the school for Mary]."

Cassatt understood Theo and Mary's anguish over losing one who was "snatched away so young and without, as far as we can judge, having fulfilled his earthly mission," but she urged them not to despair. "No doubt he was wanted elsewhere; oh! we must not lose that faith, the faith that life is going on though we cannot see it." She hoped that "you may sometime have a convincing proof" that John's soul was still alive.

After recommending a book by the spiritualist, Frederic Myers, Cassatt inquired, "I wonder if you have seen Hodgson, and Mrs. Piper. I think I would if I were you." The reference was to Dr. Richard Hodgson and the famous medium, Mrs. Leonora Piper, at the American Society for Psychical Research in Boston.

In February 1904, still overwhelmed by grief, Theo and Mary acted upon Mary Cassatt's suggestion. They arrived in Boston during a snow-storm. Standing close together on the railroad platform, the two women were a striking pair: tall, dark-eyed, chisel-featured Mary, athletic and regal in her bearing; and Theo, shorter but just as imposing.

They were met by an attractive man in his late forties. Dr. Hodgson was a professor at Harvard University and the secretary of the American Society for Psychical Research. He escorted Theo and Mary to his carriage, and, after a bumpy ride over snow-covered streets, they came to a small, plain house at 15 Charles Street in Boston's Back Bay.

Dr. Hodgson arranged Mrs. Piper's sittings, acted as the intermediary between the medium and the sitters, and kept transcripts of the proceedings. He also participated in the conversations with the spirits, who expressed themselves usually through Mrs. Piper's automatic writing and occasionally through the medium's voice.

A scientist originally from Australia, Hodgson became a spiritualist early in life. When he was a young man, the English Society for Psychical Research sent him to India to investigate the Theosophical Society and its colorful leader, Madame Blavatsky. A guide showed Hodgson the Theosophists' shrine, a wooden box that mysteriously produced flowers and messages from the beyond. To prove that it had no hidden panels, the man rapped on the box. But to his chagrin, a trap door snapped open. Hodgson questioned him, other disciples, and Madame Blavatsky herself, who finally broke down and confessed to fraud. Following this triumph, Hodgson continued his work as a psychical researcher. He came to the American Society for Psychical Research buoyed by the conviction that, in contrast to Madame Blavatsky, Mrs. Piper was a true psychic.

Hodgson ushered Theo and Mary into a sparsely furnished room. Opened curtains let in the winter sun. At one end of the room, Mrs. Piper sat on a wooden chair. She was a pleasant-looking, middle-aged matron dressed in plain clothes. In front of her was a card table, on which lay three pillows and a pad of paper. Hodgson introduced the visitors to the medium, using pseudonyms. Theo was "Miss Smith" and Mary, "Miss Bergman." Then Hodgson and the women sat down and quietly waited.

After a few minutes, Mrs. Piper's head dropped forward onto the pillows. That was the sign that she had entered the trance state. She began breathing deeply and regularly. Then, without lifting her head, she made the sign of the cross with two fingers. Hodgson rose from his chair, approached her, and placed a pencil in her hand. She took it, and, in a large scrawl, wrote a word on the pad. She tore off the sheet and threw it on the floor. Hodgson retrieved it and showed it to Theo and Mary. It contained one word, "Hail." This was the standard greeting of the spirits known as Imperator and Rector, who were the spiritual equivalents of Mrs. Piper—intermediaries who summoned the souls in the spiritual world whom she requested.

The medium turned to Hodgson for a response by holding out the palm of her hand toward his mouth.

"Hail, Imperator and Rector," he replied into her hand.

On the pad, the words of the spirit Rector appeared. "Once more we greet thee friend of earth and blessings on thee," scrawled Mrs. Piper in large letters on several pieces of paper.

Rector was an old spirit, but patient, sympathetic, and wise. Mrs. Piper asked him to try to find the soul of John Hillard so that the two visitors could communicate with him.

The minutes passed. Theo watched the snow falling outside the window. Finally, the medium wrote on the pad that John's spirit was present.

Overcome by emotion, Mary could not respond. Instead, Theo spoke into Mrs. Piper's palm. "Please try to make me conscious of you as often as you can, and I will try not to be afraid."

In an effort to engage John's soul in conversation, Theo asked, "If we camp this summer, will you come to us there, and stay with us, and will you find a beautiful place for us to camp?"

Sometimes, like the newfangled telephones, there was static on the spiritual communication line.

"Is that tramp?" Mrs. Piper's hand wrote.

"If, she says, we camp...if we *camp* this summer," Hodgson stepped in and explained.

"Oh I hear. That's good. Yes I will, surely I will." The medium rapidly wrote John's words.

After the sitting, Hodgson sent Theo a transcript of the conversation for her comments. Next to John's words, "Help me dear to keep my thoughts clear," Theo wrote, "He never called us 'dear.'"

In subsequent sittings, Theo bluntly expressed doubts that the spirit of John was really communicating. "Tell him he was always a dear fellow, but he didn't used to be so stupid as he is now," Theo instructed.

The spirit of John was insulted. "Do you feel me stupid dear. I shall prove myself to you. Do you remember saying you could not live if I went?" Mrs. Piper scribbled hastily.

"Did I say that when you were ill?" Theo asked.

In another session, John said that he loved her. Theo responded, "You never told me when you were here that you loved me."

"No but you knew I did and I feel it now."

At home, Mary had been writing automatically in a trance-like state in an effort to receive messages from her brother, but she had not been successful. John mentioned that he often was with her and Theo but they were unaware of his presence. He asked if he should tap on a table or move some object.

"Tapping on the table will be excellent," Mary responded. "We will call each tap a letter in a word, one for A, two for B, and so on. Theo and I will sit together and think of you, and then you can tap the table and we will try to talk to you."

A few evenings later, alone at Hill-Stead, Theo and Mary tried to establish contact with John. They suggested that he move some furniture. The two women waited, but nothing happened.

In March, Theo brought John's diary to Mrs. Piper. Assuring the spirit that neither she nor Mary had read it, Theo asked John to tell them some incident, and then they would look it up.

John consented, but only after he had time to think it over.

After several minutes of confusing messages, Theo addressed Rector directly. "Would it be of any help in reaching my friend if Dr. Hodgson should hypnotize me here at the next meeting? I will submit myself to anything to make conditions better."

Not receiving an answer, she repeated the question and added, "I do not mind if you kill me in the attempt."

"What you want is to split the canopy and peep through," Rector responded.

"Yes, that's really it," she agreed. "Nothing short of that."

Rector agreed to the hypnotism, but Hodgson hesitated and asked, "Would it do any good?"

"Not a d— bit," was the reply.

"Well, see here," Theo said, addressing both the living Richard Hodgson and the dead Rector. "I am not going to be hypnotized for your amusement, you know."

Theo and Mary made frequent trips to Boston, but they sometimes arranged with Hodgson to carry on without them and to send transcripts of sittings. In one such session, Hodgson told Rector that he had brought along a message from Theo in a sealed envelope. On opening it, he found a letter and a substantial check made out to him in John's memory. Theo had written that she wanted him to use the money as he thought best, but she would prefer to support the publication of his writings in which he produced evidence of a future life.

Sittings with Mrs. Piper began to progress more smoothly after John told Theo information that was almost impossible for an outsider to know, such as the name of the janitor at Andover School, which he had attended as a boy, and the name of the man who drove the boys to the station. Satisfied that she really was communicating with his spirit, Theo asked him questions about the spiritual world.

"Tell me, what you do with all the time you have on your hands now?" she inquired.

"I am really happier here, free from care and worry, helping, praying, and comforting others who are constantly coming into this world," John replied.

He told Mary, "I am living with father and mother in a home of our own. It is one of the many mansions spoken of in your bible."

"I retain my same personal appearance in a way," he continued. "I have a body in a sense but not an earthly one but a spiritual one," he explained. "I am having a good time, Mary, but very different from your pleasures."

After communication with John's soul had been firmly established, Theo asked Hodgson to try to reach the spirit of Miss Sarah Porter. On Wednesday, July 6, 1904, Hodgson was successful.

Hodgson and the spirit of Miss Porter had a conversation in which he learned that, as she had on earth, Miss Porter had founded a school for girls in the spiritual world. "Please say to Miss Pope," she told Hodgson, "I am very active in the work here and I am doing all I can to advance and help the minds of all these young girls. They are doing nicely and the school is growing fast on this side." Miss Porter then remarked that Theo "is a good soul and always well meaning, but awfully impulsive."

Hodgson agreed and then asked about Mary Hillard.

"Hillard," she hesitated. "Oh yes. I knew her. Give her my love and tell her to send me one little wee word."

Upon receiving Hodgson's report, Theo was suspicious. At a subsequent sitting, she asked John's spirit, "Was that really Miss Porter trying to communicate? It did not seem like her. She used phraseology she never used here."

John explained that it was not *Miss Porter* who had used these expressions. The spirit entities who communicated with Mrs. Piper read the headmistress's thoughts and put them into *their* words. Rector, who was Scottish, chose words like "wee." Theo was satisfied with the explanation.

During a sitting in December, John mentioned that he had observed Mary at the snow-covered cemetery in Plymouth, placing holly wreaths on the Hillard family's graves. He could not see his own gravestone clearly, however.

"You have a flat stone of gray granite just like the rest," Mary informed him, "and on it is cut the symbol that we had on the canoe."

"Symbol?" he repeated.

"Do you remember what that was?" asked his sister. "Perhaps you can draw if for Dr. Hodgson. Theo and I had it cut on the stone. We wanted it there because it means you and Theo and me."

Mrs. Piper drew a triangle with three ellipses.

Upset at his error, Theo decided she would never go to Mrs. Piper again. On further thought, though, she remembered that John had once suggested the triangle design as an emblem for the canoe, and she became even more convinced that she was communicating with his spirit.

"I endeavor more and more to be guided by my intuitions instead of by my reason," Theo asserted, and her intuition assured her that the dead lived on and could communicate with the living. Inspired to discover more about the spiritual world, she decided to consult other mediums in addition to Mrs. Piper.

John's spirit disapproved. He criticized other mediums. Mrs. Keeler was stupid and others were fakes.

"I cannot always judge if they are impostors or not, and my desire is to experiment with any light I find," Theo countered.

John cautioned that some mediums were unclean in mind and body and that their thoughts were unwholesome. But he could not discourage Theo.

"I will not leave one stone unturned that will help in this work," she declared.

During the summer of 1905, Theo and Mary traveled abroad and again visited Mary Cassatt. John disapproved of their going and was annoyed that they left despite his advice. "Neither shall I be sorry if they do not enjoy [their trip]," the spirit added petulantly.

One reason why Theo felt that she had to get away was that she and Charles had resumed their difficult relationship, and Imperator had suggested that if they were apart for a while, Charles would miss her.

In addition to personal advice, every so often Theo and Mary asked medical advice from a spiritual doctor, who diagnosed their ills and pre-scribed treatment. "Don't swallow your food whole...eat fruit...drink pure water...do not eat anything fried, eat dark breads only...no oysters.... No meat except fowl chicken and bird." The doctor did not detect any trouble in their bodies, such as an "unnatural growth," though he did tell Mary that her stomach was "all upside down."

When Theo asked, "Shall I bathe in cold water every morning as I do now?" he responded, "We do not like it. Partially tepid is less inclined to prostrate the nerves." His advice made a lot of sense, especially when he urged the women to wear loose, comfortable clothing instead of the tight corsets demanded by fashion, and to exercise daily.

As time went on, Theo became a good friend of both Richard Hodgson and William James. James often visited Hill-Stead, accompa-nied by his wife Alice, who had become a devout spiritualist after the death of one of their children. His invalid sister Alice was also a believer, but she feared spiritualism. In her diary she hoped that after she died, "the dreadful Mrs. Piper won't be let loose upon my defenseless soul." In contrast to the rest of the family, her brother Henry, although he wrote eighteen ghost stories, said he was "alien to the whole spiritualist busi-ness" and mocked spiritualism in his novel, *The Bostonians.*

Whenever Theo went alone for sittings, she stayed with the Jameses at their home on Irving Street in Cambridge. They had modest means but were gracious hosts. Despite fragile health, William did small kindnesses. Quietly leaving his guest, he would go upstairs to start a fire in the fireplace of the bedroom so that when Theo retired, the room would be warm. James considered Theo a colleague as well as a friend, though his attitude at times was patronizing. "I am sorry I said that you were not a good girl," he once remarked, "since you seem to have been such a *very* good one."

Theo's relationship with handsome and charming Richard Hodgson bordered on the flirtatious. When Hodgson grew a beard, she recommended that he shave. He responded by writing a four-stanza poem and going to the barbershop—but not to get rid of the beard. "I told the barber to make my beard more pointed, and he did it somewhat," he wrote. The result? "When I looked in the mirror, I thought I was a Frenchman."

Theo wanted Charles to have a sitting with Mrs. Piper, but she hesitated to approach Hodgson to arrange an appointment because she did not want him to learn that she was involved with Charles. Instead, she approached Dr. James Hyslop, the other vice president of the Society; however, Hyslop inadvertently let Charles's name slip to Hodgson. Perhaps because of jealousy, Hodgson refused to admit Dr. Dana.

On December 20, 1905, Richard Hodgson died suddenly of a heart attack while playing handball. According to his obituary in a Boston paper, Hodgson had stated his belief that "the departed may under certain conditions reveal themselves to those remaining upon earth, but...much less frequently than Spiritualists believe."

Though shocked and grief-stricken by Hodgson's sudden death, William James and the others at the Society, including Theo and Mary, realized that here was a long-awaited opportunity. Hodgson had left papers on which he had written information to test his spirit personality. If Mrs. Piper received that information from his spirit, it would prove the validity of spiritualism.

At the first session after Hodgson's death, William James and Theo were the sitters. "Can you suggest who would better have charge in place of Hodgson?" James asked Imperator. "To what extent could Miss Pope help?" Then he inquired most urgently, "Have you seen anything of Hodgson and had communication with his spirit?"

Imperator counseled patience. He was helping Hodgson's soul learn how to communicate with the living. He also suggested that Dr. James Hyslop succeed Hodgson.

A little over a week later, Mrs. Piper's hand shook with excitement as she wrote, "I Am," followed by unreadable scrawls.

"Bravo," William James exclaimed. "Is this my friend?"

The next words, however, were Imperator's. "Peace, friends," he cautioned. "He is here. It was he but he could not remain. He was so choked."

On January 16, 1906, the soul of Richard Hodgson communicated with Theo. "You are Pope. I see you," Mrs. Piper scribbled. "Everything all right?"

"Everything's all right, everything's all right," Theo repeated into the medium's hand. "I am working like a tiger for you."

Not until April 16, 1906, did Theo question Hodgson about the sealed envelope he had left to test his spirit. The answer he gave was correct! The envelope contained a letter that he had written after he had visited the grave of the transcendentalist, Ralph Waldo Emerson. He had written the following words: "I am grateful to God for the privilege of living and when I go over to the other side I will prove my existence to friends in the physical world by reproducing this letter."

Though pleased with this proof, William James was disappointed that Hodgson had not provided more information about the spiritual world. "Will thinks I ought to walk into the room boldly and shake hands with him," the spirit of Hodgson complained. "I heard him say 'Hodgson isn't so much of a power on the other side.' What does he think a man in the ethereal body is going to do with a man in the physical body?"

Most illuminating was Hodgson's description of the passage from life to death. At the moment of death, he recalled, "I found the light. it looked like a tremendous window, open window. The canopy—do you remember how they used to talk about the canopy? It is an ethereal veil. If your spiritual eyes were open you could see through this veil and see me here talking to you perfectly."

After Hodgson's death, arguments arose among the sitters as to who should have sessions with Mrs. Piper. Another member of the Society, George B. Dorr, had taken over scheduling the medium's appointments and had arranged for William's son, Henry James Jr., to act as a scribe and record-keeper. Anxious to communicate with Hodgson, Dorr insisted on taking times for himself that Theo had been promised, though he admitted that "Dr. Hodgson ...would probably communicate, at least at first, most readily with you."

Theo demanded the appointments. Furious, Dorr told Lucy Edmunds, a secretary, that others had been put off for Miss Pope. Lucy reported back to Theo that Dorr was "a fanatical usurper" and a back-stabber. He finally acquiesced and allowed Theo to have the appointments but gave her questions for Hodgson. But she did not ask them. "Because," she said, "it would have taken altogether too much time."

In addition to the disagreeable George Dorr, there was another problem at the Society. Dr. James Hyslop, Hodgson's successor as Mrs. Piper's manager, believed that the medium was bitter toward him. "The more I see of other psychics," he told Theo, "the less of an exception does Mrs. Piper appear to me." He wanted to bring in another medium, a young woman from Buffalo, New York. But the spirit of Hodgson disapproved, Mrs. Piper wrote, because the girl had "some hysteria and imagination."

Hyslop also resented the influence of the main branch of the society in England with their "staid old English methods." He wanted to use more strictly scientific methods. Even before Hodgson's death, Hyslop had proposed the creation of a new, independent organization, the American Institute for Scientific Research of New York, to be established in New York City and modeled after the psychology department of Clark University, which recently had begun research into spiritualism. Two Clark psychologists, G. S. Hall and Amy Tanner, were presently conducting experiments on Mrs. Piper.

Hyslop's institute would focus on two areas: abnormal psychology, especially in relation to hysteria, multiple personalities, and the trance phenomenon; and general psychical research. To help found the new organization, Theo wrote a check for $25,000 and told Hyslop that a woman friend in Europe (most likely, Mary Cassatt) would contribute $5,000.

After Hodgson's death, Hyslop increased his efforts to launch the institute, helped mostly by Theo, who became the only woman on his board of directors. By June 1906, there were 210 members and enough money. His next step was to persuade respected men of science to join his staff, a difficult task. Theo had two medical men in mind: Dr. Charles Dana and Dr. Foster Kennedy. She had recently become Kennedy's patient and friend.

William James and George Dorr agreed to close the Boston branch of the society and to support the new organization. Instead of transferring Hodgson's records, which included transcripts of Mary and Theo's sittings, James sent them to England. Hyslop had planned to publish these records, but James was opposed to making them public.

Incensed, Hyslop wrote Theo that James was "the most incorrigible idiot I have had anything to do with in this subject. All comes from listening to snobs and social sets."

Theo had also become displeased—not with William James but with Mrs. Piper. In several of the medium's "Subliminals," the moments when she came out of her trance, she had mumbled insults about Theo. In January 1906, the notes of the Subliminal read: "Looking disgustedly at T. P. again and again, whispering 'Mad, mad, mad.'"

Theo had expressed disappointment that Grandmother Theodate had never appeared in sittings with Mrs. Piper. "I have longed to talk to her," Theo said, "because my love for her is very deep." Accompanied by James Hyslop, Theo visited another medium, Mrs. Soule, whose first question was "Do you know Birdie?"

"Why that was my childish nickname," Theo cried. Only close family members knew that Grandmother Theodate had called her Birdie.

"A lady calls you by that name and holds you in her lap and kisses your sensitive tears away," the medium intoned. "A Grandma I should think with soft curls about her face gone long ago but no loss of love. Do you know?"

"My Grandmother was a Quakeress, consequently did not wear her hair in curls," responded Theo curtly. Mrs. Soule quickly changed the subject.

On December 31, 1907, during a sitting a month after the third anniversary of John's death, Mary asked him, "Do you know in what Theo and I are interested?"

"Establishing a new school. Looks like a big school. I like it very much. [Hodgson] says it seems to be a new larger and better school for girls." John noted that Alfred "was so overjoyed with [Theo]. He gave her great encouragement and was very proud of her and so am I. She is a trump Mary if you only knew it. She is one in a thousand."

John's comments thrilled Mary. "Trump" was the word that he had often used in life to describe Theo, and she felt reassured about the enormous project she and Theo were about to undertake. With the financial backing of the Whittemores and Alfred, the two friends had purchased land in Middlebury, Connecticut, and Theo had begun to design the buildings for Mary's school.

Alfred, Ada, and Theo on Hill-Stead's southwest lawn.
Gertrude Kasebier photograph. *(HS)*.

Greeting guests at Hill-Stead's carriage porch. *(HS)*.

Hill-Stead interior: living room with view to front foyer. On right, one of two Monet's *Haystacks*. Jerry L. Thompson photograph. *(HS)*.

Alice (Mrs. William) and Professor
William James. *(HS)*.

Dr. Richard Hodgson. *(HS)*.

Anna Roosevelt Cowles holding her son, Sheffield. *(HS)* .

SIX

"The fear feels good"
1907—1910

ADA AND ALFRED spent most winters in Pasadena, California, joined by Cleveland friends and Ada's relatives. Before leaving Hill-Stead, Ada instructed Earnest Bohlen, the Popes' butler, to keep her informed about Theo. Although her daughter was nearing forty, Ada still worried that Theo might do something outlandish. During the winter of 1904, Earnest had news. Moving from the O'Rourkery into Hill-Stead, Theo had invited an old school chum as a guest, and a very sick Miss Goodwillie had arrived, accompanied by a nurse.

"I think when anyone is as ill as that, they would either be in their own home or in a sanitarium," Ada fumed. "I left home with some trepidations but I did not expect my home to be turned into a hospital." If Theo insisted on carrying out wild schemes, she should do so at her own cottage, which, Ada sarcastically added, was "always open."

During the summer of 1907, Ada and Alfred vacationed in Paris, and in their absence, Theo invited 500 members of the Dairymen's Association and Connecticut Pomological Society for an outing at Hill-Stead. The invitation to the farmers and their wives extolled the attractions of the Popes' estate: "apple orchards, extensive fruit and vegetable gardens, greenhouses, a peach orchard, rose gardens, a sunken garden, a splendid dairy of registered Guernseys, modern equipment of dairy buildings, silos, a flock of thoroughbred sheep, swine, etc., electric power, fine trees transplanted at full size from long distances."

Knowing Earnest would tattle, Theo wrote Ada, "The enclosed invitation will tell you of something I did which I fear may come under the category of 'wild' but honest and truly cross my heart there was no harm done at all."

Finding shady spots on Hill-Stead's grounds, the farm folk ate picnic lunches they had brought, and their hostess supplied lemonade, coffee, ice cream, and plates of ham and rolls. Theo locked the house, but in the afternoon she invited the ladies inside to hear music and have tea.

"The day was an immense success and so many of those tired farmers' wives spoke again and again of the pleasure it had given them," she told Ada, who could not have cared less about the happiness of farmers or their wives. Ada was probably mortified when she saw the *Hartford Daily Courant's* coverage of the event, which included a photograph of Theo seated on Hill-Stead's piazza in the middle of 500 rustic guests.

That summer, Theo was also busy working on Mary Hillard's school. Since the site was in Middlebury, a town "over to the west" of Farmington, Mary named the school Westover. From the beginning of the project, Theo took complete charge. She hired a builder and workmen and oversaw all facets of construction. When Harris's father offered to engage a landscape architect, she agreed to meet with the man but warned that she would not allow him to "butt in."

Every day, Hill-Stead's chauffeur drove Theo and Mary to the site in Theo's new automobile, a Packard that they dubbed "The Yellow Peril." One evening, as the women sat in the car gazing at the half-built buildings, Mary turned to Theo and expressed apprehensions about the enormity of their project. "Be quiet," Theo murmured, "and let your spirit fill the buildings."

Theo rejected the loose arrangement of Miss Porter's School, where the buildings stood apart in no set pattern. Influenced by the English model widely adopted by many American schools and colleges, and perhaps recalling the Great Blizzard of 1888, when she and the other girls at Miss Dunning's house became isolated, Theo placed Westover's buildings in a cloister-like quadrangle with an interior courtyard. The quadrangle imparted a sense of safety and community, and it also made the school easier to monitor. The students would sleep and eat in the same buildings where they attended classes, had music and art lessons, and went to chapel.

The school faces Middlebury's center, but passersby cannot see beyond the magnificent, long, three-story rectangular main building of yellow stucco that looked ancient even when new. To achieve this effect, Theo ordered white sea sand, goats' hair, and lime, and, following a formula used by Michelangelo, the workmen stirred the mixture in wooden vats and then sprayed it on the outside walls.

Theo combined several styles in the school's design. The facade of the main building is Georgian, but at both ends appear Gothic-style wings that suggest medieval English architecture. The six-inch overhang of the second floor is characteristic of 17th-century American buildings. The roof over the third floor, with its line of dormer windows, is similar to Hill-Stead's. In its center is a large cupola.

The school entrance is through a central pavilion. Like Hill-Stead's airy interior, the halls are wide, and the rooms spacious. Most striking is the large, two-story Red Hall, which has balconies on all sides, red carpeting, elegant French doors and walnut woodwork. The back windows and doors face the courtyard and beyond it, the playing fields.

Theo completed Westover at the beginning of 1909. As Alfred had hoped, the school brought acclaim to his daughter. The Architectural League of New York exhibited photographs of Westover, and the renowned architect Cass Gilbert described the school as "beautifully designed and beautifully planned...refreshing in its charm and simplicity."

Art connoisseur Augustus Jaccaci agreed. "I look upon your work as being of the first order, in a class by itself," he wrote Theo, "and *the best* that I know of in our day."

Mary lived at the school with two other administrators, Lucy Pratt and Helen LaMonte (the students called them the "Triumvirate"). "Dear, dear, dear, dear Theodate, our blessed architect," Lucy rhapsodized. "Every peg in every closet, every latch of every door, every screw in its place sings Theodate. My sweet bedroom almost keeps me awake with the peace of its beauty."

Theo had enjoyed carte blanche to create Westover as well as to design other details, including the girls' uniforms and the school's coat of arms and crest, but it was Mary's school, and Belle warned, "The School must be an outgrowth of her [Mary's] personality, and other folks can only contribute occasionally." Belle knew that Theo had ideas about education that were more progressive than Mary's, but she believed that Westover would be "a wonderful place in which girls find real freedom to become themselves," and that they would do so without Theo's help.

Before the school's official opening on April 27, 1909, Theo went to Cuba. She explained that she must get away to a new place. When engaged in a project, she worked at a feverish pitch, and, after its completion, she experienced not elation but depression. Going off alone usually helped. "There is nothing like the diversion of travel," she professed, "for one who is mentally fagged."

Theo visited Westover often, receiving an enthusiastic greeting from the girls because her arrival might mean an unannounced holiday. Mary suggested that once a year, whenever Theo felt like it, she could cancel classes. The students jokingly called it "St. Theodate's Day."

In her mid-forties, Mary was a handsome headmistress, regally tall, with hair pulled back severely in a bun. Some Westover girls felt uncomfortable when she looked at them with her deep-set, dark eyes. During the early years of the school, the girls knew that "Miss Hillard communed with the dead, especially her brother John." They also suspected that "Miss Pope had put her up to it."

Once Westover opened, however, Mary severed formal spiritualist affiliations. Dr. Hyslop expressed regret when she resigned from his new organization, but he said that he understood the demands made upon her by the school.

In contrast, even while Theo was working on Westover, she continued psychical activities. Through Mrs. Piper, she often communicated with the spirit of Richard Hodgson, who seemed aware of everything that was happening to Theo, including a recent fire at Hill-Stead that had burned down the stable. His spirit said he had prayed that the fire might not spread, and he reassured Theo that the little dog that had died in the fire was with him in the spiritual world. Instead of replacing the stable, Theo built a small theatre, which she called "The Makeshift."

Some of Theo's friends also attended sittings with Mrs. Piper. Harris Whittemore tried to discuss legal matters with John Hillard's spirit, but John said he was interested in discussing only cosmic laws. Theo did not reveal that she was a spiritualist to Anna Roosevelt Cowles. "I still talk with reserve to her," Theo informed Rector.

At this time, Theo was in love with someone new, and, in a sitting, she asked Hodgson's spirit for advice about a man who was younger than she. At forty-two, Theo had not changed much, though she had become a little heavier.

"He will ask you to *marry him*," Hodgson responded. "He has it in his mind but he is young and timid in a way, but keep on and let things go on as they will, give him time."

Rector joined Hodgson in giving romantic advice and urged Theo to tell the young man she loved him. "He can be greatly injured by your own perplexing manner and seeming indifference," the spirit warned.

Theo hesitated. "It comes from my lack of faith in affection," she confessed. "I wish to be sure that he prefers me before I give any sign."

The young man was definitely someone in Anna's circle, for the spirit advised, "Mrs. Cowles can sympathize and *help you also*." A few years earlier Anna had tried to make a match for Theo with tall, good-looking John Wallace Riddle, a diplomat whose promising career Anna's brother Teddy had fostered. Anna urged Riddle to propose to Theo. But he was not Theo's secret love. John was not a timid, younger man. He was two years older than Theo, and no one would ever call him reticent with women.

In May 1909, Theo received more advice from the spiritual world. "Age should not count," Mrs. Piper said. The young man "fears to go too far lest you may spurn him." Theo's response, "But I wouldn't. I would work for him with absolute singleness of mind and heart," indicates that he probably was a diplomat or a politician. A likely possibility was thirty-two-year-old Joseph Alsop from the nearby town of Avon. Theo supported Alsop's political ambitions and sent him a generous check when he ran for state representative in 1908.

During the summer of 1909, Theo again felt the need to travel. This time she headed north to Canada on a camping trip. Sending postcards and telegrams to Alfred and Ada from hotels along the way, asking for money and describing the scenery from the train, Theo mentioned a companion, Mrs. Spagge, an older woman who had met her in Canada, obviously not dressed for camping in a cinnamon linen gown, fancy hat, and floating veil. Theo wrote that Spagge was good natured, but she talked *"incessantly!"*

Theo's journey on the Canadian Pacific railroad had a restorative effect. "Would you believe it—the train ride is not nearly long enough to suit me," she observed. "The monotones of it all is like a narcotic." The rugged landscape was also comforting, although in a paradoxical way. "I dread the pleasure of seeing the mountains," she realized.

After arriving at Lake O'Hara, Theo left the other tourists and Mrs. Spagge and rode off with a guide she hired. The guide's fifteen-year-old son, Courtland, and another young man, Charlie, joined them. "He has a very good profile," she noted, "and if he had a silk hat & a frock coat buttoned snugly at the waist, he would look *exactly* like the [men] of fashion in the Godey's Lady's Book."

At the camp, which was set up in a treeless canyon, Theo sometimes sat in silence with Charlie while the flies buzzed and the sun beat down on them. When the men were away from the camp, she took dips in the river, which she found "delicious." At night, alone in her tent, she killed mosquitoes and tried to sleep. Sometimes, hearing noises, she became afraid, but, she wrote in a journal, "The fear feels good. I have come for that. It is like biting on a hard rubber ring."

Although she knew they would live off the land, it sickened her to see that the men shot animals "for the pure love of killing." Killing a deer was "like shooting a woman in cold blood." Refusing to eat murdered animals, she subsisted on nuts and raisins. When Courtland shot a porcupine, took out the animal's heart and laid it on a stump, Theo protested, "We are to eat that heart for supper—those of us who can!"

She described the play-acting she engaged in to mask the horror she felt when Charlie brought a dead deer into camp. Charlie "sits down on a log and with shining eyes tells me every detail of the little tragedy," she reported, "and I put forth all the power there is in me to appear interested & proud of his *prowess*." Seeing Charlie sharpening knives to cut up the deer, Theo went to bed, missing supper. In the morning, she emerged from the tent to a beautiful day. But then she spotted the guide holding the deer's head between his legs and skinning it, and she smelled the sickening aroma of the venison frying.

While on the trip, Theo received mail, money, and packages from Ada and Alfred, and letters from friends, including Joe Alsop. "Be sure and do not fall off a glacier or tumble into the very cold lakes," Joe wrote, impressed by Theo's daring to go into the wilderness.

If Alsop was the younger man in whom Theo was interested, she faced disappointment when he married Anna's niece, Corinne Roosevelt. After the wedding, Theo received a note from Anna, who hinted that Theo had felt nervous about attending the ceremony. "Your dress was charming & your hat most satisfactory indeed. You looked your best at the wedding," Anna reassured her. "My brother [Teddy Roosevelt] was glad to see you again."

Beyond their ten-year age difference, Joe Alsop and Theo would not have been a good match. Although she was a registered Republican, Theo would have found it difficult to support Alsop's conservative political philosophy. Most of Theo's friends, including Anna, were aware that she had liberal tendencies. "Of course with that great big heart of yours," Mary Cassatt observed, "you lean toward socialism."

It was customary for women of Theo's class to do volunteer work for the downtrodden, and, for a short time, Theo worked at Lillian Wald's Henry Street settlement house for poor immigrant Jews in New York City. Impressed by the society woman's sincerity, Wald told Theo, "I should like you to consider that you had right of ownership here."

Witnessing the abject poverty of the immigrants, Theo became even more appalled by the inordinate wealth of the Popes' circle of relatives, friends, and business acquaintances—wealth that was blatantly apparent in their priceless art collections. She shared this distress with Mary Cassatt, who also came from a privileged background, but the artist disagreed with Theo's pronouncement about "the wickedness" of private individuals' owning great art. Cassatt saw "nothing wrong in a hardworking lawyer or business man putting some of his earnings in a work of art which appeals to him." In response to Theo's strong criticism of the exorbitant number of paintings owned by the Popes' friends, the Havemeyers, Cassatt argued, "I consider they are doing a great work for the country in spending so much time & money in bringing together such works of art." Although proud of Alfred's taste, Theo was embarrassed by his priceless collection, especially since, fearing for their safety, he refused to lend paintings to museums so that ordinary people could view them.

In December 1909, Theo required some kind of surgery. After the operation, a note from Anna, who wrote, "I will telephone Mr. Riddle soon to get more detailed news," indicates that the diplomat had visited Theo in her sickroom. He seemed to be taking Anna's advice to court Theo.

The following summer, Theo sailed to Europe. Ada described her daughter's travels as Theo's being "in the trail of Halley's comet." A nurse accompanied Theo, as well as the Popes' chauffeur Pratt and the Yellow Peril, their large Packard. From Southampton Theo wrote Alfred that, upon arriving on July 4, his 67th birthday, she had toasted him with champagne. "To my father," she declared, "may each succeeding day of his life be as happy as he has made each day of mine."

This trip would inspire Theo to develop a unique style of architecture and would be important to her private life. Her circle of women friends expanded, and she also began a close friendship with William James's brother, Henry.

A few months earlier, William and Alice James had gone to Bad Nauheim in the hope that the bath cures would help William regain his health. But the baths only aggravated his heart trouble, and he was recuperating in London. When Theo visited William and his wife at their hotel on Brook Street, she found him in terrible condition, wearing an overcoat over pajamas and "whimsical over his appearance and wretchedness." He listened intently as Theo told him about a séance she had attended in New York City with Eusapio Palladino, the internationally famous medium from Italy.

Theo described the hotel room that had been rented for the occasion. It was large, about thirty feet square and about thirteen feet high, with a bare floor and gray walls. In its center was a plain table surrounded by eight plain kitchen chairs. Above the table hung a single electric light bulb. At one end of the room, behind two black curtains, was a small closet, in which several musical instruments lay on a three-legged table. The middle-aged, dark-haired medium sat at the head of the table with her back to the closet. The sitters on either side held her hands and wound their feet around hers.

After a few minutes, the small table slowly emerged from behind the closet's curtains, rose in the air, tapped the wall three times, and then fell in front of Theo. She bent down and picked it up. Then using the table's legs, she tried to open the black curtains, but she felt a resisting force. As soon as she told the other sitters, she found that the force was gone, and she was able to put the table back into the closet. The table emerged again and acted similarly, but this time, Theo touched the curtain with her hand, which was seized by what seemed to be a finger and a thumb. Back at the table and holding the hands of the people on either side, Theo suddenly felt her velvet turban being lifted. Theo's hat, which had been held on with two hat pins, rose and then settled on the table in front of her.

Although both William James and Theo suspected that the medium was a fraud, James told Theo to report the experience to Sir Oliver Lodge, the head of the English Society for Psychical Research.

During another visit to the Jameses, Theo was conversing with Alice when a portly figure entered. Theo later said that Henry James stared sharply at her, "indignant at seeing a stranger," his eyes "like the barrels of a gun."

Alice left the room to announce Henry's arrival to William. Far from being intimidated by the novelist, Theo felt completely at ease. She leaned back in the chair and waited for him to speak. While Henry walked restlessly about the room, Theo remained silent. He then turned and said that he "had been following the advice of the Doctor who recommended one to chew every mouthful of his food so thoroughly that the nauseous mess left nothing for the stomach to attack."

After this comment, Theo and Henry began to converse, and their conversation became animated. By the time Alice returned, the two were chatting like old friends. As Theo rose to leave, Henry insisted that she spend the following day with him, for he wanted her to meet his friend, Mary Smythe Hunter. Theo looked forward to Henry's company on the motor trip to Eppin Forest and to meeting one of the Smythe sisters, who were known for their many talents, especially Dame Ethel Smythe, a musician, composer, and writer.

In the car the next day, Theo discovered that Henry had not been invited to the Hunters' home nor had he told Mary and her husband Charles that he and Theo were coming to see them. When Theo asked what they would do if the Hunters were not at home, Henry replied that their butler knew him well and would invite them in for tea.

Unfortunately, both the Hunters and their butler had gone out, and, not knowing Henry, the footman who greeted them did not issue an invitation. Theo and Henry were about to leave when Charles appeared at the gate and graciously asked them to tea. Arriving soon after with her sister, Nina Smythe Hollings, Mary insisted that Henry and Theo stay for dinner. Later, as they were motoring back to London, Henry put one leg across his knee and with his hand on the ankle, turned to Theo and said, "Now let us frankly admit that we were a distinct addition to that delightful party."

On a rainy afternoon in London, Theo and Henry shopped for household goods at army and navy stores. Henry had asked, "Will you come with me and oversee the thrifty purchase of a sponge?" A few days later, William and Alice joined them on an excursion to Chelsea in the Yellow Peril. Acting as the guide, Henry pointed out houses of literary interest. William sat quietly. He was "too wretched to talk" and asked Theo to excuse him.

At the end of the week, William, Alice, and Henry left for Henry's home, Lamb House, in the village of Rye, where Theo noted that the family lived "incognito—not one soul saw them but myself and Mr. Howells." To celebrate their friendship, Theo bought a puppy and named it "Jim Jam" after Henry. It was a "chow chow," she wrote Alfred, "a coffee colored ball of wool with the most outrageous mischievous eyes—and afraid of nothing. Do please you & mother make up your minds to love him for my sake."

Theo received an invitation to luncheon from Nina Smythe Hollings, who asked if she would drive another guest, Countess Helena Gleichen, a niece of the late Queen Victoria. Theo thought that the countess was "great fun" and that she also "paints with real strength," especially when the subject was horses.

Theo saw a great deal of Nina and Helena. One afternoon Nina had a tooth extracted, but she was cheerful at dinner. "She's the best sport," Theo observed. "It is needless to say that they are not the typical English women," she concluded, "or we would never have gotten on together."

Theo made a short trip to France, leaving Jim Jam with Nina and shipping the Yellow Peril across the English Channel. She visited Mary Cassatt and then left for Fontainebleau. On the way, "the very devil got into the car," she recalled. They were motoring along "one of those damned lonesome roads lined with poplars," when the magneto broke. At a village, Theo bought a new battery for the car, but it did not help. "We snapped and popped and exploded into Paris," she reported. Leaving the car there for repairs, she moved into a respectable hotel, where the people looked "very staid and dowdy; there [wasn't] a hobble skirt staying here at all."

After checking into the Hotel Ritz in Paris, Theo wrote Alfred about the "godforsaken" villages she had motored through, whose inhabitants she suspected "have gold in a stocking hidden away but spend nothing toward homey beauty in house or dress!" She despised the French. "Their selfishness and avarice is appalling!" she wrote. "France is rotten to the core. Don't pretend it isn't."

Arriving back in England, which after France she thought "looked doubly lovely," Theo stopped at Nina's to pick up Jim Jam and then headed north to visit the Ley family. Sir Francis Ley, owner of a malleable iron company in Scotland, was a business associate of Alfred's, and Theo had visited the family twenty years earlier during the Popes' grand tour of Europe.

While in Scotland, Theo also visited the Fergusons, whose son, Robert Munro Ferguson, she had met at Anna's home. Before Anna had married Admiral Cowles, she had lived at the U.S. Embassy in England with her widowed cousin, James Roosevelt, and had become acquainted with political figures, including the Scotland Fergusons, whose family seat at Raith was a center of Liberal Party politics.

Several years earlier, handsome Robert Munro Ferguson had emigrated to America and become a Rough Rider with Teddy Roosevelt in the 1898 Spanish-American War. Bob was a favorite escort of Anna's niece, Eleanor Roosevelt, and "his charming, affectionate presence had enabled Eleanor to endure the agony of her coming-out year." Later, Ferguson married Eleanor's best friend, the brilliant, beautiful, and much younger Isabella Selmes. Isabella was the niece of John Wallace Riddle, the diplomat who, in Anna's opinion, would be a good match for Theo.

The enormous estates of the Fergusons' neighbors astounded Theo. "Sir Charles Ross where we had tea the other day owns 450 thousand acres," she wrote her parents, and "the Duke of Sutherland who has a castle fifty miles north of us—his niece whom Anna Cowles knows—owns over one million acres."

From Newberry, Theo wrote Ada of a visit to Lady Sutton's enormous Georgian house, which was situated on 3,000 acres. As Theo entered the foyer, nine Pekingese dogs swarmed around her. Before dinner, Theo was shown the dogs' room, "a room as neat and sweet and airy as a nursery," where there were twenty-one more Pekingese.

On her way back to London, Theo again visited Nina and Helena and had tea with the Crown Princess of Sweden and Princess Patricia. Nearby, at the home of the Empress Eugenia, she met the daughters of a local duke and "one of the prettiest girls I ever looked at, but quite empty headed."

The following day, Theo went to Southampton to see Nina's son's regiment leave for India. Listening to the band playing "Auld Lang Syne," "The Girl I Left Behind Me," and finally "God Save the King," Theo noticed that the poor people were weeping. In contrast to the sons of the rich who could quit the service whenever they wished, the sons of the poor had to serve for fourteen years, and their families knew they might never see them again.

Theo contemplated not returning to America. She had made good friends, and she loved not only the landscape but the architecture of England, most particularly that of the picturesque Cotswold area. She adored the medieval look of the cottages and admired the handmade methods of construction. She wrote Anna Cowles that, were it not for Alfred and Ada, she would have preferred to live in England like the expatriate Henry James.

"Theodate you are too fine to become one of that large class of homeless Americans," Anna replied. "There is so much to do for one's own
country & people & so few to take up the duties & responsibilities of good
citizens & when as in your case you have the money & the mind necessary
it is dreadful even in a casual way to think of being homeless. [It] is, at best
making a home among people where you would be a stranger."

From Henry's Lamb House, Alice James wrote Theo that, after being
severely ill, William had begun to improve. The Jameses planned to sail
back to America, but, in early September 1910, William died suddenly.
Viewing his death as "a dreadful loss" to her personally as well as "to the
intellectual world," Theo returned to America a week later.

After she arrived home, she received a real commission. Impressed by
the beauty of Westover School, Joseph Chamberlain, a Columbia
University professor, asked Theo to design a house for his family in
Middlebury.

Influenced by the medieval cottages of the Cotswold area of England,
Theo created for Chamberlain a house with a high steep roof, an exteri-
or chimney, and flat-topped dormered windows. She also followed the
philosophy of the British Arts and Crafts movement that stressed the
importance of having house and landscape connect. Architectural critic
Judith Paine points out that Chamberlain House and its garden form a
"single design," and, almost as if it were a living entity, this beautiful
home sits "calmly on the hill overlooking Lake Quassapaug."

At this time, Theo established an office in a small house, which she
called "Underledge," on the Hill-Stead estate. Her stationery and the
door of the office announced "Theodate Pope, Architect," followed by
JIL. Hill-Stead, Westover School, and now Chamberlain House attested
to Theo's considerable gifts as an architect. Perhaps other projects were
on the horizon.

The Joseph Chamberlain House, Middlebury, Connecticut. *(HS)*.

The Dairymen's Association and Connecticut Pomological Society's
picnic at Hill-Stead. *(HS)*.

Theo and friends at Westover School site. *(AOF)*.

Courtyard of Westover School. *(HS)*.

Henry James. *(HS)*.

Theo holding Jim Jam, puppy named
for Henry James. *(HS)*.

Countess Helena Gleichen. *(HS)*.

SEVEN

"A grievous shock and strain"
1911—1913

THEO TRIED to keep busy. She looked in on the cooking and sewing schools she had established in Farmington and visited Mary at Westover. She made frequent excursions to New York City, where she saw friends, consulted mediums, met with Dr. Hyslop at the American Institute for Scientific Research of New York, and sat in her Manhattan office hoping that the telephone would ring.

Mary Cassatt advised Theo to work for a worthwhile cause while she waited for another architectural commission. "I do hope you are going to be interested in the suffrage," Mary wrote. "Mrs. Havemeyer wants to know if I haven't talked to you on that subject, you must talk to her." Mary could not understand why a professional woman like Theo refused to become involved. Theo openly stated that women should have the right to vote, but she would not become a suffragette because she did not want to upset Alfred or alienate her friends in Farmington.

Anna Cowles expressed the sentiments of most of the Farmington valley set. "I feel the most important work for the women of this country is to make happy homes and set high minded standards," she pronounced. "As for the Suffrage, I feel & have always felt that when the majority of women in the country wanted it they ought to have it." The majority, she argued, did not want it.

The friendship between Theo and Anna had progressed to the stage where the two women spoke honestly with each other, even though Anna had little sympathy for spiritualism, socialism, or suffrage. "I am always deeply interested in all that concerns you and always love to have you tell me of your news and interests," Anna told Theo, "but, dear you can hardly expect me to change my opinions just because I care for you."

When Theo suggested that if women voted, there would be no more wars, another good friend, Marianna van Rensselaer, dryly commented, "My father used to say that during the Civil War the most pugnacious people were the women and the parsons."

Even Ida Tarbell, the famous "muckraker" writer who visited Theo at Hill-Stead, spoke against suffrage. Tarbell had gained enormous public stature by writing exposés of giant capitalist monopolies, but she expressed regret that she had forsaken the traditional female role, and she encouraged other women to remain at home and not to seek careers.

"I am most grateful that I belong to the generation of almost equal rights and almost equal sacrifice," Ada asserted. She saw nothing wrong with the position of women—especially that of the women of her class. "My life has been lovely," she declared.

Most discouraging to Theo was Alfred's belief that women's having the right to vote would harm the country. Despite supporting his daughter's ambitions and those of her friends, Alfred contended that woman suffrage threatened the most important values of society.

On April 5, 1911, at the State Capitol building in Hartford, a leader of the suffragettes, Katharine Martha Houghton Hepburn, wife of Dr. Thomas Hepburn and mother of the future film star Katharine Hepburn, was allowed to speak on a proposed Woman Municipal Suffrage Bill. Theo observed the proceedings. Mrs. Hepburn was "regal" in appearance and persuasive in her arguments, but the House voted against the bill as anti-suffrage onlookers applauded.

On June 1, 1911, an anti-suffrage petition was published in the *Hartford Daily Courant.* Anna signed it, and there were other prominent names, including that of Mrs. Charles Dudley Warner, the wife of the writer and editor. An asterisk appeared next to Theo's name, and, at the bottom of the page, a statement explained that her opposition was limited to the next ten years. By signing the petition, Theo appeased friends and family, but the stipulation asserted some independence.

Theo's strongest political convictions concerned the economic inequities she saw around her. She believed that socialism was necessary to eliminate excessive wealth, which was the evil that harmed both the poor as well as the spoiled, unhappy rich. She promoted socialist ideas to anyone who would listen, despite Alfred's disapproval. "If you don't stop talking about Socialism," Ada warned, "your father is going to leave you out of his will." On a summer evening, Theo held forth on the benefits of socialism as she, Alfred and Ada, and their dinner guests sat on the wide verandah at Hill-Stead. "I could see my father getting red in the face," Theo recalled. "Then I said, suddenly, 'Why, Father, you think that I invented Socialism, and that if I just shut up there would be no Socialist Party.' Everyone laughed, even my father."

Despite egalitarian sentiments, Theo enjoyed the friendship of those who considered socialism and the suffrage anathema. As evident in his novels, Henry James had little interest in people without money or high social class. Henry also did not favor woman suffrage. Writing about successful women, the novelist dubbed them "forceful ladies" and admitted that they intimidated him. Why give them more power?

After William's death, Henry returned to America to visit his brother's family in Cambridge and to travel about in the Northeast. He lunched with Theo in New York City, and she invited him to spend a week at Hill-Stead.

In response, Henry inquired whether he might bring along his valet Burgess, who was "very small and very humble-minded, very inoffensive and self effacing." Theo had no objection, and Henry announced that he would arrive with the "little attendant" on Saturday, May 20, 1911.

Theo also invited Charles Dana and Augustus "Gus" Jaccaci, the art connoisseur and former art director at *McClure's Magazine.* Jaccaci was a dark handsome man, who was said to have painted the murals in the Havana Opera House and to have killed an enemy in a duel. Theo and Jaccaci became friends during the building of Westover. He helped design the school emblem and worked with Theo on other artistic details associated with the school.

On an extremely hot Saturday afternoon, Jaccaci met Henry and Burgess at the Hartford railroad station and drove them to Hill-Stead. According to James's journal, the next day he lunched with Admiral and Mrs. Cowles, and during the week, there was "much motoring—to Hartford and elsewhere."

Hill-Stead's chauffeur Pratt drove Henry, the valet, and Theo in the Yellow Peril to New Haven, where she and Henry lunched with Yale people. A few days later, they rode to the home of Henry's cousin, the artist Bay Emmet, in Salisbury, about forty five miles from Farmington. On route, they stopped at Middlebury to visit Westover School, which Henry pronounced a "very charming place."

When the elegant, open automobile arrived at the school, the valet leapt out. Henry handed him the soft cap he had worn for the trip, and Burgess gave Henry a Panama hat. As the students watched in awe, their beaming visitor looked around, "made stiff bows, and waved the hat." When asked his first impression of the town of Middlebury, James replied, "It keeps its distance so well." Shown the school's medieval chapel, he murmured, "Quite right, quite right, so civilizing."

As he entered the Red Hall, where the students had gathered, the girls applauded loudly. "My mind has been undermined," James pronounced. According to a student, "On he went from there felicitating us upon the felicity of dwelling so felicitously in this felicitous setting." And then, with "much waving of hand and hat," he left the room, leaving "his last sentence unfinished."

Mary Hillard introduced the novelist to young Nancy Robinson and asked him to give the child something to help her remember this special day. Reaching down, James pinched Nancy on the ear and said, "If she thinks of a sharp pinch that really hurts, it will help her."

The extent of his flowery expression was apparent in the letter Theo received from Henry after the visit: "It was a wonderful and admirable day one of those blest boons that abide with one always and become subject to endless refiguring and overhauling, for the wealth of impression and the fondness of reminiscences that they contain," began Henry's epistle of gratitude.

His note, of course, included the word, "felicity." "Yet your generosity over the whole affair, your surrender of time and strength and beautiful invention—to say nothing of precious gasoline (how I winced in silence over the grim renewal of the ebbing fluid, on Pratt's part, at the place that came after Pomfret!)—already begins to affect me as fabulous, mythical and well-nigh incredible; falling in, indeed, thereby with all the beauty and irresponsibility and lavish felicity of picture that tended to make the perpetual adventure just the most masterly of summer's day fairy-tales."

James had especially enjoyed being chauffeured around in the Yellow Peril, to which he compared his ride back to Cambridge "in a prosaically-acquired car that was as to our fairy-godmother's gold-colored chariot—well, as is a scrap of newspaper to a page of Keats."

Henry ended by saying that he had become aware that Theo was ill. "I quite dread to learn that you may, like the King of France, have simply 'marched down' again," he remarked. But he knew that Alfred and Ada were "ready to pour every bit of balm on fatigue."

James was correct. Theo was not well, but her condition was more serious than fatigue. In early July, she had another operation. Whether it was related to the surgery she had undergone the previous year is unknown. According to Anna, Theo had been undergoing treatments in New York for a lump. The tumor was in a delicate spot, as evident in Theo's embarrassment when she learned that the doctor Anna recommended was unmarried. "I supposed I had made a mistake as to which Dr. Curtis it was as I know the Madison Avenue one was married," Anna apologized. "I cannot see what you are to do in view of being in the midst of your treatment unless you firmly take your maid as a friend with you when you go to his office."

Anna said that she would have moved into Roosevelt Hospital to be with Theo if she had known the seriousness of Theo's condition. "An operation of that kind must be a shock to one's whole system, a nightmare. I grieve that from what you say I imagine the operation was more radical than I had hoped & yet my beloved Theodate the joy that it was not malignant." The operation involved more than the removal of the tumor. "I cannot bear to think of your courage which I know you had when you heard what the operation had been," Anna declared. "To have any part of oneself [gone] is so difficult to accept."

Mary Hillard's letter indicates that the operation was a hysterectomy. "In even the little things that hamper a woman with the most hateful and discouraging frequency," she wrote, "it is more than worth while to make the effort for freedom." A benefit of Theo's operation was the cessation of menstruation, but, at the same time, knowing that many women felt less womanly after losing their uterus, Mary continued, "Just now you doubtless need reassurance. And so I want to tell you that both Helen LaMonte and Lucy in speaking of you since your illness have both of them dwelt upon *how lovely* you looked to them. Do not for a moment drift into thinking you are other than what we all know you to be—full of charm and loveliness."

Theo had escaped the most serious consequence, had the growth been malignant. She would live, but she felt depressed. She doubted that she would get another architectural commission, and her spiritualist work had become frustrating after the death of William James.

Mrs. Piper had moved to London, and her health was failing. "Have you heard that Mrs. Piper does not go into trances anymore?" Alice James wrote. In this letter, Alice also thanked Theo for sending a copy of a *Times* article that reported a message another medium had received from the soul of William James. Alice looked "in vain for one characteristic word" in her husband's message. She observed that "the verbiage is so *unlike* [his]," it would be "abhorrent to William."

Henry was enraged when Theo sent him the same article. "I return you the dreadful document," he replied, "pronouncing it without hesitation the most abject and impudent, the hollowest, vulgarest and basest rubbish I could possibly conceive." What most angered Henry was that Theo or anyone of culture and taste could possibly believe that the words were William's, for they were "utterly empty and illiterate, without substance as sense, a mere babble of platitudinous phrases, and it is beneath comment or criticism, in short, beneath contempt."

"The *commonness* of it simply nauseates," he sputtered. Henry despised "those people for whom such lucubrations represent a series of *values*, or who spend their time, and invite others to spend theirs over them." He blamed "new kinds and degrees of commonness" on America, which had produced "a flatness of level and thinness of air" that lacked "criticism and comparison and education and taste and tradition, and the perception and measure and standard of—well, again of more things than I can name to you." Unfortunately, he believed, America had also affected Theo. Although she was a person of "fine and true quality," she had demonstrated the audacity "to pass on such a tissue of trash."

"See how you make me write," he charged, "as if I were writing *at* you!" It was her fault that he was so upset, not just about the message supposedly from the beyond, but because she would consider taking it seriously. Had he misjudged her? He was filled "with a bewildered sense of strangeness through which I look at you as over the abyss of oddity of your *asking* about that thing to which I hate to accord the dignity even of sending it safely back to you!"

Finally, Henry ended his attack. "I see you again in that charming light of last summer and of all the Farmington hospitality and beauty," he recalled, "and of the wondrous motor-days in particular." He now expressed affection: "I embrace you tenderly and respectfully, if you let me."

Changing the subject, Henry remarked, "I saw Countess Helena Gleichen a little some time ago and found her as hard as all the nails of old Jewry put up to auction." Even Helena, he sighed, still upset about the article, "wouldn't have sent me that document, no; but she would have sent me cold poison and then charged me Ten Pounds for it."

Ending the letter by expressing the wish that he could be back at Hill-Stead, where he "could sprawl on the red cretonne," Henry signed it, "your affectionate friend," and added a P.S.: "I should like to send my very best love to the beautiful, bountiful, graceful parents."

Stunned by the onslaught of Henry's criticism of Americans, particularly those foolish enough to take spiritualism seriously, Theo was speechless. She did not react to his nasty remark about her friend Helena. She knew that the robust countess considered Henry a pretentious, effete Anglophile. Helena wickedly commented that she "loved having my mind put tidy by Henry James and found the long pauses while he hunted for the exact right word *most* restful."

Theo was angry—not at Henry but at herself. She had known that he disapproved of his brother William's interest in psychical research, and she had read Henry's satire, *The Bostonians,* which mocked feminists and spiritualists. She never should have sent him the article. She replied to his lengthy diatribe by printing "WHOW" in the center of a piece of notepaper.

At the end of August 1912, Theodate received a formal-looking document. It was an invitation to take part in the competition to build the Loomis Institute, a school that an old Windsor, Connecticut family planned to found. The invitation stated that the school would cost

$300,000 or more and that there would be twelve competing architects, three who were specifically invited and nine from the open field. Theo was thrilled to be one of the nine. At last, she might have another opportunity to work.

Theo did not win the competition, but in early February 1913, she did receive a commission to build a house in Locust Valley on Long Island for Charles and Elizabeth Gates. Theo designed what she called Dormer House, which she intended to be "a rambling English house, somehow cozy, but dignified at the same time."

The approach to Dormer House is through several acres of forest up a long road, bordered by oak, beech, and tulip trees. Like Hill-Stead and Chamberlain House, it stands on the crest of a hill. The English Arts and Crafts influence is present in the design. Dormer House is basically a long Norman Tudor with a red brick facade. The most striking feature is the roof, which has a row of protruding dormers across its front. Like the roofs of Westover School and Chamberlain house, the roof is high and steep with shingles that seem to cascade down the slope. Another unusual feature of the house is a large wing added onto the main house at a 120-degree angle.

Architectural critics have pointed out that Dormer House testifies to a significant characteristic of Theo's art, the "ability to let the nature and texture of the materials themselves become the decorative elements of the composition." The texture and color of the red brick exterior contrast with the roof's "overwhelming presence." The brick facade also reflects the Arts and Crafts' mandate that the artist use natural materials like wood, brick, and stone to create the effect of a medieval cottage or castle.

In this, her fourth project, Theo again demonstrated her awareness of the importance of connecting the house to the landscape. The attached wing is "ingeniously shaped to conform with the surrounding trees." Theo created the entire setting, which includes smaller buildings on the grounds, drives, and areas she designated to become gardens. She oversaw every stage of the construction and directed the workmen on-site, wearing knickers and boots when the mud became ankle deep.

The beauty of open space is evident in the interior rooms. Theo was also concerned with the decoration of the rooms. She conferred with Elizabeth Gates about choosing carpets and wallpaper. No detail was minor. After discovering that the painters had shellacked the floors, which she had not specified, Theo ordered them to remove the shellac and to stain the floors the proper color.

The house was completed in early 1914 at a cost of approximately $50,000. Theo received $3,000 for her services. The Gates family later sold Dormer House to Isabella Dodge Sloane of the Dodge automobile family. In 1933, the Sloanes added a large extension with an indoor pool; in Monica Randall's *The Mansions of Long Island's Gold Coast,* the house was described as a "play palace," where a stream of guests attended Gatsby-like parties. The house's name also changed. It became known as Lockjaw House, which spoofed the pompous manner of Long Island's uppercrust, who spoke with rigidly-set jaws.

During the time that she worked on the Gateses' house, Theo lived at the Renaissance Hotel, but she returned frequently to Farmington. From the window at the back of the O'Rourkery, she liked to look up the grassy slope and watch Alfred play golf on Hill-Stead's small course. When the Popes had guests, Theo usually moved into Hill-Stead. She had overcome her youthful aversion to "society" and shared with Ada the pleasure of entertaining in their home. Ada and Theo now enjoyed a fairly peaceful, affectionate relationship.

In New York City, Theo participated in social functions and attended dances, dinner parties, luncheons, and the opera. New York's wealthiest families, which included the Havemeyers, van Rensselaers, and the Vanderbilts, welcomed her. Theo's new friend, Emily Jay, belonged to "the ultra exclusive old time New York set," Anna Cowles told her. "So when she calls on you, it is because she *really* wants to know you." Miss Jay sought Theo's company because she "admires clever people." Emily, added Anna cattily, "is not clever herself."

Although Theo had strong attachments to various people, her love for Alfred always surpassed any feelings for friends, other relatives, or men and women with whom she thought herself in love. Showing considera-tion for her mother, Theo informed Alfred and Ada, "Do not either of you forget ever that it is you two who make this happiness in my life. I hope we three may be spared for one another for many years to come."

From the time when Theo was a schoolgirl, Alfred had been the most significant person in her life, and Theo was at the center of his world. Ignoring Ada's disappointment, he had calmly accepted Theo's rejec-tion of Harris and her decision never to marry. And, despite Ada's disapproval of Mary Hillard, Alfred had given Theo's friend financial support to build Westover School. If not for Alfred, Theo would not have pursued a career as an architect.

Father and daughter looked alike, and in some ways they thought alike, especially about art. Their temperaments, however, were almost completely opposite. Alfred was always prudent, politic, dignified, and reserved, while Theo had difficulty trying to control mood swings and impulsiveness. Theo disagreed with Alfred about woman suffrage and socialism, but she respected no one's opinions more than her father's, and she usually followed his advice.

Sometimes the affinity between Theo and Alfred was dramatically apparent. Shortly before Alfred's seventy-first birthday on July 4, 1913, Theo went into Hartford to buy him a gift. Looking at an exhibition of engravings at Kennedy's Print Shop, she suddenly stopped in front of a picture, turned to a clerk and asked the price. "I am sorry," he explained, "but that mezzotint has just been sold to Alfred A. Pope of Farmington."

Alfred enjoyed excellent health and led an active life, but on Tuesday morning, August 5, 1913, he suddenly suffered a cerebral hemorrhage. He did not regain consciousness and died before the day ended.

Alfred had resided in Farmington since the beginning of the century, but he had made arrangements to be buried in Salem, the small town in Ohio where he had lived as a boy. The journey and the funeral were a blurred nightmare for Ada and Theo. On their return to Hill-Stead, they refused to receive any visitors except Harris.

Even Anna Cowles was not allowed entry. When she tried to visit, the Popes' butler Earnest said that Theo was refusing to see anyone. Anna had planned to go on vacation with her husband and their teenage son, Sheffield. "I simply hate going away," she wrote Theo, "and I would wait a little longer," but Will and Sheffield would not leave without her and she hated to disappoint them. She said that she would return immediately should Theo need her. The next day, after expressing further regrets, Anna rationalized, "Probably when I get back I may be more useful than now."

From a hotel in Albany, Anna wrote, "In the face of such sorrow it seems absurd to say it, but I feel it is a deep personal loss to me, for I always felt when I needed a friend your Father would always be there for all three of us." She continued to send letters daily.

Other letters of sympathy poured into Hill-Stead. From Scotland, Lady Alison Ley and her husband Sir Francis, Alfred's friend and business associate for over thirty-five years, extended their sympathy. Eight years earlier Sir Francis had experienced a stroke similar to the one that killed Alfred, and he assured Ada and Theo that he would have preferred to have died rather than to live on as he was, paralyzed on his left side.

Letters from other friends arrived. From Ohio, Belle wrote that she understood Theo's loneliness, but she advised going on with life and establishing a stronger relationship with Ada: "I have had real faith that you two would build together better than you dare hope." Belle also spoke of Alfred's wisdom, "You know I quote him to myself often."

"I did not know how much I loved you until I heard of your terrible loss and thought of your suffering," Marianna van Rensselaer sympathized. And from Hull House, Jane Addams's settlement house in Chicago, Dr. Alice Hamilton described Alfred as "a very unusual and lovely person."

From France, Gus Jaccaci observed, "He lived as a most perfect, the most beautiful example I have known in the greatest of all arts, the art of living, a *simple, unostentatious, noble,* and *true* life."

Theo was touched by the story that Isabella Selmes Ferguson told about how she had first met Alfred. Isabella, her husband Bob, and their six-weeks-old baby were on a long train trip, and, when night came, they could not quiet their child. "We were all so tired and so dreadfully embarrassed by Martha's unending wails," Isabella related. Then a dignified older man approached them. The stranger was Alfred, who asked to see the baby. He then told the young couple of a trip he had taken with Theo when she was a child. "He almost made us feel he liked hearing a baby's weary cry," Isabella claimed. She realized that the incident was "a little thing," but it was a moment that told of Alfred's gentleness and kindness.

"You have had your dear father for twenty five years longer than I had mine," Corinne Roosevelt Robinson reminded Theo. "I have always wished that my father might have lived long enough for me to have a mature friendship with him as well as having experienced a great, girlish passion for him. You have what I missed."

Several months earlier, Henry James had written Theo about his own poor health. He said he had been "put into durance by my Doctor, who has also placed on guard of me a mild dragon of a Nurse." He complained, "I am rather in a minor key—so that I can't raise any very high note." But when he received a cable from Theo telling of Alfred's death, he immediately responded. "I devotedly share in your sorrow," he began. "May I venture to say that your Father's admirable hospitality and cordiality to me, with the sense of his generous loyal nature and all his delicacies of taste and tact, left me with a feeling of affection for him beyond the mere measure of our too few contacts." Henry was saddened by his vision of Hill-Stead, "your beautiful, your exquisite palace of peace and light and harmony overdarkened and shaken in a grievous shock and strain."

William James's daughter Peggy wrote that she knew "the valley of desolation through which one has to walk," but the young woman was "so thankful that you believe in that other life." Theo's spiritualist beliefs, however, did not assuage her grief. "No matter what faith what certitude we may have," Mary Cassatt commiserated, "we feel the separation terribly."

Dormer House, Long Island. *(HS)*.

Theo and Alfred. *(HS)*.

EIGHT

"My architectural work, psychical research,
and little Gordon"
1914—1915

ALFRED LEFT $5.5 million in assets, not including land and his art collection. Hill-Stead's household goods, which three years earlier had taken 300 pages to catalogue, and other property went to Ada, who received forty percent of the estate with ten percent to be invested in trust; $500,000 was to be invested for income for Theo. Other bequests included property in Cleveland left to Western Reserve University's School of Law and generous sums to relatives. Apparently the income from Alfred's plan of investments was insufficient, so Harris, as executor of the will, went to probate court and arranged an increase.

A few weeks after Alfred died, workmen digging in the peach orchard came upon bone-like objects that looked like vertebrae, but the disks measured over five inches. They reported their discovery to Theo, who contacted Yale University's Peabody Museum. A team of specialists arrived and identified the bones as those of a gigantic mastodon—a rarity on this continent.

The ensuing flurry of paleontological activity on Hill-Stead's grounds contrasted with the sadness of the mourners in the house. Finding the remains of a prehistoric era, however, might have struck Theo as symbolic. Indeed, in its Edenic beauty, Hill-Stead always seemed a place where time stood still. Outsiders remarked that Alfred, Ada, and their daughter appeared never to age. And Earnest Bohlen, now in his fourth decade of service, looked the same. But Alfred's death was dramatic evidence that the years go by, and the world changes.

In a condolence letter, Theo's cousin Alden Brooks wrote that he was certain that, "however deeply wounded inside," his grief-stricken Aunt Ada "would go on, head high, fighting bravely to the end." His words were more hopeful than true. Crushed by Alfred's death, Ada retreated into self-pity and depression.

Although it meant leaving Theo alone, Ada explained that she must get away from Hill-Stead. Taking along Earnest, Pratt the chauffeur, several maids, and Theo's old fox terrier, Silas, Ada went to Augusta, Georgia, to stay with Brooks relatives. She wrote pathetic letters telling Theo not to worry—she was not worth her daughter's time or energy.

Becoming increasingly concerned, Theo engaged a physician in Augusta to attend her "darling little Mother." Petulantly, Ada responded,

"I do not need him and I know I could use the three dollar visit to better advantage. Doctors do not heal broken hearts."

"Do not fasten a doctor on me," Ada warned, "or I shall go so far away that you cannot reach me." She also had advice for Theo. "Do not plunge into work!" she pleaded, believing that rest was the best way to deal with grief.

Alfred had always embraced the opposite philosophy. "He seemed to think I'd never see him again," Alden wrote, recalling the last time he and Uncle Alf were together. "But I pooh-poohed this idea out of our conversation as best I could. Then, finally, after we had teased each other a little, he put his hand on my shoulder and said, 'Well, Alden, work, work, work, and concentrate, concentrate, that's the secret always.'"

Theo followed Alfred's counsel and the example of his life. Although grief-stricken and suffering from shingles, she plunged into a whirlwind of activity. She seemed to have become liberated. Since she no longer could or needed to seek Alfred's approval and did not care about anyone else's, she forged ahead in several directions simultaneously.

In October 1913, she opened a new architectural office on East 40th Street. She decided not to wait for another commission but to build three double cottages in Farmington for the farm workers at Hill-Stead. The modest, picturesque homes were simple and comfortable with partially enclosed front porches so that, on summer evenings, the families could sit and watch passersby. Characteristics of Theo's previous work appeared in their design, though on a much smaller scale, including steeply-sloped, dormered roofs that overhang the first floor.

Almost immediately after finishing the workers' houses, Theo was asked to design the Hop Brook School, a public elementary school in Naugatuck, Connecticut. The Whittemores were the most prominent family in town, and Harris managed to get the commission for Theo.

Theo took great care to make the school fit into its charming New England setting. She set it far back from the road, and, as with Dormer House, used brick for the facade. The design is a long rectangle for the upper grades that connects by means of a curving wall to a small wing for the youngest children. On the small wing's door appears a whimsical carving, "ABC." Behind the curved connecting wall, hidden from the front, is the playground. Compared to the imposing seriousness of most multi-storied, square public schools with their rows of blankly staring windows and dark, asphalt playgrounds, the effect of Hop Brook's spacious front lawn, arched doorways, and simple design is pleasant and welcoming.

In a letter to Ada, Theo said that, in addition to work on the Hop Brook School and her involvement in Dr. Hyslop's institute, during the past week she had attended a State Central Committee meeting of the Progressive Party in New Haven, lunched with Anna in Farmington, and conducted a séance in the apartment at the Hotel Renaissance in New York. The exciting news was that another medium, a society woman whose name she did not mention, had recently contacted Alfred in the spiritual world; Theo, however, did not relay his message.

Feeling released from her promise to Alfred, Theo became active in the woman suffrage movement. To help Louisine Havemeyer, a fervent suffragette who was organizing an art exhibition to raise funds for the cause, Theo tried to persuade Ada to exhibit four of Hill-Stead's paintings. Though there was little risk to the pictures, Theo said she would understand if Ada did not want to lend Degas's *The Quarrel*. "If anything happened to that," she wrote, "we could not make it up to Harris," who had given the painting to Alfred.

Ada refused to lend any pictures. "I know you will be disappointed, but I have many reasons," she explained. "One great one is that your father was very much opposed to woman's suffrage. He looked so sad once, when he said if I ever followed you in that, he would feel he had lived for naught—[and] the pictures are so much a part of him."

"The pictures were his, they are yours and it is for you to say," Theo responded. But she went on to inform Ada that the dangerous political situation in Europe was a consequence of women not having the vote. "This is a man's world thus far," she observed, "and they are making fine fools of themselves over there." German women "have permitted the Prussians to develop into the brutes that they are," she said, adding that the women were too weak-willed to fight for the power to exercise a civilizing influence.

Theo had more to tell her mother. In April 1914, acting on a resolution that she had made almost thirty years earlier when Ada refused to adopt an orphan, Theo had taken in a child: two-year-old Gordon Brockway, who had been abandoned by his parents.

Ada was shocked and outraged that Theo had brought an outsider into their small family, even though Theo tried to convince her that the child was not going to change their lives. Gordon would stay at the O'Rourkery with Mr. and Mrs. Stewart, a couple she had hired, who would bring him to Hill-Stead only at specific times. She assured Ada that the boy was beautiful, normal, and healthy. Theo's friend and physician, Dr. Foster Kennedy, had thoroughly examined him.

Even more compelling was the promise of Miss Guy of the New York State Charities Aid. She told Theo she "could take the boy for a week, month or three months, any time I choose, and return him at any time, and that she will be sure to place him in some home that would be entirely satisfactory, so that I would not feel that he was being neglected if I found he did not prove the kind of child I wished." One rarely received that kind of guarantee even when purchasing a dog.

Ada was not persuaded. She was so enraged that she could not find words to argue with Theo. Surprisingly, Mary Hillard agreed with Ada. "Your mother thinks it your own affair and your right (if it be called that) to have the child," she wrote. But "she thinks it her right not to have the child imposed upon her in any way whatsoever. (And of course that is what all your friends think too)."

According to Mary, Ada would accept the situation only "if she need never see or hear of the child save by the chances that will come up of themselves." But Ada feared that Theo would not be able to hold herself back from "'springing' the child onto her." Mary warned that, because of the child, Ada might move from Farmington, and "if she does not return to Hill-Stead, all the servants are going to leave, including Earnest."

Ada would act the martyr and remain in Farmington only because the staff's leaving would be "too terrible" for Theo. If Theo did not meet Ada's condition about keeping the child out of her life, however, "she will definitely and permanently turn the house over to your care and leave Farmington forever. She will in that case live in Salem or Cleveland."

Theo must have expressed disappointment—or worse—to Mary for taking Ada's side. Less than a week after Mary's letter, a Westover student wrote Theo, "I think it is too bad that the custom of having you give us a holiday is going to be stopped and I don't see why Miss Hillard wouldn't let you give us one."

Theo's friends were astonished not only that she had taken in a child but also that the child was a boy. Marianna van Rensselaer "could not understand why, with all your 'feminist' sympathies and ideas, you did not choose a little girl and show what could be made out of her!"

To complete the new family she was creating, Theo now considered adding a husband. Her choice was John Wallace Riddle, the handsome, cosmopolitan diplomat Anna had introduced to her eight years earlier. Curiously, he had almost the same name as the hero John Ridd in *Lorna Doone*, Theo's favorite novel as a girl.

Over six-feet tall, slim, and dark-eyed, John Riddle at fifty had thick gray hair and sported a full mustache. A Harvard graduate and a member of several elite clubs in New York and Washington, he was a popular house guest because of his intelligence, charm, and elegance in manners and dress. He had a remarkable facility for languages and was fluent in at least a half-dozen. Riddle owed much of his success as a diplomat to the support of Teddy Roosevelt. There were rumors, however, that he was a womanizer and had lost his last post as ambassador to Russia because of gambling. Though he lived well, he presently had neither a position nor much money.

After Alfred's death and throughout 1914, Theo and John met frequently. He wrote flowery letters such as the one that recalled a rainy picnic at Hill-Stead: "Notwithstanding the leaden sky and the dreary downpour, that day stands out as the brightest of all my Farmington memories." He realized how busy she was and how difficult it would be for her to take "a day or two out of [her] interesting occupations." He added, "If there is going to be a time in the next week or two when you have nothing to do and can devote all your time to me," he wanted to be with her.

Although the sophisticated diplomat was not a spiritualist, he sent Theo a book on psychical matters because he "thought it looked interesting and that you might find something suggestive in it for your researches."

During the summer of 1914, John wrote Theo an eloquent letter from The Breakers, the Vanderbilts' palatial home overlooking the ocean in Newport, Rhode Island. "From my corner room there is the most enchanting view over the sea in two directions," he observed, "and absolute stillness except for the breakers on the shore."

A few weeks later, John told Theo that he was planning to leave soon for England but had heard that she might be visiting the Vanderbilts at the end of July. If so, he would postpone his trip and meet her in Newport. "Only I should not brook any rivalries of new architectural creations or village parties," he teased, "but should expect you to continue your philanthropic efforts by devoting all your mornings to me and the lovely surrounding country."

Theo spent July 22-30 at The Breakers with John. Because of the war in Europe, John delayed his trip not only to be with Theo but also because he thought it "more prudent to wait until the first panic is over and the great crowd of American refugees had evacuated London."

The outbreak of war was no surprise to John nor to anyone else who was aware of recent events. Earlier that summer, on June 28, Archduke Francis Ferdinand, Crown Prince of Austria, had been assassinated in Sarajevo. In response, the Austro-Hungarian government declared war. During the first week of August, Germany went to war against Russia and began its march on Belgium.

Germany attacked Belgium on August 4. Because of its treaty with Belgium, Great Britain then declared war on Germany. The next day, the United States proclaimed its neutrality, followed by a statement that all the belligerents should agree that the open seas were to remain neutral areas.

Theo felt strongly about the war between Great Britain and Germany. "Whatever else could [the Germans] expect when they have insulted England for years, and she is now simply and honorably keeping her agreement with the Triple Alliance?" she demanded. "If they wanted England's help against the Slavs, they have been taking a very queer way to get it after the last twenty-five years." She hoped that Germany would be destroyed "beyond recognition."

Several young men she knew immediately volunteered to fight, including Christopher Ley, the son of Sir Francis and Lady Alison in Scotland, and Nina Hollings' two boys. When Germany declared war on France, one of several students whose education Theo was financing wrote that he must return home and join the French army. "If I die, you lose the money you lent me," he apologized.

Too old to be a soldier, Gus Jaccaci established a center in Paris to help Belgian refugee children, and the novelist and expatriate, Edith Wharton, became involved in his project. Gus wrote Theo of the misery and suffering of the orphans and thanked her for the money she was sending.

Theo received other letters from abroad. Nina and Helena were working in hospitals and soliciting contributions from Americans. In November, Nina thanked Theo for a generous contribution. She also wrote, "My poor boy Jack is badly wounded and missing." Her other son was coming home for one day to be married— "no wedding feast or anything (naturally)." Countess Helena desperately wanted "this ghastly war" to end, but she contended, "we mustn't leave off until the Germans are smashed or it will begin all over again in a few years' time."

The war was especially problematic for Theo's German-American friends. Marianna van Rensselaer's sister and family lived in Munich, and Marianna's nephew was serving with the German army in France. Her relatives were "filled with joy over accounts of great German victories," Marianna told Theo, and were "full of confidence that their 'righteous cause' must win."

To help the war effort, Theo initiated a money-making activity in Farmington. At Hill-Stead's Makeshift Theater, built in place of the stables that had burned down, Theo showed movies every other week to the townspeople for a small admission fee, and then sent the money abroad with her own contributions.

From the start of the Great War, psychics became deluged with messages from the spiritual world. A young medium Theo had recently met received the admonition: "Under no circumstances, whatever, should the United States participate belligerently in the European conflict." Theo forwarded the message to President Wilson. Another medium sent Theo a warning, "There will be a battle in Switzerland and on the Austrian border. Send this to Hyslop, because he must know."

Theo was having difficulty, however, with Dr. Hyslop. In order to make certain that he was employing valid research techniques, she had persuaded Foster Kennedy and Charles Dana to verify Hyslop's work. Kennedy and Dana were medical men, not spiritualists, but both were interested in Hyslop's experiments as they might relate to certain mental diseases. But Dr. Hyslop resented what he considered their interference.

Though known for dedication and hard work, James Hyslop listened to no one. He was quick to insult others and to take offense. He especially resented suggestions that he be more prudent in publicizing psychical experiments. Fanatic in his attempt to prove the validity of spiritualism, he did not care about the consequences. "I want facts and the truth," he said, "[even] if they take me to hell."

Hyslop refused to worry about his own image or the reputations of supporters. "No materialistic prejudices will ever hinder me trying experiments," he announced. "Darwin played a bassoon to his plants! I am not above that sort of thing. This is not a time or place for materialistic dignities."

He became increasingly angry about the physicians Theo sent to oversee his experiments, mostly because he was hostile toward members of the upper class, whom he considered materialists. He felt uncomfortable with Kennedy and Dana. "I have had no chance to get at either of them, in fact, no time to feel into the inner mental states of that class as a whole," he complained. In fact, he hoped that the truths he discovered would torment the rich physicians and "prove a nightmare to the materialist. He deserves it, and, perhaps, if he had a few of them [the truths], he would awake to the fact that the medical world needs to rest on ethical and not on an economical basis."

During 1914, Theo met Edwin Friend, a spiritualist with an impressive academic background. Still in his twenties, Friend had received bachelor and master of arts degrees from Harvard. He had taught classics and Indian philology at the University of Berlin, followed by two years teaching at Princeton University and a year at Harvard. When Professor Friend said he was willing to risk his scholarly reputation by devoting himself to psychical research, Theo offered him a position at

Dr. Hyslop's institute. She also invited Edwin and his wife Marjorie, a promising young medium, to live in a cottage on the Hill-Stead estate.

Dr. Hyslop was not receptive to Theo's protégé and tried to block Friend's working at the institute. He believed that Theo was trying to gain further control through Edwin. But those at the spiritualist headquarters in London shared Theo's enthusiasm for the young man. "I am glad to hear that you have enlisted another active worker," wrote the English Society's secretary, Alice Johnson, "and especially one connected with Harvard."

Despite the war raging in Europe, Alice asked that Professor Friend come to London to meet with leaders of the Society: Mrs. Sidgwick, Mr. Piddington, and Mr. G. W. Balfour, Britain's former Prime Minister. Since the head of the society, Sir Oliver Lodge, was presently in Australia and would return to England in September 1914, perhaps Edwin could make the trip then.

Theo was becoming further alienated from James Hyslop and more devoted to Edwin Friend. She suspected that for years Hyslop and his colleague Dr. Bull had been circumventing her wishes, though they cleverly tried not to antagonize her, fearful of losing financial support. When she learned that Hyslop had no intention of allowing Edwin any real role in the organization and might even try to discredit the young man, she decided to act.

Theo looked into the financial records of the institute and concluded that Hyslop and Bull had misappropriated funds in their acquisition of a new office. There might be enough evidence to bring a suit against them. Theo contacted a lawyer, Charles Neave, who, instead of initiating a lawsuit, tried to heal the breach in the organization.

Neave said that Hyslop agreed to work with Edwin and to accept him on the board of trustees, but only if Theo stepped down. She refused. "I do not know just how the trouble will end but it is not disturbing me," she told Ada. "It has simply kept me rather busy."

In the ensuing battle, Theo revealed an iron will. To fight Hyslop, "who," she informed her mother, "has not a drop of gentle blood in his veins," Theo resorted to blackmail, bribery, and threats.

She directed Neave to find "Dr. Hyslop's vulnerable spot," something she could "hold over him with a threat of publicity." Next, Neave was to explain to the institute's trustees that she wished to remain on the board with them and that she planned to make a bequest to the institute of not less than $200,000.

Along with this bait, Neave should also warn the board that Theo would sue Hyslop "if she has any more trouble about the office, and would, in that case, have Hyslop examined for mental instability."

Finally, Neave was to see to it that the trustees pass bylaws that would "ensure E.W. Friend's retention" and make him "secure from dismissal by Hyslop." If they refused, Neave should mention that Theo was thinking of leaving the institute and asking Mr. Friend to help her establish a new Society for Psychical Research in Boston.

In response to these orders, Neave asked, "Will you permit me to go outside of what might be considered strictly my functions as your legal adviser and make some suggestions based upon the impressions I received from our interviews with Doctor Hyslop and Mr. Friend to-day?"

At Theo's assent, Neave went on to say, "Doctor H did not impress me at all favorably and Mr. Friend did." He believed it would be a waste of effort for Theo to continue to work with Hyslop and advised sending Edwin to meet with the English leaders, so that Theo and Edwin could establish another organization.

Realizing that Theo was serious about leaving the institute, Hyslop proposed initiating a journal with Edwin Friend as editor, supported by funds she would contribute. "This is a sop thrown to us to maintain my financial interest," Theo retorted and destroyed her will, which contained a large bequest to the Institute. She then wrote a proposal to found the "Organization of the Massachusetts Society for Psychical Research."

The next step was for Edwin to meet with the British Society's leaders, convince them to break their ties with Hyslop, and obtain authorization for the branch in Boston. Theo would have liked to accompany the young man, but she was working on the final details of the Hop Brook School.

The noted architect, Charles A. Platt, had recently suggested to the editor of *Town and Country* that he see Theo's colored rendering of the school, which was being featured in an exhibition. When the editor saw the drawing, he exclaimed, "Bully; bully; bully!" He asked Theo for photographs of Dormer House so that he might incorporate pictures of both projects for an article he planned to write about her.

Theo had already decided what her next project would be after she completed the Hop Brook School. Since Alfred's death, she knew that she could best honor his memory by using her architectural ability. She considered building a public gallery to exhibit his art collection, though she doubted that Ada would part with it during her lifetime. Then inspiration struck with such force that she later confided to Harris, "My courage to live and act came when I had decided what form the memorial to my father should take." She would design and found a school for boys in honor of Alfred.

In the presence of Harris, Theo revealed the idea to Ada. Her mother sat dumbfounded. When Harris said, "She can do it," Ada nodded in agreement. She approved of the project, even after Theo admitted that she would have to borrow money and that "the interest on this indebtedness will amount to about the same sum" that they spent each year on Hill-Stead.

"I find the subject has taken hold of mother's imagination," Theo rejoiced. She and Ada searched the area near Hill-Stead for a site for the school and settled on a 3,000 acre parcel of land a few miles away in the small town of Avon. Then, chauffeured by Pratt, the two women drove throughout New England to look at boys' schools, including St. Paul's, St. Mark's, and Middlesex. Theo also visited Pomfret, Groton, Hotchkiss, and Andover. "They all illustrate exceedingly well," Theo wrote Harris, "the things which I wish to avoid."

To Harris, who had become her most trusted friend, Theo confided, "Besides my care for my mother, I have three interests in life which will take my time and much of my income: my architectural work, Psychical Research, and little Gordon."

As Theo had hoped, the presence of two-year-old Gordon Brockway helped alleviate the sadness at Hill-Stead after Alfred's death. The angelic-looking child, with light blond hair, fair skin, and blue eyes, had won over Ada, whom he called Auntedda. Because Theo did not legally adopt the boy—he was her ward—she did not think it proper for him to call her "mother" though she referred to him as "son." She was Aunt Theo.

Theo sometimes brought Gordon along to her Farmington office. The child was delighted when she took out architectural pens and paper and drew pictures for him. In truth, though, Ada assumed more responsibility for the child. Little Gordon adored Auntedda, but when she asked his favorite question, "Whose little boy are you?" he always replied, "Aunt Theo's darling boy."

Whenever Theo and Ada were away from Farmington, Gordon seemed content to stay with his caretakers, Mr. and Mrs. Stewart. "The rascal probably does not miss us at all, being quite sufficient unto himself," Theo wrote Ada. Mrs. Stewart told them not to worry about the child—"he is so very healthy and happy." However, when Theo remarked that she had to return to New York, the child tearfully begged, "Aunt Theo no leave Gordon."

For various reasons, Theo's protégé Edwin Friend had postponed the trip to meet with the leaders of the English Society for Psychical Research, and, in March 1915, Theo decided to accompany him to London. The Hop Brook School was just about finished, and Ada would stay with Gordon.

Theo was aware of the risk of traveling during wartime, but it did not matter to her. She courted danger and adventure. On a sudden whim, she had once taken an airship to Quebec. "Anyone that has enough nerve to go up in an airship I call a sport," Betty's young son, Brooks Emeny, wrote, "and you are the best kind of sport." Without any qualms, Theo made travel arrangements to sail on the magnificent luxury liner, *Lusitania*, which would depart from New York on May 1, 1915.

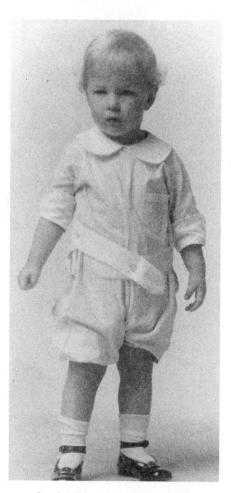

Gordon Brockway, age two. *(HS)*.

John Wallace Riddle. *(HS)*.

The Hop Brook School, Naugatuck, Connecticut. *(HS)*.

NINE

"A damned dirty business"
1915

LIKE THE *Mauretania* and the ill-fated *Titanic*, their sister ship *Lusitania* was palatial. The length of its deck was a quarter of a mile and its height was six stories. It was a magnificent floating hotel with handsome tapestries, expensive carpets, and an exquisite white-and-gold first-class dining room.

Theo reserved two cabins: an outside saloon deck room for herself and her maid, Robinson; and a single room for Edwin Friend. Her stateroom had been reduced from $500 to $350, and Edwin's room from $150 to $137.50. She wasn't certain whether the reduction was due to her late purchase of the tickets or because the Cunard Steamship Company was trying to increase business. Because of the war, voyages to England had become less popular, and there were many empty cabins on the ship. The *Lusitania* could accommodate 2,300 guests served by a staff of 900, but when it sailed on May 1, 1915, there were only 1,959 aboard, including 129 children.

The United States had declared neutrality for international waters, but many Americans were afraid to sail on a British ship through a war zone. The *Lusitania's* passengers believed that German submarines would not dare attack a luxury liner carrying American civilians since such a barbarous action would provoke the American government into entering the war. Besides, it was not likely that a submarine could sink such a leviathan. German torpedoes had trouble sinking much smaller ships.

The Cunard Line sent Theo a brochure that featured a lovely picture of the *Lusitania* and listed Theo's fellow saloon passengers. Its "Information for Passengers" did contain a warning: "Notice. Passengers are informed that Professional Gamblers are reported as frequently crossing on Atlantic Steamers, and are warned to take precautions accordingly." It did mention the European war: "During present Hostilities passengers of foreign nationality are, under the Aliens Act, only permitted to land at certain approved ports, of which Liverpool is one."

Theo did not know that the German Embassy had been trying to warn the *Lusitania's* passengers that the ship might be attacked. Ten days earlier, George Viereck of the embassy had attempted to place a notice in fifty newspapers. The notice first reached the *New York Sun,* whose editor contacted the State Department. He was told to wait before he printed it until its authenticity had been verified. The *Sun's* editor informed the United Press of the State Department's position, and the notice was suppressed throughout the country.

After five days, Viereck went to the State Department to try to find out why the warning had not been published. He told Secretary of State William Jennings Bryan that the *Lusitania* was known to have carried munitions on previous voyages. "'More important,' he [Viereck] informed him [Bryan], 'no fewer than six million rounds of ammunition were due to be shipped on the *Lusitania* the following Friday and could be seen at that moment being loaded on Pier 54.' Bryan picked up the telephone and cleared the publication of the notice. He promised Viereck that he would endeavor to persuade the President publicly to warn Americans not to travel." President Wilson, however, did not issue a warning.

In addition to munitions, it was rumored that J.P. Morgan was secretly shipping gun cotton to England in the *Lusitania's* hold. Gun cotton posed a considerable danger if a torpedo struck the ship. According to a chemist, who later testified in the *Lusitania* inquiry, if sea water came into contact with a certain kind of gun cotton, "immediately a chemical change takes place...causing a sudden explosion."

A few weeks before she sailed, Theo formally resigned from Dr. Hyslop's Institute for Scientific Research of New York. She also informed the medium, Mrs. Halsey, that she was taking transcripts of sittings to show to the English Society for Psychical Research. She told Reverend Cleaveland, whose wife was the medium "Mrs. Smead," that she might be interested in underwriting the cost of publishing his book, *The Religious Aspects of Psychical Research,* but he would have to wait a few weeks until she returned from her trip. Last, she wrote Peggy James that she was sorry that the young woman could not accept her invitation to go along on the trip.

May 1, 1915, was a perfect spring day. A band played and the crowd noisily milled about on Pier 54. In the group boarding the ship were well-known, wealthy, and celebrated figures, including young Alfred Vanderbilt and short, plump Charles Frohman, the most famous and successful producer on Broadway. Swarming about were reporters asking the passengers their reactions to the German Embassy's warning, which had finally appeared in the newspapers that very morning.

Ada had come to see Theo and Edwin off. They had not read the notice, and they ignored the reporters. They also were unaware that the Cunard manager was at the pier trying to reassure the passengers. "The fact is," Charles Sumner told them, "the *Lusitania* is too fast for any submarine." He did not reveal that when the war began, Cunard had shut down a boiler room to save money and that the ship would not be using all its power.

As the two women boarded the ship, they exchanged pleasantries with Captain Turner, who greeted the first-class passengers. Then Ada accompanied Theo to her stateroom, where they said their good-byes.

After the *Lusitania* pulled out of the dock, Theo, Edwin and Theo's maid, Robinson, went to the writing-room of the ship, where Theo read aloud the German Embassy's notice in the *Sun*. Turning to them, she remarked, "That means, of course, that they intend to get us." She outlined what they should do if anything did happen. To avoid their running around trying to find each other, Edwin and Robinson were to meet her on the boat's deck.

At first, Theo was unable to get a good night's sleep because a noisy family with young children had the stateroom next to hers. After noticing that there were quite a few empty cabins, she asked the purser to change her room. Within a few days, she felt rested and relaxed.

The voyage was smooth and pleasant. Theo spent every afternoon sitting next to Edwin on deck while the intense young man read and translated passages from Henri Bergson's *Matière et Mémoire* to her. She enjoyed listening to Edwin and felt inspired by his devotion to spiritualism. She told him that if anything terrible did happen on this voyage—if the Germans dared to attack them—she hoped that he, at least, would be saved to carry on their important work.

On Thursday, May 6, the *Lusitania,* now close to the war zone, traveled slowly in a thick fog, blowing her foghorn. Meanwhile, close by, the steamer *Candidate* emerged from the fog into the path of a German submarine that was traveling above water. The U-20 submarine fired its deck guns and made a direct hit. The young German commander, Kapitän-Leutnant Walter Schwieger, allowed the *Candidate's* crew to abandon ship. The U-20 then tried to sink the ship with a torpedo, but it remained afloat. Schwieger fired a dozen rounds from his deck guns and after several hours, finally sank it. When an English patrol boat arrived to pick up the *Candidate's* crew, the U-20 allowed it to do so.

An hour later, the submarine attacked another steamer, the *Centurion,* which first escaped into the fog. Then at 1:00 p.m., the U-20 fired a torpedo that struck her. The steamer's crew abandoned ship, and again there was no loss of life. The single torpedo did not sink the *Centurion,* so the submarine fired another at point-blank range. Even then, the *Centurion* took an hour and twenty minutes to go down. That afternoon, in a war diary, Kapitän-Leutnant Schwieger noted, "There are only 3 torpedoes available, of which it is my intention to conserve so far as possible two for the return trip."

The sinking of the first ship, the *Candidate*, was reported to the British Admiralty at 11:00 on the morning of May 6. But not until 7:50 that evening, as he was about to go down to dinner, did the *Lusitania's* Captain Turner receive the message: "Submarines active off the south coast of Ireland."

At dinner, Turner informed the passengers about the submarines and requested that they not light after-dinner cigars outside on the deck. He reassured them that they were safe and said that in the morning the *Juno*, a cruiser, would shepherd them into Liverpool. "There is no need for alarm," Turner said calmly, "On entering the war zone tomorrow, we shall be securely in the care of The Royal Navy." At that moment, the U-20 lay submerged 120 miles away from the *Lusitania*.

The next morning, at 11:02, the *Lusitania* received a message that Captain Turner decoded as instructions to divert the ship into the port of Queenstown on the coast of Ireland. At noon, Kapitän-Leutnant Schwieger spotted the *Juno*, the ship that Turner thought would be escorting the *Lusitania*. But England's First Lord, young Winston Churchill, had recalled the *Juno*, leaving the luxury liner completely unprotected. Having changed course, the *Lusitania* was slowly heading toward the Irish coast and would come within forty miles of the U-boat.

By noon the fog had cleared, the sun was shining, and the sky was a cloudless blue. Theo and Edwin went below for lunch. The orchestra was playing "The Blue Danube." At their table sat a young Englishman with a dish of ice cream in front of him, waiting to be brought a spoon. Looking ruefully at the ice cream, he said, "I would hate to have a torpedo get me before I eat it." Theo, Edwin, and the others at the table laughed. Then they noticed that the ship was running more slowly. They wondered if the engines had stopped.

The *Lusitania* was southwest off the rocky coast of Ireland near the Old Head of Kinsale, just seventeen miles offshore and twenty-five miles from its destination, when Kapitän-Leutnant Schwieger spotted it. He told the pilot that there was a steamer with four funnels heading toward the coast. "Either the *Lusitania* or the *Mauretania*," the pilot replied, "both armed cruisers used for trooping." Indeed, at that moment, the luxury liner *Mauretania* was loading troops at Avonmouth to be sent to the Dardenelles.

After lunch, Edwin and Theo strolled on deck B. The morning fog had lifted, and the day was clear. Theo thought that the sea was "a marvelous blue and very dazzling in the sunlight." They leaned over the railing, and she wondered, "How could the officers ever *see* a periscope there?" At that moment, the U-20 was within attacking range, and, a few minutes later, Schwieger ordered a torpedo to be fired at the ship.

When the torpedo hit the bow, Theo and Edwin were on the starboard side toward the stern. The impact sounded, Theo thought, like "an arrow entering the canvas and straw of a target, magnified a thousand times." A second, more powerful explosion occurred, which sent up a geyser of water, coal, and debris. The torpedo might have hit contraband munitions, or perhaps the rush of sea water had caused the second explosion when it met volatile gun cotton. As water and debris flew past them, Friend struck his fist in his hand and said, "By Jove, they've got us."

Theo and Edwin ran into a small corridor. The boat listed severely, throwing them against a wall. They struggled up to the deck, which suddenly looked nightmarish because of the crowds of shouting, hysterical people. An officer fended off desperate passengers and tried to stop the lowering of the lifeboats because of the ship's heavy list. Theo watched in horror as a boat tipped, spilling out half its occupants into the ocean. The scene was utter chaos. Lost children were screaming for their parents, who were running frantically around the decks looking for them. A woman clutching a small child fell and slid along the deck. Lifeboats crashed onto the deck, smashing into people.

Steerage passengers, "white-faced and terrified," made their way onto the deck. Others from below had become trapped in the electric elevators that had stopped when the generators failed. Screams could be heard as those inside beat their fists on the elevators' elegant grilles.

Holding onto each other's waists, Theo and Edwin pushed through the crowd. On the port side of deck A, the crew was having more success in lowering the boats. Because the waiting crowd contained women and children, Edwin would not get into a lifeboat. He urged Theo to do so, but she also refused.

Only four minutes had passed, but the foredeck was completely under water, and the sea was pouring into the ship. In six minutes, at least 1,500 tons of water entered through the open ports. Captain Turner tried to head toward land, which was so close that the passengers could see it, but the ship was going down nose-first. The front of the ship was completely underwater, and its rudders were almost out of the water. As the bow sank lower and lower, the stern rose farther out of the water. The bow would soon hit bottom, and the ship would stand upright, and then fall over on its side.

Suddenly, Theo saw her maid in the crowd, a smile frozen on her face. Theo reached out to the dazed woman and said, "Oh, Robinson."

Over the noise and chaos, Edwin shouted, "Life Belts!" He and Theo ducked into nearby cabins, where they quickly found three lifejackets. Edwin helped Theo and Robinson, and then tied one on himself. Glancing at the young man, Theo noticed how straight he was standing, and she thought, "The son of a soldier."

There was little time left. People were sliding down the deck into the water. Those above grabbed onto wires and ropes and, in their rapid descent, shrieked as their hands and feet were flayed. People grabbed children and started throwing them overboard. The list of the ship was so severe that Theo knew they had to jump.

Theo asked Edwin to go first. Without hesitation, he stepped over the ropes, shimmied down an upright, and reached the rail of deck B. Then he jumped. In a few seconds, he emerged from the water, looked up at Theo, and shouted encouragement.

Telling her still-silent companion, "Come, Robinson," Theo tried to follow his example, but she slipped. Then she found a foothold on a roll of canvas, closed her eyes, and jumped. Her next sensations were that she was deeply immersed in the ocean, unable to reach the surface, and swallowing salt water. Instead of terror, however, she felt strangely apathetic. She opened her eyes and saw through the green water that she was lying between the submerged decks of the ship.

She closed her eyes again and heard herself saying in her mind, "This is of course the end of life for me." She felt strangely calm and unafraid. The thought occurred to her that bringing little Gordon into their home against Ada's wishes had been wise. Her mother had come to love the boy, and now the child would console Ada after the death of her daughter.

Although the temperature of the water was cold, about fifty-two degrees Fahrenheit, Theo perceived it as being surprisingly warm, probably because she was in shock. Reaching the water's surface, she found herself surrounded by an unspeakable chaotic inferno, amid jagged parts of the ship, broken furniture, clothing, draperies, unrecognizable pieces of objects, and hundreds of people, many dead or badly injured, some dazed and others frantic and screaming. A survivor later wrote: "In places the wreckage was so thickly clotted that it formed 'an undulating horrible mattress of deck chairs, oars, boxes, and human heads.' Many bodies had been 'mangled and disfigured in the surge and grinding of the wreckage so as to stain the ocean with blood.'" Those still alive grabbed onto anything, including corpses.

Theo waited for death. She closed her eyes and counted the buildings she had designed. She thought about her friends, and finally she prayed wordlessly. Then she received a blow to her head and lost consciousness.

After Junior Third Officer Albert Bestic had tried unsuccessfully to launch the port boats, he left the deck and went back into the ship where, in the ship's nursery, he found Alfred Vanderbilt and the theater producer Charles Frohman tying lifejackets to small beds that contained crying infants. Officer Bestic urged the men to stop and to save themselves, but Frohman and young Vanderbilt ignored him and kept to their task. As the water flooded the ship, Frohman spoke lines from *Peter Pan*, "Why fear death? It is the most beautiful adventure in life."

As the stern went into the ocean, a boiler exploded, blowing off one of the ship's four funnels. When the steam cleared, there was no sign of the *Lusitania*. It had disappeared into the water. Only eighteen minutes had elapsed since the ship was hit.

The sea was filled with wreckage and people, dead and alive. Of the almost 2,000 who had been onboard, few were in the six lifeboats that had been successfully launched. The other forty-two lifeboats had broken against the sides of the liner or on the decks at launching and had killed and maimed their passengers. Alfred Vanderbilt and Charles Frohman's lifejacketed infant beds sank in the turbulent water, and the cries of the babies were silenced.

Theo regained consciousness, and a man with no lifebelt and insane with fright grabbed onto her shoulders. She didn't struggle against him but merely said, "Oh, please don't." She then sank under the water and again lost consciousness. A few minutes went by and when she opened her eyes, she saw brilliant sunshine and blue sea. She was floating on her back. Looking around, she saw that other people were drifting apart. There were wider spaces between them. The man on her right had a terrible gash on his forehead. On her left, there was an old man who must have been treading water, for he was upright. She called to him and asked if he saw any rescue ships coming.

At 2:15 p.m. the *Lusitania* had sent an SOS: "Come at once—big list." On receiving the message, Vice-Admiral Sir Henry Coke ordered out the cruiser *Juno*, the fairly large ship that was originally supposed to have escorted the *Lusitania* but had been recalled into the Queenstown harbor. Shortly after the *Juno* left, the lighthouse keeper on the Old Head reported that the *Lusitania* had sunk. Vice-Admiral Coke immediately sent out everything that would float and asked the harbor masters at Kinsale and Oysterhaven to do the same. Then he reported the ship's sinking and his actions to the Admiralty.

Learning that the *Juno* had been ordered to the scene, Admiral Lord Fisher recalled her, ostensibly because he feared for the ship's safety.

Perhaps the U-boat was still in the area. In the water, some survivors saw the *Juno* approach and, to their horror, turn back.

Almost two hours elapsed before rescue boats and ships arrived. Fishing sloops, cutters, and naval patrol craft searched for survivors until dark.

Continuing to lie on her back, Theo heard occasional shouts and close by, a man chanting in Italian. Suddenly, she spotted an oar. Thinking that she could help the old man nearby who was not wearing a life jacket, she grabbed the oar and pushed it toward him. At the same time, feeling her heavy clothes dragging her down, she put a leg over the oar and held it with one hand. Then she again lost consciousness, but the oar worked its way up and caught under her skirt, which enabled her to remain floating on her back. Miraculously, she stayed afloat for several hours, even during periods of unconsciousness.

Theo was the last survivor rescued by the *Julia*. The crew fished her unconscious body out of the ocean with large boat hooks and pulled her on-board. Because she was suffering from severe hypothermia, which made her pulse so weak as to be undetectable, they thought that she was dead and laid her on the deck with the corpses. A fellow passenger, Belle Naish, whose clergyman husband had died that day, came over and touched Theo. Her body was so stiff with salt water that the woman later said it felt like a sack of cement.

But Mrs. Naish thought she saw Theo's eyelids flicker. She pleaded with two crewmen to help. They succeeded in restoring Theo's breathing, but she remained unconscious. One of the men ran to the dining saloon of the ship, returned with a carving knife, cut off Theo's clothes, and wrapped her in a blanket.

When Theo awoke, she was lying in front of a fireplace in the captain's cabin. The first thing that she saw was the opening of the fireplace grate, which, she thought to herself, measured about 18 x 24 inches. She next noticed a pair of gray trousered legs by the fireplace and a man leaning over a table and looking at her. The man said, "She's conscious." Two women approached her. Theo's first words were to ask them their names and to inquire if they were sisters. She could hardly speak, however, and was shaking from chills and fever.

When the ship docked, a doctor arrived. He asked two sailors to make a chair with their hands and, still with only the blanket around her, they lifted and carried Theo off the boat, shouting "Way, way!"

The next thing Theo knew was that she was riding in an automobile. The car stopped, and Theo insisted on getting out and walking by herself, but she collapsed and had to be carried inside. Lying on a lounge in the lobby of what she later called "a third-rate hotel," she glanced around at a room filled with survivors, mostly men, dressed in all sorts of strange garments. The Englishman who had been waiting for a spoon to eat his ice cream came over to her. He was wearing a woman's pink dressing gown. "Have you seen Mr. Friend?" she asked. He shook his head.

Theo shared a hotel room with three others from the ship. She could not stop shivering, her teeth were chattering, and she was perspiring so much that the blanket was soaked. A woman in the next bed, Mrs. Duckworth, left the room to get Theo a dry blanket and a glass of brandy. After Theo drank the brandy, she felt better. Before Mrs. Duckworth went back to her own bed, she warned Theo not to look at a mirror because her face was swollen and discolored from the blows she had received in the water.

During the night, Theo waited anxiously for news of Edwin. Every time the door opened, she expected to see him, but instead, all night long, men kept coming into the room, snapping on the lights, taking telegrams, getting the women's names for the list of survivors, and bringing children in for Theo and the others to identify. Theo managed to send a telegram to Ada with the one word, "Saved!"

A fellow passenger from a town near Farmington offered to search for Edwin. He went to hotels, hospitals and private houses and reported back to Theo—but to no avail. Robinson's name, meanwhile, appeared on a list of survivors. But both Friend and Robinson had been lost.

The news of the disaster quickly reached America. *The Boston Evening Globe's* headline screamed, "LUSITANIA SUNK" followed by "Not Known How Many Passengers Saved" and then "TORPEDOED BY GERMANS REMAINED AFLOAT 12 HOURS." New York's *Evening Telegram* announced, "LUSITANIA BLOWN UP BY GERMANS; LOSS OF LIFE REPORTED SLIGHT."

The next day, *The New York Times's* headline was smaller and longer and almost correct: "LUSITANIA SUNK BY A SUBMARINE, PROBABLY 1,260 DEAD; TWICE TORPEDOED OFF IRISH COAST; SINKS IN 15 MINUTES; CAPT. TURNER SAVED, FROHMAN AND VANDERBILT MISSING; WASHINGTON BELIEVES THAT A GRAVE CRISIS IS AT HAND."

The *Times* had the number of torpedoes wrong—there was only one— the ship sank in eighteen, not fifteen minutes, and the number of dead was sixty-five fewer than reported. Seventy-eight years later, researchers estimated that the figure was 1,195 dead, which included ninety-four children and 123 Americans.

All night, under gaslights, survivors searched for friends and relatives in the piles of water-soaked bodies on the piers in Queenstown. The dead children were laid next to each other, some with name tags pinned to their clothing. Most were unidentified. Throughout the next days, residents of three Irish villages along the coast looked for bodies. The Cunard Company and relatives offered rewards: £1 for any body, £2 for an American body, and £1,000 for Alfred Vanderbilt. Frohman's body was found, but not Vanderbilt's. After a few days, the Irish buried the dead in three mass graves on a hillside outside the city.

Although exhausted, Theo had difficulty sleeping. Whenever she did fall asleep, she had a recurring nightmare of trying to find Edwin. Devastated by his death and by the loss of children and others, Theo was not grateful for being one of the few who survived. Later she told Ada, "I truly believe there was no one on the ship who valued life as little as I do."

Photograph of Theo taken after the *Lusitania* disaster. *(HS)*.

TEN

"Unthinkable, unthinkable"
1915—1916

AS THE TRAIN neared the Belgian border, the conductor told Dr. Alice Hamilton to throw away the English newspaper. She had bought it to see if Theo's name was listed as a survivor of the *Lusitania* disaster. At the hotel in occupied Belgium, Alice and a companion, Miss Kittredge, were barraged with questions: "Had we heard of the *Lusitania*? What did we think of it? What would the U.S. do?"

Alice joined Jane Addams in Berlin, where articles in the *Berliner Tageblatt* exulted in the sinking of the luxury liner. With few exceptions, Alice saw that the Germans felt no remorse about the *Lusitania* incident. After all, the ship was carrying munitions, and the German Embassy had warned the passengers.

On the day that the *Lusitania* was torpedoed, Ada was still in New York City because her niece, Betty Brooks Emeny, was scheduled to undergo surgery there. Betty died before the operation could be performed, however, and was buried on May 7. After the funeral, Mary Hillard was visiting Ada at the Renaissance Hotel when the maid rushed in and told them that the *Lusitania* had been sunk.

Ada later confided to Theo that on first hearing the news, she was "overcome by the thought, that now I was indeed alone in this world and how was I to face it." Immediately, she telephoned the Cunard offices. To her relief, the officer who answered the call said that all aboard were alive.

As the newspapers' headlines began to report that there were deaths, Ada became terrified. Then she received Theo's cablegram with the one word, "Saved." She still worried that Theo was badly injured or had pneumonia, but once she learned that her daughter was all right—except for shock, a head injury, and grief over the death of Edwin Friend—Ada turned to practical matters. Theo had lost all her clothes when the ship went down, and Ada expressed great concern about the purchase of a new wardrobe.

A spiritualist friend of Theo's, L. Hollingsworth Wood, cabled a friend in Dublin to find out where Theo was staying. Wood's friend then contacted the Haughtons and the Newsoms, two working-class, Quaker families in Cork, and asked them to help.

The Haughtons searched for Theo at the hotels where survivors were being sheltered, finally arriving at the hotel in Queenstown. Still wrapped in a blanket, Theo told the middle-aged Irish couple that she appreciated their offer, but she refused to go to their home.

Mr. Haughton did not argue. He responded, "You will need money." Theo shook her head. She said that she had already made arrangements with the British Embassy to secure funds. "You will need something now," Haughton insisted, placing several silver coins in her hand. He told Theo to let him know when she was willing to leave the hotel, and he and his wife would return.

Three days later, on May 11, Theo sent word to the couple that she had decided to accept their kindness. To dress for the short journey to the Haughtons' home, she made selections from baskets of clothing that the Irish citizens had contributed for survivors. If she had looked in a mirror, she would have seen a short, sturdy woman in ill-fitting, motley attire, her face swollen and discolored green and purple.

A bizarre, pathetic figure, Theo greeted the Haughtons, who were impressed by her composure. Theo had maintained what appeared to be an heroic calm from the moment that the torpedo hit the ship. But this seeming strength owed much to the numbness that sometimes accompanies shock. During the hours of drifting in and out of consciousness in the sea and during the nights and days of waiting and hoping for news of Edwin Friend, Theo had felt detached, as if trapped in a surreal dream.

Four days after she had been rescued from the frigid Irish Sea, Theo arrived at the Haughtons' modest house and entered the guest room, which she described as a "little room with its mahogany furniture against the white walls, the window boxes with tulips, and a flapping, snapping coal fire." She felt a rush of emotion. "I dropped into a chair," she later recalled, "and, for the first time, cried my heart out." She felt bewildered "in that quiet room." After witnessing so much death and destruction, she was overwhelmed to be in "such a safe place on earth," a home.

She undressed, put on the clean nightclothes Mrs. Haughton had provided, and lay down on the soft bed. As the days went by, letters and telegrams covered the bedspread. She was touched by Henry James's message of "tenderest love and blessing." "You have been through more than is knowable or conceivable," the novelist sympathized. From now on, he and other friends would take "infinite care" of her "beyond any now you have known...henceforth!"

Theo answered Henry's letter, but in a distracted state, she forgot to insert the note into its envelope. When he received it, Henry knew that the envelope came from Theo. The postmark was Cork, and he recognized the handwriting. Seeing that the envelope was empty, or, in his words, "hollow—a gaping void without contents," he was filled "with a sense of the unthinkable shock you have suffered. Unthinkable, unthinkable."

Dr. Foster Kennedy sent a cable from Belgium, where he had volunteered to take charge of a "flying hospital," a corps of physicians and nurses who lived in trucks and set up tents for operations on the battlefield. After reading Theo's name in a list of survivors, he contacted Ada and learned that Theo was staying with the Haughtons. Kennedy told Ada that he would go to Ireland and take Theo to London.

Theo stayed with the Haughtons for four days. Then she moved to the home of the Newsoms, whose children solemnly greeted "the lady from the boat." On May 16, Mr. Newsom took Theo by train to Dublin, where she was met by Foster Kennedy.

Theo was grateful to Foster for his concern and appreciated his saying he was proud of her "great display of heart and courage." Late in the afternoon, they crossed the Irish Channel to England. The small boat went at a tremendous speed and kept changing its course to avoid becoming a target for torpedoes.

Kennedy had reserved rooms for Theo at the Hyde Park Hotel in London. Henry James telephoned every morning and visited almost every afternoon. Theo later recalled that she was "in such a state of exhaustion and shock that I would frequently fall asleep when he was with me." On opening her eyes, she would see Henry sitting in the room, "his folded hands on the top of his cane, so motionless that he looked like a mezzotint."

Another loyal friend also appeared at the hotel. Upon learning that Robinson had died in the disaster, Theo's former maid, Elizabeth Riddell, sailed to England. Although she was enrolled in a nurse's training program in America, Elizabeth gave up her studies and made the dangerous voyage to take Robinson's place.

Two weeks later, Theo gathered enough strength to ask about her cousin Betty. She had not inquired earlier because she knew that she could not bear it if Betty's operation had not gone well. When Elizabeth responded that Betty had died, Theo reacted stoically, struck by the coincidence that, on the same day that she had been rescued from a watery grave, her beloved cousin and best friend from childhood was buried.

Theo worried about Betty's sons, and she also was lonesome for three-year-old Gordon. Ada wrote that the first thing that the boy did when he came for luncheon at Hill-Stead was to run to Theo's room. Seeing that she was not there, he would shake his head sadly and say, "No Aunt Theo."

Ada reassured Theo that Gordon was "well, happy and adorable" and "never still a minute." He was "not noisy" though he "talks all the time." Ada was pleased that he "is so good and is showing so much character of the right kind," and she enjoyed his energy. "His little straight legs are fly-ing from one end of the house to the other, when he is not out of doors."

As the weeks passed, Elizabeth kept Ada informed about Theo's condition. Her worst trouble was "a nasty cough which exhausts her & also helps to keep her from sleeping quickly." Dr. Kennedy came often to see Theo. "He understands her so well," Elizabeth reported.

Theo agreed. "When I tell him my head feels unholy with misery," she remarked, "he takes me to a play instead of giving me medicine."

Like many medical men at the time, however, Foster prescribed rest cures for depressed women, and, despite Theo's protests, he insisted that she do nothing. Foster "will not listen to any plan I may put forth for trying to *work*," Theo argued, "and thus free myself." She knew that work would be a distraction from remembering the horror she had experi-enced and from feeling guilty about Edwin's death.

"I hope you do not censure yourself a moment for taking him over," Ada admonished. "It is just what he most desired to do." She reminded Theo of all that she had done for young Professor Friend. "You made it possible for him to marry, and were giving him advantages that he could never have had, if he remained at Harvard. You also were helping him to work in a line, most interesting and absorbing to him." Ada's advice was "Do not be crushed by it." She added, "I know you are actually suffering more than Marjorie."

A letter from Anna Cowles confirmed Ada's impression that Edwin's widow was neither overwhelmed by grief nor angry at Theo. Anna praised Marjorie's "courage and sweetness" and said that the young woman had expressed an intense desire to see Theo. After the disaster, Marjorie wrote Theo, "Let's just thank God with all our hearts and souls, that He gave us the understanding to know that Edwin is safe and free before He took our dear boy away from us."

"We meant perhaps more to him than anyone except his mother," she continued. "Your mother has been a perfect angel and so has Mrs. Cowles. When you come back you will find us in the little housie so glad to see you and have you back safely that we won't be able to half tell you how we feel."

Addressing Marjorie as "My darling Girl," Theo replied, "Your letter of wonderful courage has just come and it breaks a spell that has hung over me." Theo continued to dream that she was searching for Edwin, but she said that she now accepted his death and wanted to try to reach him through spiritual communication. "If not, we will wait until we see him face to face."

Almost immediately after the disaster, Marjorie received messages from Edwin's spirit. Theo learned that Edwin had also communicated through Mrs. Chenoweth, the famous English medium whom the poet and occultist William Butler Yeats consulted. In a deep trance, Mrs. Chenoweth moaned, "Oh, it's the ocean. Oh, Oh, I'm dead. Friend. Friend is here." Two days later the soul of Edwin promised, "I will do what I can to make my identity a good case. Edwin." After another week, the medium called out, "Marjorie" and then "Theodora, Theodora," and "I keep looking for her all the time."

While Theo recuperated, Marjorie and her twin sister Natasha remained in the cottage at Hill-Stead, and Theo instructed Ada to provide for their support. Ada replied that the sisters "had only forty dollars in the bank, and a number of bills, amounting to one hundred and fifty dollars." After paying the debts, Ada gave them an extra fifty dollars for a trip to Boston. "I am going to be very frank with you," she wrote Theo. "I think they are both irresponsible and [have] no idea of the value of money."

During the summer, Ada was scandalized by Marjorie's appearing in public obviously pregnant. Commenting on the young widow's "notice-able" figure, Ada noted that Marjorie seemed "perfectly unconscious about it, and never hesitates to go any place." Marjorie was "to be sick" in early October and wanted to move to Boston so that she could raise the child near her family. Asked to pay the rent for an apartment, Ada consented, irate about the expense but glad to be rid of the sisters.

In June, Dr. Kennedy thought that Theo was well. "For a while after she came to Ireland and to London she was rather emotional, given to tears and a gloomy view of all things & was rather less capable than before," Foster told Ada. "Now she laughs long and heartily, is much interested in all things, and right glad to have her friends around her." He still believed that Theo should not work and advised ignoring friends who were urging her to become involved in causes, "refugee children and the like."

Kennedy felt that the traumatic events that she had experienced would not scar Theo; in fact, the experience might improve her charac-ter. Surviving the disaster "contained potentialities of much mental pain," but could "do much to give her a truer sense of proportion in all things." In other words, because she now knew how terrible life could be, she might not succumb to the tendency of women, especially those who were rich and privileged, to overreact to minor crises.

Theo did not resent Foster's insensitivity or condescending attitude. Still shaky, she needed his strength and appreciated that he had left his work to care for her. He advised Theo to go home, but she decided to stay in England. She feared making the voyage, she said, because of the threat of German U-boats. The truth was, despite Marjorie's assurances, Theo dreaded seeing Edwin's widow. Logically, Theo knew that Edwin's death was not her fault, but she felt the irrational guilt that survivors often feel. For the rest of her life she would have difficulty sleeping, being awakened by the terror of not being able to find Edwin and by the images of horror and the sounds of screaming when the *Lusitania* went down.

Ada was worried about Theo's remaining in England because the American papers reported that bombs were falling in London. "I do not even feel safe here," she declared, "with a population of 15,000,000 Germans in this country."

"You can have no idea of the war atmosphere here," Theo responded. "It is suffocating, it is so—not depressing—but so constantly in the thoughts and on the lips of everyone."

Theo visited the medium Mrs. Verrall and also Mr. and Mrs. Sidgwick at the English Society for Psychical Research, but they spoke little about spiritualism. Mrs. Sidgwick, the sister of the former prime minister, believed the war to be far more serious than most people realized. "The government seems slowly awakening to the fact," she told Theo, "that this is a life and death struggle."

A few years earlier, the British woman suffrage leader Mrs. Pankhurst had visited Theo at Hill-Stead, where they had discussed women's rights. When Pankhurst came to see Theo in London, she announced, "This terrible war has changed our work. It is impossible to work politically for the suffrage until the end of the war." Pankhurst was certain that the patriotic endeavors of women "will bear fruit when the war is over." Male politicians, she believed, would recognize and reward the unselfishness, courage, and hard work of women and give them the vote.

"This war takes all wish for painting out of one's head," confessed Helena Gleichen. Helena and Nina had become involved in an unusual war effort. With Theo's financial help, the two women had purchased an ambulance and were driving about on French battlefields, picking up fallen soldiers and taking them to a Paris hospital.

Helena and Nina also bought a portable Röntgen Ray machine, an early x-ray device. After a French doctor taught them how to use it, they traveled from hospital to hospital, x-raying wounded soldiers to find bullets in their bodies. From the war zone, Helena painted Theo a word picture of the scene: "a big marsh with brown weeds, golden poplars growing in the water and the bluest of blue mountains with a snowline beyond and white puffs of cotton wool (meaning shells) bursting every minute over it." Helena showed an artist's perspective as well as spirit, courage, and humor. "We had a shell burst just behind our private car." It was "*much* too near as it gave both Nina and me splitting headaches."

"The *London Times* pounds away every day urging conscription and the necessity for more munitions especially high power explosives," Theo wrote Ada. "There are thousands of soldiers everywhere billeted in towns and going to and fro on crowded trains—the streets and houses even here darkened at night—people informed that the sirens will blow if Zeppelins appear."

Every evening, from the suite at the Hyde Park Hotel, Theo heard a band playing light, peppy music to buoy the spirits of the Londoners. The contrast between the cheerful tunes and the grim realities of war "startles me," she said, "as much as I would be were I watching a corpse which suddenly smiled at me."

After spending a month in England, Theo went to Mary Cassatt's villa in the French countryside. Theo confided that she had lost all interest in living. "Dear Theodate your courage will return I am sure," the older woman promised, if for no other reason, because of the war. "Even I am absorbed by this great drama."

In Paris, Theo visited Gus Jaccaci and the Belgium refugee children he was caring for. Finally, she made arrangements to return to America. Jaccaci planned to accompany her, but he came down with ptomaine poisoning. Fearing to be mistaken as Theo's lover, Jaccaci admitted he was glad that work and illness prevented him from going, "because things in our world being as they are it is best for a woman not to put herself and not to be put by her friends in a position which evil ones might use in their gossip."

Jaccaci did not know about John Riddle, who wrote Theo a love letter that she received while she was in Paris. Though not a Quaker, John used the Quakers' old-fashioned pronouns to please Theo. Writing that he would not leave New York City for his family's home in St. Paul, Minnesota "without thy touch and thy dear blue eyes!" he also professed a belief in spiritualism. "Theo darling, I do not believe in death any more. I am *just as sure* it is not true! But the waiting is a stern, hard trial!"

When he thought that Theo had died in the *Lusitania* disaster, John realized that he loved her so much that he had contemplated suicide. "Almost losing thee out of this world brought thee so much nearer," he declared, "for in the hours of agony when I thought thee gone, I felt, now indeed I can be with her at will—and there is no more separation." He proposed marriage and described a wonderful future. "Just think what flights we shall some day take together, Theo."

126

John signed the letter, "Toto," Theo's pet name for him. Towering above her at 6'2", he reminded Theo of a totem pole. He rather liked the name, he joked, because totem poles were "objects of reverence."

After three months abroad, Theo left on the *Espagna,* arriving in New York on August 1, 1915. John was not there to greet her. Instead, former suitors Harris and Charles met her at the dock. Harris brought along a note from Ada, who thought it best that she and Gordon welcome Theo at Hill-Stead.

Theo discovered that, as a survivor of the *Lusitania,* she had become a celebrity. Photographs and articles about her appeared in newspapers across the country. They mentioned that she was an heiress and a successful architect, but most newsworthy and sensational was that she was a spiritualist.

Glad to be back in Farmington with Ada and precious Gordon, Theo answered the correspondence pouring into Hill-Stead. Before Theo returned home, Ada had responded to 175 letters from an enormous stack that continued to accumulate. Theo took over the task, dictating replies to her secretary, Elizabeth McCarthy, who kept neatly typed carbons.

Some letters were from friends and relatives, but many were from strangers. A neighbor from a less affluent section of Farmington wrote that she had kissed Theo's picture when she saw it in the newspaper. The publisher Henry Holt, who was planning to include Marjorie Friend's automatic writing in the next issue of his spiritualist magazine *The Unpopular Review,* wanted "to hear how this world looks to you after being so nearly on its outer edge. Did you get any glimpse into another [world]?"

"I am distressed beyond measure to hear of the sorrow you are going through in the loss of your little son," Theo responded to another correspondent whose five-year-old child had drowned a few weeks earlier. The grief-stricken woman told Theo of futile attempts to communicate with the child through automatic writing. Theo replied that the death of the boy would provide "a strong emotional quality between you and the next world," an "emotional connection," and she encouraged her to keep trying.

"I have been making special researches in 'Metaphysics' and 'Psychic Science' for some years past and have invented and *very successfully* demonstrated a 'Psychophone' or 'Spirit Wireless Telephone' which reproduces the voices of our 'Spirit' friends as clearly as the voices of our Mortal friends are now heard over the ordinary Bell telephone," wrote Professor William Craig, Jr., of Philadelphia. Professor Craig wanted to perfect his extraordinary instrument, but he had run out of funds. Would Theo send him $125? She would not.

Theo had lost interest in establishing a branch of the Society for Psychical Research in Boston because she did not want to name a replacement for Edwin. "Utter discouragement and depression over the loss of Mr. Friend," she said, had made her "unwilling to make any plans for the future in regard to ways in which [she could] help the work."

"Your life was given back to you for a purpose," a fellow spiritualist admonished and urged that she "continue the work for which Edwin gave his life."

"My dear heart, do not thee feel that thee is balked of life work by the loss of Mr. Friend," John Riddle counseled. "Thee has been saved for a real use and vision will be given thee."

Theo realized that she must take steps to make certain that Edwin's death had not been in vain. But she searched for another way rather than the project she and Edwin had planned. Years earlier, she had contributed to the Richard Hodgson Memorial Fund at Harvard University, which provided support for psychological and psychical research in honor of the spiritualist leader. Theo's first thought was to establish a similar fund in Edwin's name. Then she decided to endow a professorial chair for psychical research at Harvard. The scientist who held the chair would study what she and Edwin had been most interested in—"the alleged supernormal psychical and physical phenomena connected with the state called 'trance.'"

Although the impetus for creating the position was connected to furthering Edwin's work, Theo planned to name it the "Alfred Atmore Pope Chair for Psychical Research." She was not abandoning the plan to build a boys' school in Alfred's memory, but that would take many years to complete. In the meantime, the Chair would honor both her father and, indirectly, Edwin.

During the late fall of 1915, Theo contacted Professor James H. Woods of the department of philosophy and psychology at Harvard. Enthusiastic about the proposal, Woods knew someone willing to carry on the kind of research she described: Dr. Leonard T. Troland, a brilliant young scientist who was presently working at the Nela Research Laboratory in Cleveland. In his mid-twenties, Troland had completed his undergraduate work at M.I.T., and in 1915 had received a Ph.D. from Harvard, where he had conducted research in psychophysiological optics.

On December 13, 1915, Professor Woods contacted Dr. Troland and described the position that Theo planned to fund. Initially, Troland would be appointed as an instructor in psychology at Harvard with a yearly salary of $1,500. He would be expected to teach one psychology course, and there would be a "peculiar condition," that he would give half his time to "an investigation of trance and other similar phenomena of abnormal psychology." He would be expected to devise tests for the subjects—mediums who were mostly women. At the same time, Troland could investigate a special interest of his own, color vision, by studying the trances of these subjects.

Assuring Troland that he "would not be required to hold any belief pro or con with regard to these cases, and your conclusions might be altogether negative," Woods urged the young man to accept the offer, which eventually might lead to a permanent position at Harvard. Furthermore, "all the Professors in the laboratory approve of the plan, and would give you a hearty welcome."

On May 9, 1916, Professor Woods informed Theo that President Lowell of Harvard and Leonard Troland had agreed on a contract, "with the exception that the Instructorship should not be named, and that Dr. Troland's salary would be $1800."

"As the University did not come out in the open and designate the Chair as being for Psychical Research," Theo later asserted, "I decided to support it for three years" rather than to endow it permanently because she knew "how apt a University is to divert the funds into side channels."

Pleased with the choice of Troland, Theo corresponded with the young scientist. She directed him to contact Professor Henry Lane Eno, who was conducting psychical research at Princeton University. At a dinner party in Bar Harbor, Theo had told Professor Eno about Troland, and "he most generously offered to explain his work to you." Because meeting Eno was so important, Theo would pay all traveling expenses.

Leonard Troland visited the Princeton professor, whom he believed to be "a man of clear scientific judgment" because Eno agreed that "if psychical research problems are to be made scientifically reputable, they must be studied under laboratory conditions."

At Harvard, Troland carried out telepathic experiments on six people: "four normal subjects, one suspected of being slightly dementia praecox, and one showing signs of being a 'sensitive.'" He used "the cruder methods already employed by the Society for Psychical Research," which involved "stimuli, such as numbers, playing cards, diagrams, etc.," and he also introduced an apparatus he had designed, the Electric Stimulus Shuffler. Though there were some extraordinary successes, his experiments produced mainly negative results.

Referring to the Electric Stimulus Shuffler, Theo told Troland, "It is my belief that you could experiment with an electrical device for one thousand years and still have only negative results unless, unless, unless you are able to produce a sufficient emotional stir in the mind of the agent."

The young man, however, did not believe that "emotional stimulation is necessary in order to induce telepathy. I see no *a priori* case for the importance of the emotions."

Theo and Troland argued about other subjects as well. After reading an article the young scientist had written, "Philosophy and the Present War," Theo considered it profound, but she challenged his pacifism. "When there is a spirit abroad like that of German militarism," she asked, "does it not argue well for the future of the human race that so many nations rise in arms to kill, now and forever if possible, that evil?"

"I am not perfectly sure that the cause of the Allies is fundamentally that of a hatred of militarism," Troland replied. He maintained that "the French and English are fighting for self-preservation, and France is fighting for Alsace and Lorraine. As for the other Allies, it seems pretty clear that they are in it for the spoils, or to avoid becoming themselves, the spoils."

"No one can accuse me of being other than contra-German," he protested, "but I seriously doubt that Teutonic human nature is radically different from the average."

"Would you be willing to admit," Theo asked the scientist, "that even with the great losses of the best type of man, the world at large still seems to improve? Are not our ethical standards better than they were?"

Theo's optimism, though naive, and her renewed enthusiasm about psychical research were signs that she had emerged from depression. She also had planned something that no one—not even Ada—suspected. In February 1916, right after Theo's forty-ninth birthday, she announced that she was going to marry John Wallace Riddle.

In a note to his future mother-in-law, John demonstrated charm and diplomatic skills. "I feel like a culprit," he admitted. "I fear you must regard me as an interloper, but I can only say in extenuation that I fully realize the great happiness which has come to me and shall try to deserve it."

"We did forget 'John Riddle' did we not!" Mary Hillard exclaimed, taken aback by Theo's news. "And now he is never again to be forgotten."

Though Mary's colleague at Westover School, Lucy Pratt, sent wishes for "great happiness," she told Theo she was "shaken to the foundations at the thought of you as no longer of the Household of Spinsters to which we have forever belonged!"

"Dear Miss Theodate," Earnest wrote, "I have your note announcing your engagement to Mr. Riddle. Stunned, I was of course. But after a little thought, Why not."

130

ELEVEN

"The voice of Little Blue Feather"
1916

"NO ONE ever spent a dull moment with John Riddle," a friend re-marked. He was "the cause of many a school girl's giggle and *roué's* chuckle." John liked traveling, fine food and wine, witty conversation, the theatre and opera, playing bridge, gambling, and beautiful women.

Born in Philadelphia on July 12, 1864, he was the only child of John Wallace Riddle and Rebecca Blair McClure Riddle. His father, a medical student at the University of Pennsylvania, died from an unknown illness seven months before his son's birth.

A highly educated woman, Rebecca knew several languages, including Italian and French, and had translated a Norwegian novel, *Professor Lovdahl,* published in 1904. The young widow had a strong, independent spirit, and in 1870, she and six-year-old John moved to St. Paul, Minnesota. A year later, she married Charles Eugene Flandrau, a widower with two daughters. In 1867, after his wife's death, Flandrau had sent six-year-old Patty and one-year-old Sally to live with their maternal aunt in Kentucky. When their father married Mrs. Riddle, Patty and Sally did not return to St. Paul. The girls never were fond of their stepmother, who they claimed was "manipulative."

Originally an attorney in New York, Flandrau, like many young men in the mid-19th century, had gone West to make his fortune. He succeeded in gaining wealth, power, and even some fame as an Indian fighter and the author of several books and articles on frontier history. He became a Minnesota Supreme Court judge and ran for governor but lost the election. Theodore Roosevelt, although thirty years young-er than Flandrau, became a close friend. It was rumored that Teddy fell in love with Flandrau's daughter Patty when she was already married to Tilden Selmes.

In the first year of marriage to Judge Flandrau, Rebecca gave birth to a son, Charles Eugene, who later changed his middle name to Macomb; four years later, she bore another son, William Blair. The judge did not legally adopt John Riddle, who kept his father's surname, but, like his two younger half-brothers, John called Flandrau "Papee."

In 1880, Rebecca took sixteen-year-old John, nine-year-old Charlie, and five-year-old Blair to Europe, where they remained for a year. Judge Flandrau stayed in St. Paul. Most likely, Rebecca was bored in St. Paul, and she might have wished to separate from her husband because of marital problems. In addition, she wanted to give the boys a cosmopolitan experience.

After they returned, John left home to begin studies at Harvard, but, a few weeks later, wrote his mother that he was ill. Rebecca immediately boarded a train, rented a room in Cambridge, and took care of her favorite son. When he recovered, Rebecca and John embarked on an extended vacation to Egypt and Italy, returning to America in the spring. John re-entered Harvard the following fall.

Rebecca initiated and fostered John's love of travel, but a wealthy Harvard friend, John Vanderburgh, introduced him to the extravagant pleasures of Europe. Because Vanderburgh had lost a wager to John, he had to treat him to a trip abroad during the university's summer recess.

In Genoa, John reported finding "some of the finest women imaginable." A week at Monte Carlo was enchanting. John wished he and Vanderburgh could stay longer because of the delightful climate, superb restaurants, and pretty women. John also won almost $300 at the gambling tables.

The two Harvard men continued on to Budapest, which John described as a "paradise of the amorous." There he flirted with a seventeen-year-old girl and, in a letter to Charlie, asked, "What would Mother say if I brought home a Romanian bride?" He then retracted his mock threat. "When I marry," he promised, "I will present a patrician to the family."

Although he was developing sophisticated tastes, John was not above enjoying crude pleasures. He went to the Moulin Rouge to see Paris's reigning sensation, a man who imitated volleys of artillery and played tunes on "his natural wind instrument."

Upon returning to Harvard, John studied languages and wrote compositions. His essays reflect his character, sense of humor, and facile writing style. In one composition he poses the question, "Is man necessarily a bear and a pig if he does not always give up his seat to a woman in a street-car?"

His conclusion? "A man must always give up his seat to an old woman or to a hard-working woman. To a young, pretty and attractive-looking woman he undoubtedly will give it, so that case does not enter into the argument." But, John contended, "there is surely no need of his resigning it to a young, healthy-looking, buxom cook or housemaid going on an afternoon's outing," though a man might offer such a woman his seat if he is "endowed with so much inborn chivalry that he finds it impossible to be comfortable while one of the weaker sex is uncomfortable."

John was describing his own nature. He would never sit when a woman, even one from the lower classes, was standing. He always acted the gentleman.

John's gracious personality, talent for learning languages, and love of travel, along with Judge Flandrau's political connections, led him to pursue a diplomatic career after he graduated from Harvard in 1887. In order to prepare himself, he first attended Columbia Law School, graduating in 1890. He then entered the *Ecole des Sciences Politiques* in Paris. Rebecca soon arrived in France with Charlie and Blair. Then, with John joining them, the four went on to Russia where they saw the czar, whom Charlie described as "a big jolly man who yawns a good deal."

In 1892, while John was still studying in France, Rebecca came alone for an extended visit. Throughout John's career, she would travel any distance to be with him. John returned her devotion. Whenever they were apart, from 1883 through the nearly three decades until her death, he wrote long, affectionate letters to Rebecca every week. At times, mother and son corresponded in one of the foreign languages they both knew.

John's relationship with "Papee" was cooler, most likely because Rebecca's husband thought her son financially irresponsible. Attorneys Eller and How once called to Judge Flandrau's attention a $56 debt of John's that had not been paid for over a year.

In 1893, through Judge Flandrau's connections, John obtained his first diplomatic position, serving, for the next seven years, as secretary to the U.S. Legation in Constantinople, a city he called "a hotbed of intrigue." While John was there, the Armenian Massacre occurred. In a letter to Charlie, now a student at Harvard, John reported a raid in a café, where "sixty or eighty were brained with clubs or gashed to pieces." To horrify his brother further, John added that the assailants "were in such a hurry they did not have time to indulge in the favorite method here—gently crushing testicles between flat-irons until the victim succumbs." John concluded with a description of "carts filled with naked bodies rumbling away into the peaceful moonlight." It was "possible the swift currents of the Sea of Marmora have carried some more off to the westward."

John's vivid observations of the massacre also appear in a journal. Out on the street, at first he was unaware of what was happening around him. "As the killing was done with cudgels and knives, there was little shooting," he noted, "and the only sounds were the distant puffing of the steamers on the Bosphorus and the occasional faint echo of a remote cry when some wretched victim was run to earth."

Besides witnessing atrocities, John learned what it was like almost to lose his life. On a November night in 1896, he left Constantinople to sail to Italy, where he planned to meet Charlie for a brief holiday. Suddenly, the ship collided with another vessel. John was able to get off the ship before it sank, but he spent several hours in an open boat in a rough sea.

In 1901, John left his position in Turkey and sought another diplomatic appointment. "Theodore [Roosevelt] is in Oyster Bay but will probably be back here off and on and I shall tackle him when I have a chance," he wrote Charlie. "I know Roosevelt's sister Anna will do whatever she can. In the meantime Papee might write him a letter on the subject as they are such friends."

Again, through social connections, John received his next appointment as secretary to the U.S. Embassy in Russia. Arriving in St. Petersburg, he felt that he had "landed on another planet." What was most alien was the lack of light. "For two or three weeks in midwinter, the sun does not rise until 9 and it sets before 3," he lamented. "Even during the hours of daylight the sun is nowhere to be seen, as the sky is covered with such a thick leaden pall."

In contrast to the drab physical world, John discovered that life for the upper class was bright and colorful, with parties at the Winter Palace that lasted from New Year's Day until Easter. Entertainments were staged for thousands of guests, who were served elegant dinners featuring such delicacies as fresh asparagus.

"Most people have thirty or forty servants living in their cellars," John discovered. "Every wealthy Russian family has an English nurse, a French Governess and a German companion or tutor." As one who spoke nine languages, John found it fascinating that "English is the first language learned by many Russian children, coming even before their mother tongue, and it is English which is spoken by the Emperor and Empress with their children."

In 1903, John left Russia and became a diplomatic agent and consul general in Cairo. In Egypt, he found "general prosperity which is enjoyed by the smallest farmer." Then, from 1905 to 1906, he was Envoy Extraordinary and Minister Plenipotentiary to Siberia and Romania.

John reached the pinnacle of his career when he was appointed the United States minister (ambassador) to Russia in 1906. He obtained this position through influence as well. Before the appointment, President Roosevelt, writing to his sister Anna, referred to "a most interesting letter of Riddle's" that she had sent to further John's career.

Some said that John "divided his time between bridge and diplomacy," both of which required finesse. An anecdote that made the rounds of diplomatic circles exemplified his quick thinking, courtesy and wry sense of humor. In Russia, he unexpectedly came upon the Tsaritsa bathing in the nude. "I beg your pardon, Sir," John calmly apologized to the startled woman.

John relished the social whirl of a diplomat's life. He wished he could always live the way he had for three months at the Summer Palace Hotel in Therapia, where he attended parties, dances and other social events. He wrote that he hardly ever got to bed before five in the morning on Saturdays and "more than once rowed home in a three-oared caique towards the gray dawn."

In 1908, John left his post in Russia, supposedly because of illness. According to Charlie, "John doesn't seem in the least cast down at not being reappointed although he wouldn't have resigned (they never do)." Blair's wife Grace later said that John's diplomatic career in Russia ended because he had "cavorted about with dissolute grand dukes and gambled for high stakes—losing most of his fortune, and greatly annoying the President." In fact, he gambled "like a lunatic."

During the winter of 1910, John arrived in St. Paul and moved in with Rebecca and Charlie, who had become a successful novelist, short story writer, and essayist. Judge Flandrau had died several years earlier, and Blair was married and living in Mexico. John felt comfortable in St. Paul with his mother and brother, though Rebecca was unwell, and Charlie, who spent most of his time writing, did not share John's interest in attending parties, carrying on flirtations, gambling, and engaging in what Charlie scorned as frivolous conversations.

Redheaded Charlie exhibited a contemptuous attitude toward those he considered fools, and he also had a violent temper, which had been evident from childhood. At age eight, he had tried to kill Papee with a red-hot poker, and at fifteen, he had heaved a heavy silver inkwell at John. Charlie now expressed rage at the world in clever, biting satires. His scandalous, cynical, and hilarious *Harvard Episodes,* published two years after he graduated in 1895, was a great success. During the first years of the 20th century, Charlie's stories and articles appeared in *The Saturday Evening Post* and other magazines. From 1915 to 1920, he was the music and drama critic of the *St. Paul Pioneer Press and Dispatch,* where his commentary was described as "witty, urbane, and sometimes acerbic."

John soon became bored in Minnesota. Charlie described his older brother tiptoeing about the house "in his characteristic way—smelling books in one room, taking the parrot for a ride on his finger in another, disturbing me at my work in another and then settling down to the study of some unknown vocabulary in his own." In search of excitement, John made what Charlie called "an appalling number of calls on everyone." Life in middle America was a "perfect monotony" for John. "How peaceful it all is," he dryly told Charlie.

Unable to "rest from travel," John persuaded Charlie to go with him to Brazil, and during the following summer and fall, John wandered about alone in England, Paris, and Vienna. He spent a brief time in New York and St. Paul, then sailed again to Europe where he visited friends in France, Switzerland, and Italy.

In late 1911, John returned to Minnesota because he was suffering from an eye infection and because Rebecca was extremely ill. When she died in December, John said that her death was a terrible wound that would not heal.

After the funeral, John stayed on in St. Paul. During the summer of 1912, the infection recurred and John spent several months at Dr. Pagensteacher's Eye Hospital in Wiesbaden, Germany. As soon as he was released, John visited "a Russian princess here and an Austrian Arch-Duke there," according to Charlie. During the next few years, John made the rounds in New York, Paris, St. Paul, Newport, Bar Harbor, and Long Island. He seemed not to have employment of any kind, except that of being somebody's guest.

"For last night I had five dinner and one opera invitations; for the night before, nothing for anything. Oh the injustice and inequalities of this world!" John jokingly complained to Charlie. "On Tuesday night I sat between two Mrs. Vanderbilts at dinner, last night, next to only one—and so it goes."

In June 1914, John wrote Theo that he was considering a new job that was "merely 'volunteer service.'" He mentioned that if he accepted the offer, he "might serve the cause," an indication that it was an unpaid political position. John also professed hope for a future with Theo. "What I want to communicate on," he began, "is you and your boy," referring to Gordon. "I know why he is there, but I want to *hear* from *you* how far ahead you see him—and yourself. As for you," he continued, "never forget I have to look in your eyes once in a time." He signed the letter, "Yours—and your mother's—and I hope the boy's one of these days."

Six months after he wrote this letter, John was enjoying the company of other, not particularly reputable women. "John," Charlie sighed, "was unable to tear himself away from the flesh-pots."

In early 1916, John announced to his family that he intended to marry Theo. He expected disapproval from the cantankerous Charlie but did not worry about Blair's response. The youngest of the three brothers was weak and non-confrontational. "There has always been something rather immature and pathetic about Googoo," Charlie once observed to John, "which has added to his charm even when it has given us trouble and irritated us extremely."

As a boy, Blair had been expelled for drinking from Phillips Academy in Andover, Massachusetts. A weakness for liquor continued throughout his life, and most people knew he was an alcoholic. Blair was admitted to Harvard but never completed his studies, probably because of gambling debts. In 1904, he used the money Rebecca advanced him from his inheritance to buy a coffee plantation in Mexico. In 1909, home from Mexico for a short visit, he met pretty, nineteen-year-old Grace Hodgson at a party and fell in love. The two married, and Blair and his bride left St. Paul to live in Vera Cruz. In 1910, the Mexican Revolution began, and Blair's hopes of making a fortune crashed.

Remaining on their plantation became extremely dangerous, and Blair insisted that Grace leave. She returned to St. Paul and lived in the Flandrau home with Charlie, who had inherited the house after Rebecca's death. Blair stubbornly insisted on staying in Mexico to defend his ranch, but by 1916, he was forced to flee the country. His adventure ruined him but profited Charlie, who wrote *Viva Mexico!* a novel based on Blair's experiences.

Even though Charlie was not attracted to women, he adored Blair's wife, a pretty, petite, flirtatious brunette who loved stylish clothes. "Grace is a charming and remarkably intelligent girl—one can really talk to her about pretty much anything," Charlie declared. "She has one of the best minds I know either in man or woman." He believed that the marriage of Blair and Grace was unusually happy, which was astonishing because "they are really not in the least alike." Not only were they far apart intellectually, but "Blair is typically 'Mid-Victorian,' and Grace is anything but—."

An accomplished violinist, Grace also had a talent for writing. Recognizing her potential, Charlie urged Grace to compose stories and novels. With his help, she began writing with determination but found it difficult to concentrate because of migraine headaches, anxiety about Blair's safety in Mexico, and depression over her husband's alcoholism and their lack of money.

Grace was also concerned about the seeming impropriety of living alone with her brother-in-law. She had moved in with Charlie because she did not get along with her mother. Although Grace's family was well-to-do, and she had received a fine education in St. Paul and Paris, she never felt accepted in St. Paul society. She suspected that people in town whispered that she was her father's illegitimate child. Grace craved love, approval, and admiration. Fear that people were gossiping combined with worry about Blair to finally cause her to collapse. Grace was in such a bad condition, Charlie complained, that his house had become a hospital.

Upon learning of John's impending marriage, Charlie asked Grace to come into the gas-lit study. "I called you in," he announced, "to inform you and Blair that my half brother Riddle has lost his mind." Charlie was upset because John's fiancée was a spiritualist, a crackpot who "believed in spectral trumpets and the voice of Little Blue Feather speaking from beyond the tomb." Charlie and Grace knew that John agreed that spiritualism was "the ultimate in charlatanism and vulgarity." What John "thought of spiritualistic seances," Grace said, "could not be printed."

Charlie understood why his brother wanted to marry a rich woman with a mansion in Connecticut and an apartment in New York. "John, like all of us, is 'getting on' in years," Charlie confided to his half-sister Patty Selmes. "He has no real home of his own and while mine would always be completely at his disposal, he has out here no real interests."

John's "perpetual existence of clubs, however comfortable and good," Charlie sympathized, "must eventually become a rather hollow one." Although unsure about the advisability of "a very poor man [marrying] a very rich woman," Charlie observed that it "often works entirely well," especially if a man has expensive tastes. Whenever John bought new clothes, he went to London, even though he could buy a good looking suit at Brooks Brothers for only thirty-three dollars.

The gossip columnist of the St. Paul newspaper bluntly noted that "John Riddle, while not particularly rich in worldly goods, has birth, breeding, position and erudition to offer his bride," who, the writer mistakenly added, was "a survivor of the *Titanic*."

Charlie admitted that he did not know whether his brother was in love with Miss Pope, but the couple certainly should feel comfortable with each other. For years they had traveled in the same circles and had known the same people, including Mary Cassatt, Gus Jaccaci, and various van Rensselaers and Vanderbilts. The main link between them was the Roosevelt family, both the Oyster Bay and the Hyde Park branches, and their most important friend in common was Anna Roosevelt Cowles.

Because few people were aware of Theo's romances with Harris Whittemore, George McLean, and Charles Dana, and did know of her close friendships with Mary Hillard and Belle Sherwin, they had assumed that she was not attracted to men. During that more Puritanical era, they would not have said what, in modern times, the architectural critic Brendan Gill publicly stated: that Theo was a lesbian. Gill believed that Theo's marriage to John Riddle was a platonic arrangement, and he credited her success as an architect to her not having been tied down by a husband early in her career.

Others thought marriage to John would help Theo fight the hostility and condescension of men as she competed in a field that they dominated and controlled. With a husband like Ambassador Riddle, she would be in a stronger position as an architect, for she would command more respect.

That Theo married John for reasons other than love was a common perception, and some friends and relatives shared this opinion with the bride-to-be. John's stepsister Sally Cutcheon said that she approved of marrying "for a good disposition rather than love," for it was "safer for one's happiness."

"I'm so glad you have a '*companion*,'" wrote a friend who thought Theo had made a wise choice. "What a fund of experience and knowledge of human nature he must have acquired in his unusual career." This background would stand John in good stead, the writer joked, for "it looks as if he might, in time, understand *you!*"

Theo's choice of John might also reflect loneliness for Alfred, whom John resembled. Like Alfred, John was soft-spoken, highly intelligent, reserved, and gracious. John might also have chosen Theo because, like Rebecca, she was impulsive, strong-willed, and independent.

There was another possible motive for Theo's marrying at almost fifty. As a young woman, she had lacked confidence and had been frightened of marriage, but now she feared little. Perhaps Theo viewed marriage to John as an exciting new adventure with a man she trusted, admired, and even loved. She did not doubt his love for her or suspect that he might be marrying only for money, for there were many other heiresses he could have courted.

Whatever Theo's reasons, Ada heartily approved of the match. Always adverse to having strangers in her home, Ada had greeted Gordon with a coldness that only the child's innocence could melt, but she warmly welcomed her prospective son-in-law. And, like Gordon, John charmed Ada—and also called her "Auntedda." Ada looked forward to having a man at the head of the family again. She expected John to be an ally and hoped that, as Alfred once had, John could temper Theo's imprudence.

"I hope that your marriage will not diminish your interest in Psychical Research," worried Mrs. Sidgwick of the English Society. Theo believed that John would not hinder but rather help in spiritualist activities. Recently he had accompanied her to a sitting with the medium, Mrs. Halsey, in New York, and he had previously given Theo spiritualist books.

Those in Theo's social set, as well as John, probably expected an elegant wedding with hundreds of guests, but Theo invited only those people she cared about, even to the point of ignoring the etiquette of including their spouses. She asked Harris but not his wife Justine, explaining that she wanted just a small, intimate group and adding that she hoped for Justine's "loving thoughts that day." Harry Pope and Joe Alsop—but not their wives—also received invitations. She asked John's stepsister Patty Selmes and her daughter Isabella, but not Isabella's husband, Robert Munro Ferguson, an arrogant man whom Theo disliked, though she had been his parents' guest in Scotland.

Those invited realized how special they were, but some declined. "You can't begin to know what it would mean to be one of the honored few you have asked to be with you that day—I know of nothing these many years that I have longed so to do," responded Isabella, who was "quite broken up at not being able to be with you and Uncle John."

"Bless you for wanting Isabella and me to come to you," replied Patty, who sent regrets, but "the fact that you wanted me at your wedding, of a dozen, is precious to me."

Theo invited both Anna and Admiral Cowles, but Anna pleaded a previous engagement. She added, "I feel very cut off from you." Highly sensitive to slights, Anna probably resented that, during the past few months, Theo had been too busy to make regular calls on her. Charlie, Blair, and Grace also refused their invitations.

The wedding took place on Saturday afternoon, May 6, 1916, a day short of the first anniversary of the sinking of the *Lusitania*. In the morning, it rained, but just as Harris arrived, the sun came out. After a luncheon at Hill-Stead, Ada, John, Mary Hillard, Belle, Harris, and about thirty other guests left Theo alone to dress and walked down the hill to the O'Rourkery.

At the cottage, Reverend Sedgwick, an Episcopal minister who had been a classmate of John's at Harvard, and the guests gathered in the dining and sitting rooms. Some remained outside. Gordon sat on the sofa. When Theo appeared at the top of the hill, John went up to meet her, and the two walked down together. Theo wore a light-blue afternoon dress with a matching hat, and she held a bouquet of lilies of the valley. In her other hand, she carried the silver-tipped cane that she had begun using after the *Lusitania* experience.

The ceremony began at 3:00 p.m. Theo and John exchanged vows standing next to the sofa near blond, blue-eyed Gordon, who looked on in wonder. Afterwards, all helped themselves to wedding cake and wine. Theo noticed that girls from Miss Porter's School were watching from across the street, and she directed that cake be brought over to them.

In front of Hill-Stead's sunken garden, a photographer took a formal portrait of Theo and John. Then he took a panoramic photograph of the couple, Gordon, and Ada, in the middle of a line of guests that included Hill-Stead servants, two young girls, a baby, and two small dogs held by men sitting cross-legged on the grass.

After posing for the photographs, Theo went back into Hill-Stead and shortly reappeared wearing a dark blue dress. As she and John walked over to the gate where their car was parked, the guests showered them with rice. To the Miss Porter's girls who were still watching from across the street, Theo called out, "Come nearer, come over here." She threw her arms around Ada and said, "Remember us in your prayers."

A few days later, Theo wrote Ada from the Hotel Puritan in Boston. "I must write my very first married note to thee," she said. "What a wedding day and wedding!" Sounding like a woman in love, she asked, "Does every bride think she has married the finest man in the world? This one thinks she has. I feel as if I were in a dream and that I will soon awaken and come home as Theodate Pope."

On their honeymoon, a week-long motor trip throughout New England, Theo read Charlie's books, which she called "enchanting." On their return, Theo and John were glad to see that friends who had not been invited to the wedding did not seem to harbor hard feelings. Invitations poured into Hill-Stead, so many that Theo and John refused a few, including a dinner invitation from one of his favorite hostesses, Mrs. Cornelius Vanderbilt.

In June, Charlie finally made the trip to Farmington to meet his new sister-in-law. Theo was thrilled. "Charlie Flandrau my brother—the last words are unnecessary but I love to write them—is dining with us tonight."

Charlie's visit was a success. He reported to Patty that he had charmed Theo to the extent that if he "hadn't been exceedingly firm... I should be at Hillstead yet." He still was concerned, however, about his brother's marriage. He told Patty that he didn't know Theodate well enough, but he worried about whether she would go along with the kind of life that John preferred. Could she tolerate "an existence of perpetual visiting?" he asked. If so, "all will be well."

The following year, Charlie returned to Hill-Stead and reported that it was "beautiful and luxurious" and that John and Theodate were "hospitable and kind." He had affectionate words for Ada. "I got to like Mrs. Pope very much," he wrote.

But Charlie now "felt sorry" for John and Theo. He thought that their relationship was "placid enough, but entirely artificial." He observed that "the two have absolutely nothing in common." He thought that the Riddles "fundamentally bore each other dreadfully." John, of course, was "always the extreme of politeness and patience" with his spouse.

Disingenuously, Charlie insisted that he was "really extremely fond" of Theo, but "her entire life consists of changing fads, 'isms', and tiresome, useless, semi-scientific and semi-philanthropic activities, that rarely arrive anywhere. With the girlish idealism of fifty," she was trying to change John's "entire character, tastes, ambitions and habits." Charlie admitted that Theo was "not in the least a fool" but thought she was "self-deceived."

The real reason for Charlie's diatribe was that he was angry about the way Theo had treated his chauffeur, William Dundee Clark. Not realizing that the relationship between the men was more than that of employer and servant, Theo had not offered Clark accommodations at Hill-Stead. Instead, she made arrangements for Clark to stay, according to Charlie, in a "not particularly reputable roadhouse," which, most likely, was a perfectly respectable inn.

"Theodate, with the inconceivable denseness of most women with money," Charlie grumbled, "actually planned to have Clark leave the car in the Pope garage and then take six rides of five miles each in a street-car jammed with stinking Italian laborers every day, for the privilege of eating his meals in the Pope kitchen."

"Theodate, I prezume, is bravely hacking her progressive way through the unresisting family entrails," Charlie continued, no longer hiding his rancor. "Well, my various organs are no doubt poor things at best—but are still mine own," he muttered, unhappy that the rest of the family disagreed. The union of John and Theo, he pronounced, was a "strange, and to my mind, tragic marriage."

Theo and John (6th and 5th from right) and their wedding guests
at Hill-Stead. *(HS)*.

Wedding photograph. *(HS)*.   Young John Wallace Riddle. *(HS)*.

TWELVE

"Through the eyes of boys"
1916—1918

SOON AFTER they were married, John went to New York. He wrote Theo that he was so lonely for her that he had not even gone to the theatre. He ended the letter, "Love to Antedda and Gordon and with a great deal of love and a kiss for little Effie," and signed it, "Your Boy." No one had called Theo "Effie" for over thirty years. She placed the note in a silk box, where she saved her most precious letters and souvenirs.

One summer night in 1916, Theo and John returned to Hill-Stead from a trip to Bar Harbor. As soon as they entered the house, they went to the third floor, tiptoed down the hall, and opened Gordon's bedroom door. Theo never forgot the image: the adorable child sitting up in bed, "blinking" and "angelic." In the morning, Gordon came downstairs and crawled into bed with Theo. As he ate a piece of toast from the tray that Earnest had brought up, Theo thought that the boy looked pale.

For the child as well as for herself, Theo faithfully followed a spiritualist regimen, which stressed the importance of fresh air, exercise, loose clothing, and natural foods. At the end of July, taking the child to the Alsops' home in Avon to play with other children, she insisted that he go barefoot as a health measure. In late August, because the poliomyelitis virus was highly contagious in the hot summer months, Theo decided against vacationing at the seashore or the mountains, believing it safer to keep Gordon close to home and away from crowds. But, despite all precautions and an isolated, sheltered life at Hill-Stead, Gordon became ill. Ada's sister concluded that he must have become infected by contact with a worker who carried the germ from Hartford.

The progression of the disease was unstoppable and terrible. On a paper in Theo's silk box appears the beginning of a sentence: "DEAR SANTA CLAUSE. PLEASE BRING GORDON A LITTLE" written in a very young child's awkward capital letters. The sentence continues in Theo's handwriting: "Christmas tree and a little red drum." A note explains, "Printed by Gordon a few hours before he died and then printed by me knowing what my darling wanted." Gordon was four years old.

Letters of condolence arrived at Hill-Stead, some from relatives and friends who had also lost children. Alice Brooks hoped that Gordon had not suffered and imagined that "he and little Chad [Theo's cousin's child] will find each other and be little friends" in heaven.

Few relatives and friends visited the mourners at Hill-Stead, which was empty and silent without the child running through its beautiful rooms. "No one can go to you—every one is afraid of this deadly disease," Aunt Nora explained in a note.

Anna Cowles said that her thoughts were constantly with Ada and Theo "through these days of torture" and that she *would* come to them if "either of you were alone and really needing me."

"Perhaps you would rather be alone," suggested another writer.

Theo did not prefer being alone. John's brother Blair and his wife were spending Christmas with friends in Connecticut when Grace was called to the telephone. The soft, steady voice of Earnest said he was speaking for Mrs. Riddle. He announced that a car had been sent for Grace and Mr. Flandrau. Unaware that Gordon had just died, Grace told Earnest to tell Mrs. Riddle that Mrs. Flandrau was sorry but they were engaged for the weekend. A few moments passed. Then Earnest responded, "Madame says the car will be there in two hours."

John then came to the telephone and told Grace of the child's death and of Theo's great distress. Putting aside fear of becoming infected, Blair and Grace went to Hill-Stead. The young woman comforted Theo, who sat in the corner of a room, her eyes filled with tears.

In January, Ada left for Pasadena, and Theo and John moved to their New York apartment on East 47th Street. Occasionally they returned to Hill-Stead for a few days. "I like to go home," Theo wrote her mother. "I love the associations. I feel his little spirit is there."

John felt that Theo should stay away from Farmington and lose herself in the whirl of New York society life. But Theo did not have the heart to go to luncheons and dinner parties. "Everything I do here I do perfunctorily," she confided to Ada, "but it is right that I should go with John, for his sake."

After returning from the theatre, Theo admitted, "I really don't know the name of the play nor of the playhouse." She went only because "John is so dear—and he feels that it diverts me and it probably does."

On February 2, 1917, Theo's fiftieth birthday, she received a gift from John. The accompanying card made her smile. He had written, "T.P.— With love—from T.P." The first T.P was for Theodate Pope. The second T.P. stood for Totem Pole, the silly name she affectionately called him.

In March, still in New York, Theo told Ada that she and John "gave a little—a tiny dinner for Mrs. Cornelius Vanderbilt," who was still in mourning after the death of her son Alfred in the *Lusitania* catastrophe. But after a while, social engagements were more than just difficult for Theo. They became "accursed."

John realized that what Theo needed was neither rest nor dinner parties nor the theatre. What always revived her spirit was work—involvement in an architectural project or psychical research. When Gordon had first become ill, over six months earlier, Theo had put aside designing the school in memory of Alfred, and after the child's death, she was unable to get back to it.

Remembering a book on psychical phenomena that Theo had mentioned wanting to read, but could not because it was written in Italian, John offered to translate Bottazzi's *Fenomoni Medianici,* and suggested that they try to have the translation published to benefit other spiritualists. Every morning for the next month, Theo sat in the parlor of their New York apartment and wrote as John dictated. She then sent the handwritten pages to Hill-Stead for her secretary to type.

After they finished the book, Theo sent the translation to her friend, Henry Holt. Henry's response, that he was no longer publishing book-length manuscripts on psychical topics, did not matter. Theo was ready to resume her life.

Theo said that she could never lose interest in psychical research. The amount of money that she had already invested in it was considerable, and, after Gordon's death, she changed her will to provide more support. Dissolving a $100,000 trust fund she had set up for the child, she created a new fund. "I give to Harris Whittemore [and two other trustees] the sum of $500,000.00 in trust to hold and invest the same and to expend said income in any part hereof in such manner as in their judgment will best promote the advancement of human knowledge in the field of Psychical Research."

A short time later, Theo became worried that the bequest was too general. She asked advice from Leonard Troland, the young psychical researcher she was supporting at Harvard, who warned that top scientists would not accept the bequest if she made it too specific and restrictive. "The amount of limitation which a scientific man will endure," Leonard explained, "is inversely proportional to his ability."

"The danger that your bequest will be misapplied," he went on, "is less than that it will not be applied at all. The principal endowments for psychical research in this country: the Seibert fund at the University of Pennsylvania, the Hodgson fund at Harvard, and the money left to Clark University and to Leland Stanford… have all lain practically idle, or have been expended sporadically by scientifically incompetent men."

Theo appreciated Troland's honesty, respected his opinions and character, but did not follow his advice. In her will, she stated that the bequest would be granted only to a researcher who investigated "the

146

alleged supernormal psychical and physical phenomena connected with the state called 'trance.'"

On April 2, 1917, America finally declared war on Germany. "We are entering this War with the most superb motives," Theo asserted, not caring that, to pay war-related expenses, the government would institute an income tax. In May, the navy asked Professor Troland to participate in the psychological testing of aviation recruits. A few weeks later, he wrote Theo that this commitment was making impossible demands on his time.

"I fear you may be overdoing," Theo concurred and advised him to concentrate on his health and the "big bit of work you are doing for your Country" even if it meant some lessening of research on psychical topics.

Troland became "extraordinarily busy" working on the problem of submarine detection. By mid-August, he knew he could not conduct psychical research and take on another task the navy had assigned him—devising psychological tests to select men to operate the submarine detectors.

Because he would not become a member of the military establishment, Troland had refused a government commission. He did not want to lose the independence he had as a scientist at Harvard, but, in order to work for the government and remain at Harvard, Theo would have to pay his salary and not require him to do any psychical research.

Theo released him from psychical research obligations and continued to support his position. Upon being informed of her generosity, Harvard's President Lowell sent words of appreciation and praised Theo's patriotism.

Troland's government research reflected his ability and promise as a scientist. In addition to the submarine detector he developed, the navy adopted many of his tests, using them on aviation recruits. One of Troland's experiments involved an early lie detector, or, as he called it, "a psycho-physiological method for detecting the intention to deceive," which was remarkably successful.

Theo's original agreement with Harvard was to support Troland's position for three years, but after a year-and-a-half, Troland gave up all research and became a half-time psychology instructor. He wrote Theo that "the new arrangement will permit the University to return to you a portion of your gift, should you so desire."

Theo stopped funding the psychical research position at Harvard. Even before Troland began concentrating solely on war-related projects, she was disappointed because his investigations of telepathy produced only negative results. She told him that she was frustrated that he had depended solely on machines and omitted the emotional element. "Until experiments are tried in which the agent's mind is excited, in

147

which case it can be compared more or less justly to a dynamo," she argued, "experiments are doomed to failure."

During March 1917, when the czarist government collapsed and a provisional government was established, Theo and John had become concerned about the chaotic political situation in Russia—John, because he had friends there from the time when he was ambassador, and Theo, because she approved of socialist/communist ideas. "I do believe," she predicted after the Russian Revolution, "we will live to see the day when we shall be given points in democracy by Russia; and Heaven knows we need it!"

A well-known Russian spiritualist, Madame Catherine Breshkovsky, contacted Theo and asked for funds to create a printing office that would disseminate socialist ideas to the Russian people. Theo responded favorably and enlisted Mary Hillard and the Westover students in a project to send money and goods to the activist. As the situation worsened in Russia, John arranged to have Breshkovsky smuggled out of Siberia. A few weeks later, wearing boots, a heavy coat, and a babushka, Madame arrived in Farmington. Asked by Mary to become a member of Westover's faculty, Breshkovsky consented and went to live in Middlebury.

Ada said she would never object to Theo's helping foreign war orphans, paying for the education of strangers, or being the godmother to scores of children of friends and relatives, but, after the death of little Gordon, Ada did not want any other children brought into the family. She feared that, after leaving Hill-Stead in January 1917, "in an emotional flight," Theo would take in another child. A few months later, Ada returned to Farmington and saw that her fear had materialized. Another "waif" was living in her home.

Ten-year-old Paul Martin later recalled that he had been looking out the window of a New York City orphanage when a large, elegant automobile came up the drive. It stopped at the entrance, and a uniformed chauffeur stepped out and opened the back door. A fancy lady leaning on a silver-headed cane emerged, glanced up, and saw him. Thin, blond Paul waved at the woman, and she smiled and waved back. Theo entered the building and, in a meeting with the director of the orphanage, said she wanted the boy who waved from the window.

Ada admitted that she partially overcame feelings of resentment because she pitied the child and saw that the boy meant so much to John as well as to Theo. "I became accustomed to seeing Paul about," she told John, "although my heart cried out for Gordon. No one could take his place."

During the summer of 1917, Theo and John took Paul to a camp in Pennsylvania where Brooks and Lathem Emeny, the sons of Theo's cousin Betty, spent their vacation. Theo spoke to the camp director and to the doctor, and explained "everything that the boy had been through in the way of shock and sorrow, and... the night tremor and night-mares." Since there is no other information about the boy in Theo's letters or journals, the child's history is unknown.

After the first night in the cabin that he shared with Brooks and Lathem, Paul was happy to be at camp. Theo noticed that "his cheeks were flushed and the pupils of his eyes looked black." A few months earlier, she had made an important discovery. "Seeing life through the eyes of boys," she realized, "seems to comfort me more than anything."

Satisfied that Paul was in good spirits and would be well cared for, Theo and John left for Switzerland. In Lucerne, Theo met with the psychologist, Carl Jung, and described to him various out-of-body experiences, from the first time when, as a child, she was frightened, to subsequent, more pleasant episodes.

After they returned to Farmington, John received a commission to work for the executive division of the Military Intelligence Branch at the War College in Washington, D.C. His main job would be to translate documents having to do with espionage and counter-espionage. In Theo's silk box, where she kept her most precious possessions, are several documents that John kept after the war, such as "*Notes on the German Spy System in Europe,* translated from the Italian by John Wallace Riddle."

Other members of John's family were also called upon to serve. His stepsister Sally's husband, Frank Cutcheon, became a legal adviser on General Pershing's staff. Blair was first put on a civilian construction job in Iowa. Then, in January 1918, he was transferred to a military base in Norfolk, Virginia. Once again, Grace moved in with Charlie in St. Paul. Charlie tried to enlist but was turned down because, at 47, he was too old.

Hearing that Anna's seventeen-year-old son, Sheffield, had volun-teered for the Marines, Theo sent the boy a sizable check, which, Sheffield said, "will make all the difference in the world to me when I am over there." As a future officer, he planned to purchase only "the best things" in order to "set an example to his men." Ignoring his mother's terror at the possibility of losing her only child, Sheffield exclaimed that he could hardly wait to go over, which he hoped would be by the middle of September "if we are lucky."

The year that America entered the war also saw the publication of Grace's first novel, *Cousin Julia,* which was received well and would later become a film. Instead of being elated about its success, however, Grace was on the verge of another collapse.

In December 1917, Theo took a trip west to spend Christmas with Grace and Charlie. On route to St. Paul, she stayed with John for a few days. During the war, John lived at the Metropolitan Club in Washington, D.C., and Theo remained in Farmington. They sometimes met on weekends at their New York apartment.

Theo then visited Belle Sherwin in Cleveland. Her next stop was St. Louis, where she had arranged to have a sitting with the new psychical sensation of the day, Mrs. John Curran, or—as the medium was publicly known—Patience Worth.

During the war years, as the number of casualties mounted, there was renewed public interest in spiritualism, and even the scientific establishment took Patience Worth seriously. At Washington University, a professor studied Patience, whom Mrs. Curran described as "an ego coming from nowhere (everywhere) with no body but words." The Currans became wealthy from the sales of subscriptions to the *Patience Worth Magazine*, novels (the latest was *Hope Trueblood*), and an especially designed ouija board, which John Curran sent Theo as a gift.

Theo spent two evenings at the Currans' home. When Mrs. Curran entered the trance state and became Patience, she made circles with her hand and, in a Scottish accent and dialect, rapidly called out letters that John Curran wrote down. The medium seemed to be creating poetry spontaneously.

Theo later sent copies of Patience's poems to Hamlin Garland and included an invitation to the writer to meet Mrs. Curran when she visited Hill-Stead. Garland accepted the invitation and told Theo that the poems were "astonishingly good considering their extemporary character."

"Theodate will probably turn up in St. Paul next week some time," John notified Charlie. "As she has her maid with her she will go to the St. Paul Hotel, but, needless to say, she will spend most of the day or two of her sojourn at 385 [Pleasant Street, Charlie's home]."

John said that Theo was anxious about Grace's health and wanted to see for herself how she was. Aware of Charlie's hostility toward Theo, John warned, "I write to tell you of her impending arrival so that you will not take just that time to be absent 48 hours."

Charlie later wished he had stayed away. As soon as Theo saw Grace, she became frightened by the young woman's distraught state and weakened condition. Furious at what she assumed to be Charlie's neglect of their sister-in-law, Theo turned on him, and he responded in kind. Grace said that she took no part in the ensuing battle. It was like a "summer electric storm, colors slightly livid and too bright, that grumbles and flashes sheet lightning but never really explodes."

The result was that Theo forcibly removed Grace from the Flandrau house and brought her back to Farmington, where the invalid remained for quite a while. "Life at Hill-Stead was not only gay and luxurious but melodramatic," Grace later reflected, "and it was all too easy to live under her powerful wing and do nothing."

In an essay that Grace later wrote for *Reader's Digest's* "The Most Unforgettable Character," she described Theo as the "most unique, most importantly gifted and most tumultuous woman of her time." She admired Theo's "passionate heart" and "passionate and understanding mind" but admitted that her sister-in-law could often be "gullible or mistaken."

Grace recognized that Theo's emotional nature fueled her creativity, and, though Grace did not know a great deal about architecture, she marveled at the beauty of the buildings Theo designed. Curiously, Grace also believed that "like many women of genius," Theo "had a good deal of the masculine in her makeup." To illustrate, she cited an incident that had occurred at a dinner party in New York. Theo had become so incensed at former Ambassador Henry White, a friend of John's, that she threatened to slap his face. To delicate and feminine Grace, overt displays of anger and assertiveness were signs of manliness.

Rescued from misery in St. Paul, Grace felt "irrationally happy" basking in the comfort of Hill-Stead while frigid temperatures, strong winds, sleet, and snow enveloped New England during the winter of 1918. "Our three thermometers outside registered respectively, one morning, 18, 19, and 20 below," Theo informed Ada, who was basking in the sun in Pasadena. "Aren't you sorry you are not here to enjoy it?!"

John was also absent from Hill-Stead, diligently working for the war department, where he translated documents; wrote reports about the political situation in Denmark, Austria, and Bulgaria; and corrected the carelessness of others. "John seems to be specializing now as the General Supervisor of Inaccuracies in his department," Theo commented, worried because "Totem" had lost fourteen pounds.

John explained that, although he was lonesome for Theo, it had become almost impossible for him to meet her for weekends in New York because the trains were running so poorly. It had taken a friend twenty-six hours, instead of the usual twelve, to go from Boston to Washington. Theo's neighbor, Will Cowles, teased that John was having a good time and was taking long lunches at his Washington club. Will told Theo that he had met John's secretary, who was "a sweet little thing."

Isolated by blizzards that left high drifts on its grounds, Hill-Stead was a warm, bright haven for its inhabitants, which now included some new pets: Ali Babba, a beautiful but independent cat; Ching, another chow puppy; and Pepper, a small smooth-hair terrier; as well as Theo, Grace, Earnest, and other servants of various nationalities, and eleven-year-old Paul Martin.

To Theo's relief, Paul was now "a changed boy." She saw that he had lost his "self-conscious expression" and had become "a regular boy and a very fine earnest one." At Kingswood School, a private day school in Hartford, Paul showed unusual ability in mathematics and French, the two subjects that Theo had always found impossible. Every evening, the child joined Aunt Theo, Aunt Grace, and their guests. After dinner, when the grown-ups retired to the library, he usually studied his lessons or sometimes amused himself by playing with the Hill-Stead pets.

With fireplaces in every room and thick, highly insulated walls, Hill-Stead was unaffected by the coal shortage brought about by the war, but Theo's neighbors were finding it difficult to heat their drafty mansions. In January, when pipes froze and the kitchen ceiling collapsed at Oldgate, Anna and Will arrived at Hill-Stead and stayed until the end of February. Anticipating that the ever-loyal Earnest would inform Ada, Theo confessed this latest act of hospitality. Ada learned that Anna was now ensconced in her suite and that Anna's maid was sleeping on a couch in Ada's closet. Theo assured her mother that Anna, "who is such an invalid, was absolutely the best guest and the easiest one to care for that we have ever had under our roof," and that the Admiral was "perfectly contented if he had a table and his cards, or a picture puzzle, or a novel."

Grace was Theo's grandest houseguest. The arrival of the glamorous, dark-eyed brunette caused a sensation in Farmington. Despite a weak physical condition and fragile emotional state, Grace managed to attract everyone's attention. "I seem to be quite the rage just now," she boasted in a letter to Blair, who was still stationed at Camp Dodge.

One wintry afternoon, four male members of Farmington's elite braved the snowdrifts to have tea with Grace, including Dunham "Dan" Barney, the scion of a prominent Connecticut banking family, and his former Yale roommate, Wilmarth "Lefty" Lewis. Originally from the Midwest, Lewis had settled in Farmington to get away from a domineering mother whom he said he despised. After a stint as the editor of the Yale University Press, he devoted himself to his Horace Walpole collection, which he kept in a private museum built onto his house.

Grace enjoyed their attention but told Blair that she felt contempt for her admirers—especially Dan Barney. "Of all the posing, conceited half-crazy egotists that ever lived—well, he beggars description." Even though he was married (but "horrid about his wife and babies"), Barney had asked Grace to go with him to his studio in New York. An aspiring artist of sorts, Barney wanted Grace to "sit for him, dine or lunch with him" and, most outrageous, "to take opium with him," though Grace suspected that his mentioning opium-taking was "misguided humor."

Grace also had few kind words about Lewis. Twenty-two-year-old Lewis, Grace confided, "is the man who likes me." The young man had made "such a fuss" over her, but she thought him "selfish and self centered," though "nice and amusing." "Lord," she sighed, "I'm sorry for the girl who marries him." Lewis later married Annie Burr Auchincloss, a blueblood who, he proudly notes in his autobiography, "had not the faintest trace of bluestockingism."

Brooks and Lathem Emeny were dazzled by Grace. Brooks said she was "the first woman he ever met who had the sympathetic understanding his mother would have had, had she lived." Lathem, a student at Hotchkiss, whom Grace thought "really nice... and fifty times more of a fella" than his older brother, loved to talk to Grace, who, he believed, could "solve all the problems of his existence."

When Blair appeared at Hill-Stead, the Farmington crowd was less impressed. Slim, with large, sleepy eyes, he charmed the women with his quiet, polished manners, but they gossiped that he drank too much. The men mostly ignored him. Position and wealth impressed them, and Blair had neither.

After his first visit, Blair threatened never to return. He recoiled from "having to see and talk to a whole lot of people I don't want to see or talk to and who feel the same way about me." He especially loathed the Alsops. "All the time they think they are conferring a favor on you by talking to you at all," he complained to Grace, "and you are thinking, what God awful fools these creatures are."

As much as she adored living at Hill-Stead, Grace soon became bored. Whenever the weather and her health permitted, she and Theo made excursions to the Riddles' New York City apartment, where one afternoon, Grace reported, Theo gave a "swell lunch" for Scott and Zelda Fitzgerald. Grace had known Scott since the time in St. Paul when he was Charlie's protégé. "Dear Theo is so nice," Grace wrote Charlie, and Scott was "so nice when he's sober."

Grace and Theo also dined with another St. Paul writer, Sinclair Lewis. Charlie was not fond of Lewis or his wife. "It is said that they have turned out to be I.W.W's [Industrial Workers of the World] or some such thing," Charlie sniped, "and that secret service people are on their track." Mischievously, he added, "I hope so." Theo invited the Lewises to Hill-Stead, but their visit turned out badly. Sinclair became obnoxiously drunk, and Theo had him removed from the house.

Having Paul and Grace to care for recharged Theo's spirit. She was her feisty self again. In addition to threatening to slap an ambassador's face and throwing a drunken writer out of Hill-Stead, Theo was now ready to do battle on other fronts.

After the Great War finally ended in November 1918, Theo was incensed by the suffering it had caused. Sir Francis and Alison Ley lost both their sons, and Nina's son was killed as well. "With Woman Suffrage," Theo firmly believed, "we never would have had this world catastrophe." To Ada's horror, Theo passionately and stridently committed herself to the cause. "Who can help but be converted to the Suffrage, when they contemplate the mess the men have gotten the world into?" she demanded.

Suffragettes from all over the country descended upon the nation's Capitol, some to lobby their senators, others—the followers of the radical suffragette Alice Paul—to picket the White House. They would be beaten, jailed, and force-fed when they refused to eat. At the end of April, Theo decided to join the Connecticut delegation in Washington to convince her former suitor, George McLean, to lend his support for the suffrage amendment.

Ada was appalled. She had never wavered in sustaining Alfred's anti-suffrage position. She was aghast that Theo planned to act and expose herself so scandalously. "But I feel that I want to do this," Theo countered. "There is work to be done in the world," she declared to her seventy-three-year-old mother.

Theo was specifically referring to efforts to get women the vote, but she also realized that she must resume the most crucial work of her life: her career as an architect. Other activities were important and meaningful, but they did not fully engage Theo's creative force. She must return to architecture and work on the design of the school that would honor Alfred's memory.

Gordon Brockway, age four. *(HS).*   Paul Martin, age eleven. *(HS).*

Grace Flandrau, Theo, John, and Brooks Emeny. *(HS).*

THIRTEEN

"This plan means peace to my soul"
1918—1919

FOR THE SITE of the school, Theo and Ada purchased almost 3,000 acres of woodland off Old Farms Road in Avon. Theo, however, had not yet been able to visualize the plan she would follow. She knew the reason. She must first make certain that there would be enough money to build the school. Theo had not minded the new income tax that was imposed to support the war effort, but after the war, instead of being repealed, the tax was increased and she worried that her fortune was not secure.

Earlier she had supported socialism and had spoken positively about communism. Now she saw them as a threat. What if the Bolshevists and the Industrial Workers of the World caused a revolution in America? "The menace of their actions is real," she concluded, "and if our entire economic system is overturned by them, this scheme of mine will *gang agley.*"

One afternoon, the head of the local chapter of the Red Cross came to Hill-Stead to ask for money. As the woman was speaking, Theo twice rose from her chair and paced about the room. She later said that she had felt "bouleverse and deeply stirred emotionally." As soon as the visitor left, Theo sat down in a chair in front of the fireplace and, on a small yellow pad, outlined the steps she must take to build her school:

    I. Think it out.

    II. Look for strength within and ask no support from any man.

    III. Begin work—on paper.

    IV. Provide in will.

She decided to create The Pope-Brooks Foundation, managed by John, Ada, Harris, and herself. If she were to die, the others would appoint nine other trustees. Theo then directed Ada to change her will, leaving Alfred's art collection to the corporation to avoid an inheritance tax. The trustees of the corporation would place the paintings in the school, where Theo imagined them on the walls of the library. This would be a homelike, attractive setting like the one they presently had at Hill-Stead, with the added benefit that the school's library would be made fireproof.

"This plan means peace to my soul," Theo told her mother. "I now have quiet and steady work for years to come, both in designing and in deciding the policy of the school." The last part of this statement was crucial to the project. For Theo, founding the school meant more than constructing buildings. She intended to establish an institution that educated boys according to her own educational theories. The curriculum and policies would be as original and imaginative as the architecture, and they would embody Theo's beliefs and values. She would dedicate the school to Alfred, but she would also create a reflection of herself, translated into stone buildings and educational documents.

In July 1918, John was scheduled for surgery. Charlie thought that the operation was unnecessary and that John was allowing it only because Theo had initiated it. "Dear heaven!" Charlie exclaimed. "John admits that his trouble causes him no inconvenience whatever, and I realize with extreme distaste that he is going to run all that superfluous risk merely to satisfy a whim not his own... No doubt even having one's guts amputated," he contended, "is a change from gratifying Theodate's passion for the 'constructive.'"

John underwent the procedure and then convalesced at Hill-Stead. Upon receiving a letter from him, Charlie admitted that John "seemed to be in good spirits and enjoying being an invalid."

On a warm Sunday morning, while John rested and Theo read a newspaper on the portico, she suddenly dropped the paper, stood up, and announced that she must leave. She dashed into the house, telephoned the draftsman she had hired, and told him to meet her at the field office on the school's site.

When the draftsman arrived, Theo asked him to pin detail paper on a board. Taking a piece of charcoal, she quickly drew a rough sketch of all the buildings for the school.

"From that moment, she was a possessed, dedicated, and transfigured woman," Grace recalled. "She plunged into a passion that was to be sustained for years, drawing, designing, and supervising the slow growth of the buildings, as well as developing the long document, her educational ideals, and aspirations for what human beings could and should be."

During that summer, Grace entered Cromwell Hall, a rest home in Connecticut. Theo paid all her expenses. Later, when Grace offered to repay $200, Theo accepted—to Grace's dismay. "I don't believe Theodate really wants the money back," Blair explained to his wife, "but probably is taking it on one of her 'theories' that it makes you feel better—HA!—or something like that." Taking the advice to "devote herself to work she believed in," Grace began writing a second novel while staying at the facility. She would dedicate *Being Respectable* to Theo.

Although working on the school always came first, Theo also believed that, at the same time, she must help people in need. After hearing about a family of homeless children, she quickly decided to come to their aid. The Carson children's father, a Methodist missionary addicted to alcohol and gambling, had lost the family's ranch in Africa on a bet. His wife, who was a nurse, left him, taking the three youngest children with her to America, where she obtained a position as a housekeeper for Reverend Goodell, a minister in the Boston area.

After the war ended, the influenza pandemic struck, and Reverend Goodell implored Mrs. Carson to help out at a local hospital. Working to exhaustion caring for patients, she caught the flu and died. Minister Goodell said he could not afford to keep her children. He sent the girl to live on a neighboring farm and was looking for a home for the two boys.

Twelve-year-old Donald Carson's life dramatically changed on a morning in the fall shortly after the death of his mother. He and his older brother were raking leaves, when Reverend Goodell appeared and said, "One of you is going to live with a rich lady in Connecticut." Neither Donald nor his brother wanted to leave Reverend Goodell's home, but the minister told them that they had no choice. He took out a nickel, flipped it, and asked, "Heads or tails?"

Donald, the loser of the coin toss, was put on a train with a few belongings. Arriving in New York, the child saw a chauffeur standing on the station's long platform. The man approached Donald and then escorted him into the vast lobby of Grand Central Station. Under the clock stood the rich lady, wearing a lorgnette and leaning on a silver cane. The chauffeur announced, "Mrs. Riddle is here."

The lady smiled. "Donald, did you have a nice trip?" she asked in a rich, melodious voice. Outside the station the chauffeur helped his two passengers into a grand automobile and then drove them around the block to the Belmont Hotel, where Ada kept a suite of rooms. After putting away Donald's suitcase, Theo and the boy went down to the dining room to have lunch.

Theo urged him to order dessert, but the child replied that it was too expensive. Then he changed his mind. Handing Theo the nickel that Reverend Goodell had given him after tossing the coin, Donald said he would eat an ice cream cone only if he could pay for it. Theo graciously accepted the nickel. About fifteen years later, when Donald left Hill-Stead to live on his own, Theo handed him the coin, which she had saved in her silk box.

After staying in New York for a few days, Theo and the boy boarded a train to Washington, D.C. She had asked John to meet them at the Mayflower Hotel, but when they arrived, he was not there. Theo ordered a car, and she and Donald rode throughout the city seeing the sights. At one point, they stopped and climbed the Washington Monument.

Returning to the hotel, they again waited in the lobby until finally Donald saw a tall, handsome man walking toward them. Theo introduced the child to his "Uncle John."

Donald never guessed that Uncle John was angry, for he was pleasant and friendly to the boy. But John did tell Ada that he was furious because Theo had made the decision to add Donald Carson to the family without consulting him. "I am very glad you wrote me so frankly your state of mind as I can sympathize with you completely," Ada responded from Pasadena.

John had asked Ada to try to influence Theo into returning the child, but Ada replied that she "would be glad to, but it is impossible. She always is contrary to any advice or suggestion from me. I have been startled and shocked so many times at Theodate's emotional actions that I ought to, after all these years, have become callous, but each time is a freak show."

Ada agreed that Theo had no right to bring another child into their home, but "the deed is done without any warning, no redress *for us*—but submission or fight," and Ada did not have the strength to fight. She would rather leave Hill-Stead. "My interest in Farmington has been growing less all the time... . This acquisition of another boy without any warning makes the place seem stranger and harsher than ever."

Ada told John that they could only "pray that no more waifs will be brought into our home life." Perhaps he and she might "jointly rebel sometime—and I am sure that unitedly we could get *very* mad."

After the fact, Theo explained to Ada why she had taken in Donald. First, the commitment might not be forever. "The father may of course wish to claim Donald later, but I am willing to take the boy and do what I can for him in the meantime." In addition, she thought that Donald had excellent potential. She was "glad to educate the child of missionaries, because I felt there would be good stuff in such a child and that he would have been well brought up to the time he came to me." Although she immediately saw that their temperaments were different, Theo also hoped that Donald would be a good companion for Paul, who was just twelve days younger than the new boy. Both children would live in the O'Rourkery, she assured her mother, not at Hill-Stead.

John was more than just angry at Theo. Grace confided to Blair that Theo and John were "in a terrible state." In fact, they were "very near a separation." Warning him not to "whisper this to a human soul especially Charlie," Grace appealed to Blair. "Theo feels you are the only person who can help out."

"John is taking a perfectly selfish unreasonable stand," Grace claimed and insisted that Blair tell him so. She asked Blair to meet Theo in

Washington and talk to his brother. "We must do this for her," she insisted. Whether Blair did anything is not known, but John and Theo reconciled that Christmas.

After the War College released him from his duties, John returned to Hill-Stead, where Theo waited with the two twelve-year-old foundlings, Paul and Donald, and ever-faithful Earnest. The soft-spoken, light-skinned black man, who was approaching his fortieth year of service with the family, warmly greeted the "Ambassador," the title that most people used for John. Ada was still in Pasadena.

John played a fatherly role to Paul and Donald. At dinner, Theo looked on happily, and Earnest stood back at a polite distance and listened while John recounted his adventures in the diplomatic service and at Army Intelligence during the war. The boys sat rapt and wide-eyed, fascinated by Uncle John's stories, especially those about the sinister activities of German and Italian spies.

That winter, Grace left for Paris. Theo had urged her to help Gus Jaccaci, who was still caring for refugee children. Theo's idea appealed to Grace not for altruistic reasons but because she wanted to go to Paris, especially since the Peace Conference was about to begin in the city.

The only problem Grace had was placating Blair, who had assumed that his now-well wife would live with him on the army base in Norfolk, Virginia, until he was released from the service in the near future. But Grace convinced him that being in Paris was important to her career because she planned to contact the famous novelist Edith Wharton, who had admired Grace's novel. "A few months and then *no more* separations," she promised.

A short time later, learning that Jaccaci was ill, Theo suggested to Blair, who had just been discharged from the army, that he join Grace and take over for Gus. "How would you like to be working for me, Keekface?" Blair wrote Grace. "I'd make you jump." But, determined to make money, Blair was not interested in humanitarian causes. On the way home to St. Paul, he planned to stop in Farmington. As much as he felt uncomfortable at Hill-Stead, especially without Grace there, he had an important reason for the visit.

"I'm awfully fond of Theo," he explained to Grace. "I want to talk over with her my plan of going into the automobile and garage business and see what she thinks of it." He also hoped she would lend him money to start the business, which he planned to do in partnership with Charlie's chauffeur Clark.

Theo and John were living an uneventful existence in snow-covered Farmington. There were afternoon bridge parties at Anna's, dinners at the Alsops', and evening séances at Hill-Stead conducted by Theo's most recently discovered medium. Theo and John frequently went to New York, where they dined with the Vanderbilts and others, and attended the opera and the theatre.

Most days, Theo was engrossed in designing the school. Sometimes she sat for hours seemingly in a trance, sleeping with her eyes open. She was imagining details of the buildings, which, in a rush of energy, she would later commit to paper.

In contrast, John had become bored and restless. He missed working for military intelligence, and, at fifty-four, he wanted to resume his diplomatic career. If he re-entered the world of diplomacy, however, he might be assigned to a post almost anywhere in the world. Theo did not look forward to the prospect. Were she and John to live in a foreign country, she would have to interrupt work on the school. But she was willing to compromise.

"I had a little talk with Totem, when I saw he intended to try for something," she confided to Grace, "and I said I thought we would have to manage on the fifty-fifty basis—that is, if he gets anything, I would have to spend half of the year here."

Theo and John knew that he would need considerable influence to obtain an appointment. Theodore Roosevelt, who had done so much in the past to advance John's career, had died in January 1919, but John hoped that Roosevelt's sister Anna could still help him. At sixty-four and severely crippled, Anna continued to hold court at Oldgate, surrounded by powerful politicians and diplomats. Securing a position for John would be difficult, though, and might take months or even longer—or perhaps never happen.

To pass the time while he waited, John asked Theo to go on vacation. Theo hated to leave her work and did not want to travel on a ship, but, for John's sake, she agreed to a five-month tour of the Orient. Before they left in April 1919, Theo gave power of attorney to Harris and assigned legal responsibility for Paul and Donald to her secretary, Elizabeth McCarthy.

Theo and John first traveled across the country to San Francisco. Blair, having received a loan from Theo, was still at Hill-Stead. He accompanied them part of the way, but they would not make a stop at the Flandrau home in St. Paul because Theo refused to see Charlie. She wanted nothing to do with him because, in addition to the battle over Grace, she had discovered that Charlie had urged John to divorce her when he was angry about Donald. "Theo is awful sore at Charlie," Blair told Grace. "I don't blame her."

In San Francisco, Ada arrived from Pasadena to see John and Theo off. Now in her seventies, Ada complained about being too plump, but she was still attractive. For the past few weeks, John had been suffering from an infected boil on his neck, and, Theo told Ada, the champagne she gave them was "the only comfort in life he has at present."

After a few days onboard the S.S. *Shinyo Maru,* Theo became alarmed when the infection caused John to develop a high fever. She summoned the ship's doctor, but, unable to speak English, he could not answer her questions. "The little Jap," Theo sputtered in frustration, "waved his hand weakly and showed his teeth in an imbecile smile saying never a word." Worried that John might have blood poisoning, Theo scurried about the ship in search of another doctor. She discovered an American but became disgusted with him as well. He had "lived so long with the Japanese that he seems like a half-breed," she wrote Ada. Finally, she found a retired orthopedic surgeon on vacation, who turned out to be "a tower of strength."

"Theodate has been a most attentive nurse," John reported to Ada, "so that she has been taken out of her own thoughts and memories," referring to the *Lusitania* disaster four years earlier. Theo had not forgotten the ordeal, however. "I hate this ship!" she wrote her mother.

Theo was alone below deck when, suddenly, she heard whistles blowing and gongs sounding. Seeing water shooting out of the hold, she bolted and raced down the corridor looking for John. A Spanish missionary in the hallway tried to calm her. It was just a fire drill. "Where is your stateroom?" he asked. Though she was hysterical, she was able to answer. The missionary took Theo to the room, where he stayed until the drill was over. Meanwhile, John remained on deck. "Totem...of course [was] quite unconscious that I was terrified," Theo explained to Ada. She blamed the infection. "He has troubles enough of his own these days."

"Honolulu isn't Hawaiian, American or Japanese," Theo observed in a more cheerful tone when they stopped at the island. It's "kind of a scrappy little town." When they arrived at Yokohama, no one could leave the ship for seven hours because there was a case of small pox in steerage and a suspected case in first class. After being vaccinated, the passengers were allowed to go ashore but were warned that there was a shortage of accommodations. "Poor Totem was feeling wretchedly," Theo wrote, "and didn't want to sleep in a chair in some hotel office." But she refused to remain onboard a moment longer, and luckily they got a hotel room.

After Yokohama, the Riddles went to Mt. Fuji and checked into the best hotel east of Suez, the Fujia Hotel, which had magnificent views from the top of a mountain gorge. Trips to the Orient had become quite fashionable, and Theo discovered a cousin, Gussie Brooks Bowman, and her husband George seated at a table in the hotel's exquisite dining room.

In Tokyo, their accommodations were a disappointment. Theo said that the Imperial Hotel was "very well known but terribly run down." They had to adjust to cramped quarters, sleeping in a room that, she noted, measured about 14' x 18' and did not have its own bathroom. Every night, she and John climbed over ten pieces of luggage, and then, "each had to move the bed to get in—whichever got in last!" Theo liked sharing the cozy room with John as well as playing a wifely role. On the trip, she mended clothes and cleaned their rooms.

After attending a garden party at the American Embassy, a dinner party at the Russian Embassy, and a luncheon with the French secretary and Holland's ambassador, Theo and John left Tokyo, and, in June, boarded the S.S. *Venezuela* to Manila. In Macao, John wanted to visit a gambling house. Trying her luck at Fan Tan, Theo won ten dollars but was nauseated by the man who handled the money because of his "large weak hands with nails two inches long."

Although earlier she had made bigoted comments about the Japanese doctor and the Japanese in general, Theo now approved of Japan because the people were clean. "They think we are too horrible going into our homes with soiled shoes—they think it all a part of our barbarism, and I'm not so sure but that they are right."

When they arrived in China, Theo was disgusted. In contrast to Japan, China was a "cruel, outrageous, preposterous, filthy land!" As for the Chinese people—"I hate them," Theo pronounced. She was comforted, though, because they were so backward that "they can never become a menace." Canton was a dangerous place where "the foreigners live on a little preserve of their own—an island which is shut off from the rest of the city and whose bridges are guarded by police."

Through narrow streets, Chinese bearers trotted, one carrying a bamboo chair that held a tall, distinguished-looking gentleman with silver-gray hair and a full mustache, and the other carrying a short, blonde woman, whose bright blue eyes glared at the scene around her. The bearers continually shouted at the onlookers staring at the rich Americans: "Stand back! Clear the way!"

"Oh what sights and smells," Theo wrote Ada. "Every one of our five senses were assaulted—*insulted*." What she saw was indeed a hellish scene: "Babies with running sores. Men with strange lumps on their necks or faces. Everyone sneezing, coughing, spitting, scratching—sleeping with heads on wooden pillows and mouths open for flies to crawl in—bloody meatshops with diseased looking carcasses of pigs and unknown cuts that may be dogs and cats—as they eat them—live cats and chickens carried in baskets slung on shoulders with bamboo poles—cats mewing and babies crying—the wail of babies in China! Green vegetables that come from fields that are manured by human excrement!"

If this was not enough to sicken Ada, Theo next described the Chinese practice of murdering female babies, often by burying them alive. In Nanking, which looked "as if the contents of a huge garbage can had been emptied on the plain," poor families hurled infant girls over the walls of the city.

Theo and John traveled across the country by train. Their compartment was extremely hot, mostly because the window screen was not letting in any air. Theo called the porter and pointed out the problem, but the man left without fixing it. Theo then took out a penknife and cut the screen. When the porter returned and saw the damage, he became furious. As John watched in amusement, Theo met the porter's fury with her own, and the man "slunk away."

Fortunately, Theo and John found "an oasis," a small hotel that looked like an English inn. The hotel-keeper, Mrs. Martin, was an Australian whose husband had been murdered by a former Chinese servant. "If you dismiss servants in China in any manner," Mrs. Martin informed her guests, "you are almost always assassinated!" There was only one accepted way to get rid of a servant, and that was to say, "I regret so deeply that I cannot give myself the pleasure of your continued valuable services but I must reduce my expenses etc etc etc."

"That," Theo protested vehemently, "saves their face—their altogether evil yellow face!"

John wrote more pleasant letters. He told Ada that Theo enjoyed shopping and looking at China's old architecture, though he did admit that "the fearful smells in all Chinese quarters took away her appetite."

In Peking, the First Secretary of the American Legation gave two dinners in the Riddles' honor and in honor of the present Russian ambassador. Theo left her plate untouched. For the past month, she had been able to digest only soup and dessert. "How I have longed for one glass of Hill-Stead milk!" she confided to the ambassador. The next day Theo entered a Peking hospital, run by the order of St. Vincente de Paul, to be treated for gastritis.

After Theo was released, she and John left for the Kumgang San, the Diamond Mountains of Korea, where she found the landscape "too beautiful." Kumgang San seemed like another Eden, and Theo expressed admiration for its inhabitants. "It all looks strangely as if the

164

world had only lately been created," she mused, "and that the brown people are the grandchildren of Adam and Eve."

While she and John were gazing on the scene, Theo suddenly noticed "a flow of green growth between mountains of rock that had been formed by the silt of thousands of years." The rock formation and the contrast between the rocks' color and the greenery were hypnotic. For three days and nights, Theo experienced an ecstasy that made her feel, as Wordsworth wrote, like "a living soul."

Soon after, while driving along a village road, Theo was again overcome, this time by the beauty of the yellow wheat fields bordered by pines. She felt as if she were falling into herself, and she could not remember where she was.

In this alien country on the opposite side of her world, Theo experienced a sense of satisfaction and tranquility. Despite the pain of Gordon's death that she would always feel, she was filled with love for Ada, John, and the two boys, and she was confident about her marriage. She wrote that John was "so companionable—I'm never lonesome—he never leaves me."

As their journey came to an end, Theo became more concerned about what lay ahead for her husband. Anna was trying to secure a position for John but had not yet succeeded. Without telling John, Theo asked his stepsister Patty Selmes for assistance.

"If I can ever help you or my dear Old Bud," Patty responded, she would do so. Unfortunately, she didn't have much influence with the Harding administration. "The Franklin Roosevelts are my only intimate friends."

Patty thought it absurd that she should try to help John since he knew so many people himself, but she offered to write to the Bob Blisses, who "are the whole thing at our Legation in Paris," and to obtain a recommendation letter for John from Alice Roosevelt Longworth. Patty suggested that John investigate working for the Paris Peace Conference because there was a great need for interpreters who knew both French and English.

Patty also promised not to reveal to John that his wife had contacted her. "I fully understand," she reassured Theo, "what you say stays put."

When Theo wrote Grace about the idea of John's becoming an interpreter, Grace responded that the Paris Peace Conference was not going well. People were saying that "Wilson doesn't know what he's about." France had lost its glamour for Grace, who could hardly wait to return to America. After traveling throughout the French countryside and seeing "trenches & dugouts, barb wire & sandbags & shells & duds & graves

graves graves," Grace was repelled by the poverty and despair of the French people. "I am not one bit of a reformer or philanthropist or anything else," she admitted. "I'm sick to death of all these poor people and I just want to go home."

Theo and John returned from their trip in the early fall of 1919. While they were away, as Theo hoped, Ada had become fond of Donald. She had even changed her will, leaving $5,000 each to Donald and Paul, the same amount bequeathed to her Brooks nephews.

Theo eagerly resumed work on the plans for the school. She finished the preliminary drawings, which were exhibited at the 57th Street Galleries in New York several months later. As an architect who had received recognition for several projects, Theo applied for membership in the American Institute of Architects. On the application form, she crossed out the name Riddle and asked that she be listed as Theodate Pope. "Use my maiden name," she directed. "By this name I am known professionally."

The A.I.A., however, ignored the request, and "Theodate Pope Riddle" appeared on the certificate. When she saw that, for the date of birth, "February 1877" was written instead of 1867, Theo was pleased. Those looking at the certificate framed on the wall would now think her forty-two rather than fifty-two years old.

Donald and Paul posing in Theo's Stutz. *(HS)*.

John and Paul play chess while Theo looks on and Donald looks down. *(HS)*.

Theo and John in Peking. *(HS)*.

FOURTEEN

"The Ambassadress"
1919—1923

IN DECEMBER 1919, the Women's Roosevelt Memorial Association chose Theo as the architect to reconstruct Theodore Roosevelt's boyhood home on East 20th Street in New York City. In contrast to being denied commissions because she was a woman, Theo received this opportunity for the opposite reason. The women's group wanted a female architect. In addition, the President's sister, Anna, was a member of the association's board. Upon hearing the announcement, Foster Kennedy was delighted that "the great American will have a House fashioned by one who loved and understood him."

Honored and excited about the commission, Theo set aside working on the school. She quickly hired a draftsman, Leland Lyon, and several other employees, and began work at her Madison Avenue office. Almost immediately, however, she became ill and had to have mastoid surgery.

For the next two months, she lay in a small hospital room, propped up in bed, surrounded by drawing boards and stacks of papers. She directed her staff, who went back and forth from the hospital to the office and the site. A headline in *The Hartford Courant* announced: "Illness Fails to Keep Theodate Pope from Roosevelt Work: Architect Completes Preliminary Plans While Recovering From Operation in New York Hospital."

Theo proudly wrote Ada, "You know they say in England of people riding to the hunt— 'it is no disgrace to be thrown if you keep hold of the bridle'—well, I was thrown all right but I kept hold of the bridle. I never lost control of the designing during my illness."

After another building that stood on the site of the birthplace was demolished, Theo rebuilt the Roosevelt Birthplace to make it look the way it had in 1865, the year a mansard roof was added. The house is a faithful reconstruction of the President's Victorian home: a modest, narrow brownstone. Theo cleverly reconciled its 19th-century appearance with an additional three stories by making them invisible from the street. On an adjacent site, she designed a connecting wing that has meeting rooms, a library, and a room to display memorabilia.

Theo not only designed the building, she decorated the interior, following Anna's recollections about the house when she and her brother lived there as children. "In her quest for historical accuracy," a critic noted that Theo "sought out actual nineteenth century chimney pieces and gas fixtures and had them installed throughout the Birthplace's period rooms. She also sent people motoring through the countryside to find just the right pieces of furniture, while wallpapers, carpets, and fabrics were carefully chosen to match those in the original nineteenth-century house." Theo's own tastes are evident as well. She chose the same colonial-block print wallpaper that she had used at Hill-Stead for the walls of the Roosevelt Birthplace's hallways.

In addition to architectual work, Theo conducted spiritualist and political activities from her hospital bed. She stayed in touch with the medium, Mrs. Fordice Knox, who was receiving messages from Theodore Roosevelt's spirit, and she sent $1500 to support Professor Comstock's psychical research. She also engaged in a battle over the suffrage with Connecticut's Governor Marcus Holcomb.

Before going to the Orient the year before, Theo had dashed off a telegram to the governor. "When are you going to give us your backing for the suffrage?" she inquired.

"If that question is purposed as a serious one, I reply seriously," Holcomb responded. "I should be willing to give you a backing for woman's suffrage if a majority of the women of the state voiced their desire to have it."

The governor believed not only that most women did not want the vote but also that the issue was losing momentum. "Personally," he told Theo, "I do not think that the women will be as anxious for suffrage twenty-five years from now as they are today."

A year later, Connecticut still had not ratified the suffrage amendment because of Holcomb's opposition. In the hospital, Theo composed a public letter to the governor and sent it to *The Hartford Courant,* asking that it be published and the cost charged to her account. When the letter appeared on April 2, 1920, it was preceded by a nasty comment from the editors about Mrs. Riddle's assumption that she could "buy a place in these columns."

"I am going to tell you a secret, dear Governor Holcomb," Theo's letter began, "because you do not seem to be aware of it. One of the greatest final effects of the world war will be the enfranchisement of women the world over—and our own little state of Connecticut still hesitates—or has the appearance of hesitating because you refuse to call a special session of the Legislature." She ended with the warning: "You cannot hold back this wagon of progress by holding the spokes of the rear wheels."

A few weeks after Theo recovered, she received word that Ada was ill. Theo and John immediately left for California, but, before they arrived,

Ada suffered a massive heart attack. She died on May 6, 1920, Theo and John's fourth wedding anniversary. After a memorial service in Pasadena, they brought Ada to Salem, Ohio. In her will, Ada had requested that her body be cremated and placed next to Alfred's in the family vault. In addition to other bequests, Ada left $3,000 to Earnest and $50,000 to John. Theo inherited the balance of the multimillion dollar estate.

"Thee knows, and we know that dear Aunt Ada is where she has wanted to be ever since Uncle Alfred left her," wrote a cousin.

"Your dear little mother...doubtless died happily, leaving you, indeed, but faring on, as was her sure faith, to meet again her soulmate," another relative assured Theo.

The servants at Hill-Stead had not been particularly fond of Mrs. Pope and, behind her back, called her "Ada Bo Peep," but one writer knew that Earnest was grief-stricken. "Please send me Earnest's last name," she asked, "for I want to write to him. I know it is a real heart-sorrow to him to part with dear beautiful Mrs. Pope."

From boarding school, fourteen-year-old Paul wrote Theo on behalf of himself and Donald. "I was so glad to receive your telegram, and it meant so much to both of us," he began. He and Donald felt "so sorry over Aunt Ada's death. But maybe it was for the best."

The remainder of Paul's letter mostly concerned news about school. He had joined the "Christian Endeavor" and had pledged "never to smoke Cigirattes, use Profain language or Drink." He boasted that he was up to page 302 in the book that both he and Donald were reading—"way ahead of Donald"—and, seeming to forget that Theo was mourning her mother, ended with the cheerful announcement: "To day is the first real May day we have had and it is *Mothers Day!*"

Theo realized that the boys were quite different in ability as well as in temperament. Paul was intense, serious, and bright. Donald was good-natured but slow. In a conversation with Paul about the school she planned in honor of Alfred, Theo mentioned that she wanted the students to learn to farm. She asked the boy what breed of cow he thought she should buy, a question Paul considered "a burning issue." Hill-Stead's farm was famous for its cows, especially for its prize-winning Guernsey, Anathesia Faith.

After thinking a few minutes, Paul named a breed that happened to be red, black and white. In mock seriousness, Theo replied, "No. I cannot endure the look of them."

"Is it possible that you would select cows for their looks," the boy demanded, not realizing she was joking, "instead of the *butter fat record!?*"

During the summer, Paul worked hard on the Hill-Stead farm, about four hours a day, and then he usually studied for six hours. Theo thought he had "unbounded ambition." On the other hand, there was "poor old Donald." "A cloud comes over his face when you mention the word *book*," Theo sighed. Paul read a book in a day, but Donald had to "pound away on it for several weeks."

In order to encourage the boy, Theo asked Donald to read aloud to her every evening. She despaired, though, because he seemed to lack curiosity, which, she believed, was essential to becoming educated. "How can you induce it when it is not here?" she asked, determined "to awaken him" if possible.

Donald also lacked "Will Power" and "Initiative," but Theo adored him anyway. "He is a great old darling and gives me no trouble." Her affection is evident in letters and telegrams. When he was away at school, she wrote, "I am so sorry to hear you are ill, son. My very dearest love for you dearest boy." On Mother's Day, she sent a telegram, "Beloved Donald. Just to let you know I am thinking of you today."

Theo also understood that intelligence was not limited to the academic. She was fond of repeating a story told by her secretary, Elizabeth McCarthy, who had cared for the boys while Theo was in the hospital. One night, when Miss McCarthy went into Donald's room to say, "Good night," she startled the child. "Oh, Miss McCarthy, you have spoilt the most beautiful thought I ever had," he said. "I was planning a brake for my little automobile."

In addition to a love for cars and machines, Donald enjoyed "coon hunting" with Earnest. The old servant took the boy out in the middle of the night, walking sometimes ten miles through the Farmington woods. They would come home at 4:00 in the morning, usually without having caught anything.

The two boys did not get along well. Donald was jealous of his clever "brother," and, if Donald got into trouble, he blamed Paul. When Mrs. Douglas Robinson, another Roosevelt sister, came to dinner, Donald said that Paul told him to pull out the chair just as the grand dame started to sit down at the table. She "didn't quite fall," Donald later recalled, "but she was flustered," and, of course, Theo was furious.

During the early 1920s, Donald attended the Kingswood School, a day school located in Mark Twain's former home on Farmington Avenue in Hartford. Because jumping off a moving trolley was considered good sport, Donald jumped and was hit by a car. His injuries were not serious, but the incident badly frightened Theo.

Despite the difficulties of bringing up two very different children,

Theo enjoyed being with the boys. One evening, leaving John home in bed with a cold, she took Paul and Donald to a movie. On their return, Earnest joined them, and the four, plus Yum-Yum, another Chow, indulged in devouring expensive chocolate bon-bons. The dog was allowed to eat only one.

At the same time, Theo sometimes demonstrated insensitivity toward the children. Shortly after she had taken in Paul, she and John made plans to go to their New York apartment, but the woman who was supposed to care for the boy had become ill. Explaining that she could not take him with her—New York City was an unsuitable place for a child—Theo brought Paul back to the orphanage for a brief period. She seemed not to realize that the boy was frightened about being returned to the institution.

In the spring of 1920, having received no word about a diplomatic appointment, John and Theo took another trip, this time to Europe. They brought Paul and Donald along and hired an English tutor, Mr. Holles, who took the boys on a grand tour of Europe while Theo and John remained in England.

Despite anxiety about taking an ocean voyage, Theo looked forward to revisiting the Cotswold area in England and speaking with an English architect, Alfred H. Powell, about her plans for the school. During previous visits, Theo had been charmed by the quaint, medieval architecture of the Cotswold area, and its influence was present in several buildings she had already built. On this trip, she planned to learn more about pre-industrialized methods of construction.

To create the Cotswolds' beautiful buildings, English craftsmen wielded ancient tools, including broad axes, to shape the wooden beams and roofs, and, like 16th-century workers, they arduously finished stone by hand. Rather than using plumb lines or levels, they employed only their eyes and thumbs, which resulted in imperfect, beautiful lines. Theo filled several notebooks with drawings and bits of advice from Mr. Powell and returned to Farmington ready to employ medieval methods of construction to build her school.

That fall, John spent most of his days alone—reading, playing bridge, taking trips to New York, and waiting for a diplomatic appointment—while Theo concentrated entirely on the school. She worked from her field office on the Avon site, where, as winter approached, she tramped about wearing a scarf, jacket, knickers and boots.

Because their tutor was a "pathetic survivor" of the war and could not bear the cold, Theo sent Mr. Holles, Paul, and Donald to Florida. Theo was pleased that the boys had completed two years' work in the six months that Holles had been teaching them.

In the spring of 1921, John went to Washington to work on obtaining a diplomatic post. Anna was still trying to help, but she and her husband had developed serious health problems. During the previous winter, Will had suffered numerous attacks of uremic poisoning, which partially paralyzed him and left him sluggish and sometimes unable to speak. Anna's rheumatism had almost completely debilitated her.

After John returned without getting a position, he asked Theo to go on a summer vacation, which included a cruise to Norway. Theo hated to leave her work, and, even though she had managed the ocean voyages to the Orient and to England, she knew she would suffer onboard ship. But she agreed to the cruise because she worried that John was becoming depressed.

The trip went fairly well until, sailing along the coast of Norway, Theo heard a loud and violent sound, almost as terrible as that of the torpedo's hitting the *Lusitania* six years earlier. The ship's boiler had exploded, killing five men and injuring fifteen others.

After a few more days, the ship stopped because icebergs blocked its way. About twenty-four hours later, it finally moved, very slowly. Approaching the fjords, Theo marveled at the eerie beauty of the evening sun on the promontories but was nervous as the ship swerved to avoid crashing into them.

Theo and John were lying in their berths when they heard another terrible noise. Theo got up and climbed on top of a table in order to look out the porthole. The ship had run into the rocks. Gazing down at John, Theo remarked, "This is a damn silly joy ride."

In September, Theo and John arrived at the docks to board another ship to return home. They learned that their ship had been destroyed by a fire. Unwilling to sail on a small boat sent to replace it, John used his diplomatic connections in Paris to obtain passage on a large ship that, they later learned, had been taken over from the Germans after the war. Unfortunately, the captain and crew did not know how to manage it, and the ship listed heavily during the entire voyage.

One night, Theo suspected that something was seriously wrong. She saw that the portholes were closed and noticed that the stewards and stewardesses seemed nervous. She fell asleep, but when she woke up, John was not in the room. He had gone to breakfast.

Theo lay perfectly still, frozen by the irrational fear that if she moved "even an eyelash, the ship would turn over." She could not even ring for the steward, but for some reason, he appeared. Through clenched teeth, she muttered, "Get Mr. Riddle."

After a few minutes that seemed an eternity, John entered the room. "Get me a pint of champagne," Theo whispered. A few minutes later, John returned with a glass filled to the brim. Although she had not eaten anything, Theo quickly drank it down. Later, she said, "It was the best thing to do under the circumstances."

A few months after they returned, John received a diplomatic position when President Harding appointed him ambassador to the Argentine. The date set for his departure was January 5, 1922. Earlier, Theo and John had discussed her spending half the year at whatever embassy he was assigned to and the other half in Farmington. Most likely, John had agreed to the compromise. Now the question arose: which half-year would come first? John believed it essential to begin the appointment with Theo at his side. Theo responded that she did not want to suspend the initial stages of construction of the school. She also dreaded boarding another ship.

When Grace arrived at Hill-Stead in December 1921 to spend the Christmas holidays and recover from her latest depression, she entered an atmosphere charged with tension. Since returning from Paris, Grace had lived in St. Paul with Blair for about six months, quite a while for her. She was unhappy, she said, because she was the target of vicious gossip. Although Blair's friends knew that he had been an alcoholic for years, they blamed Grace for his drinking because she had left him alone while she gadded about and wrote novels. In defiance of the talk, Grace had thrown herself into the social scene, and for a while, had enjoyed the attention of the men and ignored the cutting glances of the women. Eventually, she gave up and collapsed.

Theo attributed Grace's frequent bouts of depression to her attempt to balance "the competing demands of her married life in high society and of her own professional ambitions." Seemingly unaware that Grace initiated the social demands, Theo urged that she concentrate completely on work. "It is a sickening thing to me to observe you wasting your life," she admonished, "because that is what you are doing—throwing your great talents to the winds." Unfortunately, there were "thousands and thousands" of talented women like Grace, who for one reason or another did not use their gifts, Theo noted bitterly, no doubt thinking about herself.

At Hill-Stead that Christmas, Grace did not get the care and attention she expected. Because of the enormous amounts of money that Theo was using to build the school, the serving staff had been reduced, and guests no longer were served breakfast in bed. "Theo seems almost poor," Grace lamented. She was stunned to discover that "Theo is making over one million dollars to her school this month—*one million in cold hard cash.*" In addition to enduring a less luxurious life because of Theo's economies, Grace found herself in the middle of a fight between the Riddles because Theo was refusing to accompany John to Argentina. "The strain is awful," Grace wrote Blair. Making him swear not to tell Charlie, she confided that Theo and John were "having the devil of a time."

Finally, when rumors reached Washington that Theo might not go and, after he almost lost his appointment, John threatened divorce and Theo capitulated.

Although the battle was over, the situation was still "*pretty hot,*" Grace reported, convinced that the marriage had suffered "a serious—an almost unreconcilable breach." Theo took out her misery on everyone. Even Grace felt "on hot coals with Theo all the time." She witnessed Theo's getting "mad at the dearest person, her cousin Mrs. Trafford." She "practically fired the whole lot, Mr & Mrs Trafford & their two lovely girls, right out of the House!" Why? Mrs. Trafford had asked Theo if she was going to Argentina.

John arranged to have the date of departure postponed for two weeks and put Grace in charge of making sure that Theo was ready. Grace's primary duty was to keep Theo from breaking down, and her second task was to help purchase a new wardrobe.

"Every waking thought and moment is taken up by Theo," Grace complained. During the first week, Grace selected "out of hundreds of others—seven evening gowns, four or five afternoon & a lot of other dresses." In addition, she coordinated accessories: "fans stockings jewelry gloves etc. for each costume...hats & wraps," and bought "priceless Roman coins old French Italian & Renaissance pieces, engravings on jade, lapis lazuli, rose brilliants etc. etc."

"You can't conceive of the dresses & jewels & ornaments & furs & endless costumes," Grace told Blair, pleased that Theo had come around and was now showing an adventurous spirit. "She's determined to knock their eyes out."

The week before the ship left, Grace accompanied Theo and John to their apartment at the Carlton House. The time passed pleasantly. "When all is rosy," Grace observed, "they are vastly entertaining." Ignoring the blizzard outside, Theo, John, and their guest celebrated the couple's reconciliation. "I'm *almost dead* from the food," Grace moaned. "Pigeons, alligator pears, pate de fois, pastry champagne every night."

As the day they were to sail approached, Theo began to lose heart. Dread of the voyage caused her to collapse and stay in bed. Theo's terror reached such a peak that she begged Grace to go with them to

Argentina—and then to return to New York on the same boat. After a bout of hysteria, Theo changed her mind and told Grace it was not necessary.

On January 19, 1922, a motorcade approached the docks. Two trucks carried the Riddles' trunks, and Theo's small pieces were packed into several taxis. The group included chauffeurs, servants, secretaries, assistant architects, Theo's maid, and, bringing up the rear of the procession, Brooks Emeny and Grace. Theo gave last minute instructions to all, and then she and John waved farewell and went onboard.

John and Theo received royal treatment on the ship. The president of the line gave a luncheon in honor of the Argentine ambassador and his wife, and as he escorted them to their seats, everybody in the dining room rose. Later, in a conversation with the ship's captain, John mentioned that Theo had survived the *Lusitania* disaster and had suffered other mishaps at sea. Either in jest or truly superstitious that Theo was a jinx, the captain "mopped his brow" and replied, "Well, Mr. Riddle, I do not know how it makes you feel, but it makes me nervous."

Theo found the twenty-one day voyage to Argentina tolerable. During the first three days, she tried to learn Spanish but gave up. "I knew I did not wish to half learn it," she wrote Anna, "and I certainly know that I do not wish to throw myself into it with the same determination that I've expended in learning Bridge."

Once they reached their destination, the reception given to Ambassador Riddle was spectacular. While bands played *The Star Spangled Banner,* John "whirled away with the clatter of the hoofs of the mounted grenadiers, his escort," to present his credentials to Argentina's President. All traffic was barred in front of the Casa Rosado (the "Pink House," which, Theo told Grace, was the Argentine "*White* House"). Over 100,000 people came to see the new American ambassador, who arrived in a carriage drawn by four horses, with a coachman and footman in gorgeous livery.

Meanwhile, Theo was brought to the women's place in the Casa Rosada. She reported to Grace that she wore "your very favorite black & white with the gold necklace and heavy earrings & the very thin stockings, as per your order." Upon hearing the procession arrive, Theo and the other women dashed out onto the balcony. Theo looked down, thrilled to see her handsome husband stepping from the carriage: "Totem with his white *evening* shirt reflecting the sunlight, and the flying pennants of the grenadiers' lances."

Noticing Theo on the balcony, John stopped and doffed his hat. Then he and the others entered the house, and the company celebrated by drinking champagne. That evening, Theo and John dined alone. Suddenly John paused, his face solemn. Raising his glass, he smiled and toasted Theo: "To Her Excellency, The Ambassa*dress*."

"I wished to be Ambassador to Russia for my mother's sake," he confessed, "and my chief pleasure in this post is making you an Ambassadress." Theo was amused by the compliment. "I know that he is being a very wise bird at the chancery," she confided to Grace.

At first, Theo's letters indicated that she was "all right" in Argentina. But unable to speak Spanish and not permitted to go anywhere without a companion, she quickly became restless and bored. "I never go into a shop. Annie does it all while I loiter along trying not to be run over at the frequent crossings." She had made only one friend, "a really charming cat," who, she wrote Grace, "talks to me as I stroke her."

The State Department did not provide a house for the new Ambassador, nor did it pay John's entertainment expenses. After a few weeks, the Riddles rented a house, "the one Totem loves above all," Theo wrote, because it was beautiful and they would live next door to Madame de Castex, who "is a power here."

Theo and John attended Madame's dinner parties, at which guests conversed in four foreign languages. Not understanding a word, Theo tried to look "pleasant if not intelligent." When she mentioned, in English, her interest in psychical phenomena, people "listened politely and changed the subject."

Writing Grace "what it is like here," Theo sounded weary. "We go no place—except occasions...with Embassy people." To fill the hours, she read, and she also invented a "wonderful trouser button," which, of course, she wouldn't patent. "What would people think of the American Ambassadress busying herself about a button for trousers!"

"John manages everything—he is engaging servants etc etc—for I cannot speak Spanish," she fretted. "I have hours and hours to myself. *I have practically nothing to do.*"

She attended a meeting of the Patriotic Society of American Women, patiently listened to Mrs. McCrum read a talk on "Artistic Glass Ware of Ancient Times" and managed to keep her eyes open but only through a great effort of will.

Theo's greatest accomplishment was learning to play bridge. "You now play better than most women," John remarked, "and many men!"

"Incidentally," she confided to Anna, "I had beaten him badly."

In June 1922, the Women's Roosevelt Memorial Association wrote Theo that a Men's Association would donate $200,000 to the women's group, but only if it could have offices and a museum in the Roosevelt Birthplace.

Wanting to accept the offer, the women asked Theo to design changes in the building to accommodate the men's request. With John's approval, Theo agreed to return to New York to work on the project.

Soon after the ship left Rio de Janeiro, Theo realized that it was turning in slow circles. The captain met with the passengers and explained that a valve stem pivot had broken. For thirty-four hours the ship continued going in circles until the pivot was replaced. The next three weeks went by without incident, but eight hours from New York, the ship began to list sharply.

Theo saw an alarmed looking officer drop hurriedly down from the bridge and run to the rear. She ran onto the deck and joined other passengers who were looking over the railing at the ship's wake. The ship was again running in circles, but this time at full speed. The new pivot had overheated and jammed the rudder. Then one of the fresh water tanks burst.

Because the ship was top-heavy, there was a strong possibility that it might turn over. The captain sent a message to New York asking for help, and the crew hung two black bells on the mast, a sign that the ship was out of control. Finally it slowed down and, accompanied by tugs, made its way into New York Harbor.

When the danger was over, the captain approached Theo. He was the same man whom she and John had met five months earlier on their way to Buenos Aires. The captain recalled John's stories of Theo's previous misadventures on ships, and he intimated that he did not want to have her sail with him again.

"It seems incredible, but I had another dreadful experience at sea," Theo wrote Grace. "This whole thing has shaken my nerves so that I am on my back and I have a good deal of that troublesome rapid heart beat." Although she was certain she was going to be up soon, she was ill for three months with what Foster Kennedy termed tachycardia and low blood pressure, due to shock.

When she was well, Theo informed John that she would not return to Argentina. After making revisions to Roosevelt Birthplace, she went to Farmington and resumed work on the school. John did not argue. He seemed content to carry on alone, and Theo felt revitalized. Anna remarked that at fifty-five, her friend "never looked handsomer nor more attractive."

During the 1922 Christmas holiday, Theo and Grace met John in New York at the Carlton House apartment. John was in high spirits. According to Grace, one evening the ambassador paraded up and down the hall, wearing trousers that were too small for him and carrying a toy balloon. After attending dinner parties, the theatre, and dances in New York, the three went to Hill-Stead, where the Riddles hosted a large weekend party to celebrate their reunion. Guests arrived on every train and in chauffeured limousines.

Wearing a green dress, headband, lip salve, paint, powder, and perfume, Grace, as usual, was the center of attention. The men fawned over the slender brunette and praised *Being Respectable,* the novel she had dedicated to Theo. Presenting a box of gardenias, Joe Alsop told Grace that he was "crazy" about the book and had sat up most of the night reading it. Lefty Lewis said that Grace "was one of the really big girls—and had Margaret Deland & Susan Glascoe beaten a mile."

"*Men* like it much the best. *Old* ladies don't like it at all," Grace observed. "Theo is in a perfect frenzy of admiration." Indeed, Grace's second novel was an enormous success. There was "splendid criticism from Boston, Philadelphia, Life, New York Tribune, Detroit & elsewhere." She knew that "St. Paul hates it," because everyone there disapproved of everything she did and because the novel satirized high society.

F. Scott Fitzgerald congratulated Grace and quoted Edith Wharton as saying she liked *Being Respectable* "better than any American novel in years." Grace wrote Wharton's compliment in a letter to Charlie, who had moved to France. Having recently dyed his hair into "copper ringlets" that, he said, made returning to St. Paul impossible, Charlie replied that Wharton's assessment was "a great personal triumph." Since the "flaccid udders of the gifted Edith have never noticeably leaked with the milk of human kindness," he explained, "one feels sure she meant it."

When John's Christmas leave ended, he returned alone to Argentina. Foster had written him that Theo must never go to sea again until she felt a desire to, which would mean that she was no longer afraid. Theo was relieved that Totem proved to be "a darling." He told Theo not to worry, that she could stay home, and that he would do the traveling. The only problem was convincing the State Department that there was a valid reason for Theo's deserting the post of ambassadress.

At the end of January 1923, Secretary of State Charles Hughes requested that Theo come to Washington and explain the situation. Apprehensive about the meeting, Theo asked Grace to go with her. She also brought a letter from Dr. Kennedy that she had promised she would not read. Stating that he had taken professional care of Mrs. J. W. Riddle for ten years, Foster's next sentence bluntly asserted, "She has always been emotionally unstable."

"Her participation in the *Lusitania* catastrophe has left a scar which has not yet healed," Kennedy continued. "She has made several voyages since the end of the war—all of them with increasing difficulty, and all of them followed by tremors and sleeplessness."

As a patriotic American, Dr. Kennedy "was firm in insisting on her companioning her husband as her national duty when Mr. Riddle first went to the Argentine." But the unfortunate incident of the ship's going in circles the previous summer had caused "so much panic in her, such prolonged insomnia and terrified weeping" that Kennedy "could not undertake the responsibility of again forcing her to sea travel" because he "feared the probability of a mental collapse." In fact, she might lose her reason.

Theo handed the letter to Secretary Hughes and waited while he read it. When he finished, he looked up and spoke quietly. "You cannot travel by sea. We understand and you are not to worry." Later that evening, Theo dined with Under Secretary of State Phillips. He said that he had seen the letter and repeated Hughes's exact words to her.

Others were not so understanding. Anna received a call from Speaker Gillette, who reported, "There is much talk about it at the State Department...They simply say Mrs. Riddle didn't like the Argentine and wouldn't *stay* and *won't return* and the Argentines will be offended!"

Aware of the gossip, Theo begged John not to keep quiet but "to blaze the matter forth," to "describe in detail my experiences & tell them that I simply cannot go to sea without running the danger of ending my life in a Sanitarium shaking like shell-shocked soldiers."

During the three days in Washington, Theo said she felt "like an alley cat being chased by gutter boys." Finally she could take no more. When anyone dared to ask, "Aren't you going back to the Argentine?" she said she "bit their heads off" and acidly replied, "No, I'm not."

"Why should I die for this administration?" she protested. "Totem won't cry if he is recalled." In truth, "it isn't such a damned fine post for him after Russia & 'they' know it....I stick my tongue out at the State Department." She hoped that they *would* recall John. "We'll have a *very happy* reunion home!"

"My God she is an exhausting person—so explosive & vehement about everything," wrote Grace, worried about the extent of Theo's anger. "I should think she'd wear herself out living at such a violent pitch."

Aware that Theo had been frightened the previous summer by the possibility of the ship's overturning, Anna Cowles contended that, since nothing terrible had occurred, she saw no excuse for Theo's abandoning John. At the same time, Anna reasoned that "as long as John has a well-appointed house and entertains all the time," he might prove to be an excellent host without Theo, because he was "very popular with our large business colony in Argentina." She was worried, however, that by squandering her fortune to build the school, Theo would not provide John with enough money to keep a fine house and entertain on an appropriate scale.

There is no reason to doubt Foster Kennedy's honesty when he wrote that Theo's recent horrific experiences aboard ships had intensified her fear to the point where she could completely collapse. Grace and Anna believed, however, that the reason why Theo did not return to Argentina was that "she was so mad to build her school." Most likely, both Dr. Kennedy and the women were right

Ambassador John Wallace Riddle arrives in Buenos Aires, February 1922. *(HS)*.

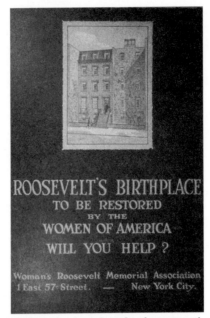

Poster asking for donations for the restoration of
President Theodore Roosevelt's Birthplace. *(HS)*.

Theo and prize-winning cow, Anathesia Faith.
Reed Hilderbrand photograph. *(HS)*.

FIFTEEN

"The lady on the hill"
1923—1926

WHEN THEO brought home Gordon Brockway, Peter Martin, and Donald Carson, some friends asked why she didn't take in girls. Perhaps the choice reflects a wish from childhood that she had been born male. Although Alfred had treated Theo almost as if she were his son, she felt constrained by society's expectations. By raising boys, she could vicariously share their freedom to experience and enjoy the world. She liked to see life, as she often said, "through the eyes of boys."

Theo founded a boys' school rather than a girls' for several reasons. Originally, she meant to honor only Alfred's memory, and she probably assumed the he would prefer a school for boys, though after Ada's death, Theo decided that the school would honor both parents. There was also the possibility that Theo did not want to compete with nearby Westover, a girls' school. Another more compelling reason might have been that she was convinced that men would continue to run the world for the foreseeable future. Thus, it was crucial to produce leaders who would avoid plunging the world into another disaster like the Great War.

In contrast to the typical elite preparatory school, which admitted students on the basis of their wealth and social standing and turned out, Theo said derisively, "pleasant little gentlemen," Theo's school would educate boys to become strong, decisive, and enlightened men who would not only maintain traditional values but also accept progressive and spiritualist ideas—the most important of which was that the souls of all human beings transcend class, gender, race, religion, and nationality.

Avon Old Farms School was to Theo what Taliesin was to Frank Lloyd Wright. Both she and Wright felt a mysterious, indefinable bond to their buildings, perhaps because of Theo's belief in spiritualism and because of Wright's quasi-mystical Celtic faith.

Both architects were also influenced by the Arts and Crafts movement, especially in the tenet that a building should appear to be a natural part of the landscape. To achieve this effect, Theo used materials from the area: red sandstone from a ninety-three-foot-deep quarry near the site and oak saplings from the surrounding woods.

To construct the first buildings, Theo brought over craftsmen from the Cotswold area of England, and she made certain that the American workers employed the craftsmen's 16th-century methods and tools. She admonished them not to use carpenter's levels or plumb lines, and direct-ed them to "dispense with all mechanical methods" and, wherever possible, work "by rule of thumb and to gauge all verticals by eye; as a natural varia-tion in line and surface was far more desirable…than accuracy."

At the peak of the school's construction, Theo's cousin's husband brought their son to visit the site. Gazing at over 500 workmen laboring with primitive tools and at the hodge-podge of unusual buildings, the boy turned to his father and pronounced Theo's work "the purest mess." Although he did not yet appreciate her genius, the scene had a pro-found effect on young Philip Johnson, who became one of the 20th-century's most famous architects.

The workers found it odd to take orders from a woman, but there were few complaints. In fact, as they built in the old-fashioned manner she insisted upon, they found Theo's enthusiasm contagious. They addressed Theo affectionately as "Miss Theodate," but in front of observers, she was "Mrs. Riddle." The site boss, a burly man from New York, did not resent occasional flare-ups of Theo's temper. He joked that "he was hired in the morning and at noon he was fired, and in the after-noon, he was rehired."

Theo's secretary at the field office said that Mrs. Riddle was "a pleasant woman to be around." Verna Deming had the impression that, despite Theo's short, sturdy figure, she was tall, because "when she walked across the floor, you knew she was royalty to a degree." But Theo sat down "just like a man" and put her feet up. "The boys got the biggest kick out of her doing that," Verna laughed, "because otherwise she was very ladylike."

One morning, Theo said to Verna, "I am concerned about something and I wondered if it is upsetting you." A worker had printed "Tilly the Toiler," the name of a cartoon character, in big letters on the field office's outside wall, and Theo worried that the message meant that she was work-ing Verna too hard.

Theo was so intensely involved that she didn't plan to meet John when he arrived in New York on vacation from Argentina. "The chauf-feur can go and get him and he can bring him up," she told Verna. "I'll kiss him when he gets home." But when the day came, she felt guilty and went to New York.

Then, Theo faced a problem she had not anticipated. Joe Alsop sent a letter alleging that she was paying workers a higher wage than the going rate in Avon—as high as $1.10 an hour for a mason. He referred to wide-spread anger because she was hiring away help at prices that her neighbors could not afford to pay. In fact, he himself had lost workers. "If this condition continues," Joe threatened, "you will have very difficult times with the people of Avon, as they are all assuming an air of exceeding hostility against you."

"You will have a great many things which you will want from the towns of Avon & Farmington, both in the way of fair treatment and in concessions and I think you will find that if the present condition continues," he warned, "the townspeople will become your active enemies." Joe sent a copy of the letter to Harris and attached a note: "If she were to ask an Avon town meeting for anything at the present time, she would be lucky to escape alive."

Startled by the accusations, Theo immediately contacted A. Milton Napier, the president of Tidewater Building Company, who was in charge of the workmen. "The statements made in the first paragraph of Mr. Alsop's letter are absolutely false," Napier replied. "We showed Mr. Alsop our pay sheets quite willingly, and proved to him that there were no men receiving pay as high as the amount" that had been indicated. Furthermore, there was no record of any men who had given Alsop's name as their previous employer. Napier also protested that it was unfair to compare the wages of farm laborers with those of the skilled workmen hired to erect buildings.

Taking Joe's letters (the one to her and the note to Harris) to Anna, Theo was shocked when, matter-of-factly, Anna stated that she did not have to read the letters because she had advised Joe to write them. "You should know what people are saying," Anna explained, assuming that she had done nothing wrong. To Theo, however, Anna's telling Joe to make threats had endangered the school.

Unaware that Theo felt betrayed, Anna later remarked, "Should Theodate ever divulge why she abruptly cut me off from her list of not only friends, but remote acquaintances, it would be amusing to hear."

"I think she is dead right to devote her whole time to that object [the school]," she added in the same icy tone, "considering the terrific amount that is being spent, entirely aside from the fact that it represents her own creation, and the thing she has probably loved most in her life."

Several weeks passed, and Joe Alsop did not respond to Napier's report. Theo wrote to Joe, addressing him as First Selectman Alsop. "The charges in your illbred letters to Mr. Whittemore and myself are untrue," she began.

She pointed out that it was not she who should feel grateful to Avon, but rather, the opposite. The establishment of the school would greatly benefit the town. Although Joe was ill-bred and a liar, "the Directors of AAPF [Alfred A. Pope Foundation] hope to have a pleasant relationship with the townspeople."

There were probably other letters sent back and forth across the few miles that separated the former friends. Their relationship ended eventually in a kind of truce. Theo saved an undated, handwritten note from Joe that read, "Your letter came last night and meant more to me than any letter I have had in years. Bless you for it." She never entirely forgave him, though, and stipulated in her will that the Alsop family was "never to have anything to do with the School."

In 1923, the town of Avon assessed the property at $107,000, an enormous sum for a nonprofit school that was only partly built. For Theo, this meant a lawsuit. In some ways, she looked forward to it. Harris, the one friend Theo could always depend upon, helped her. Anna noted that Theo consulted Harris "at every move as to the school." The buildings (half of the school) were taxed $464,265 in 1924, and Theo's foundation sued to have the property declared exempt from taxes. At the hearing, the amount was reduced to $65,000. On later appeals, the foundation was finally successful in having the property declared completely tax-exempt.

A good fight invigorated Theo, and with renewed energy, she plunged into work. "If I could only avoid human contacts," she declared. "I'm like an express train running at top speed. If people don't want trouble with me, they'd better not put stones on my track."

She could not "'serve two masters'—society & architecture." And the choice was clear. "I feel," she said, "that if I saw one of my friends around here, I'd spit at them like a cat! Not because I dislike them... but because they interfered."

Theo "gives everyone the feeling that she never wishes to see them at any stray moment," Anna observed. Whenever she telephoned Theo, Anna felt as if she were interrupting. So Anna stopped calling. She sent notes, but Theo no longer read any mail, except from Grace or John.

"No messages of any kind pass Miss McCarthy and Earnest," Anna discovered. She knew the reason for Theo's isolating herself: "she is building furiously." Anna suspected that, because of Theo's obsession with work, even Earnest dared not approach his mistress except for those rare occasions when he was "not too terrified of the lady on the hill." If Theo cared for Anna and her other Farmington Valley friends, "she would at least have allowed their messages or letters to come to her knowledge."

In a memoir written many years later, Theo referred to an incident that might have occurred at this time. She was interrupted by a call from an "insistent friend," probably Anna, who wished to see her. Intent on a design for a building at Avon, Theo refused through Miss McCarthy to come to the telephone. The friend called twice again in the same week, and the third time, Theo broke down. "I left my work, came home and went to bed where I remained for three or four days."

The incident had a strange and dreadful consequence. "Something in me was shattered, and interrupted all power of work," Theo declared. "When I was up again my back felt weak and I knew my stance was not correct and I felt as if my pelvic bones had been forced apart in some way."

Originally, Theo intended that the school include two years of college, and she referred to it as "Avon College." Then Theo decided to make it just a secondary school. She was unable to build the Brooks Quadrangle, which would house the college, and she was anxious to open the school by the fall of 1927. Grace suggested another name, "The Pope School," but Theo didn't like the way that sounded. "It is now the Avon School," she wrote Grace, "giving the short sound of 'a' as they do in England." Later, Theo included the words, "Old Farms," because a section of the tract had been called that for 150 years.

As with Hill-Stead and Dormer House, a long winding road leads to the campus of Avon Old Farms School. The sense of isolation is more intense than in Theo's previous buildings because a thick forest surrounds the flat clearing on which the school stands. The overall effect of the cluster of buildings is almost eerie. The mostly red sandstone buildings, with leaded glass windows, timber framing, and red slate roofs, seem to exist in a place outside of time. Rather than the solitary, Edenic atmosphere of Hill-Stead, there is a magical aura about Avon Old Farms.

To a young boy leaving his family to live with strangers, the school must seem fantastic. His boyish imagination would be stirred by the surrounding forest, the school's farm and animals, and the medieval, quixotic architecture. He would feel like Harry Potter arriving at Hogwarts. How adventurous it would be to live in this strange, new world. At the same time, he would feel secure and safe in his comfortable room in a building with thick stone walls and rounded archways. He would not be just another student in a small, square room down a narrow hallway in a cold, sterile, institutional-style building. At Avon Old Farms, he would be a member of a self-contained, somewhat democratic community that existed on a mysterious and beautiful plane, apart from the ordinary world.

Arriving at the school, the boy would notice first a tall, brick water tower, "a hulking mass that looks like a medieval Castle Keep." Then he would see the Station House, situated next to railroad tracks that run through the property. Next he would come to other non-academic buildings: a forge, a carpenters' shop, the school's garages, and the estate manager's Tudor house. Ahead stands the Pope Quadrangle, a group of stone buildings with sloping, sagging roofs; two-foot thick exterior walls; narrow, leaded glass windows; bas-reliefs, gargoyles, and other statues.

The entrance is through the arched passageway of Diogenes, the juniors' dormitory, which has the largest bas-relief. Two sturdy farm boys, one on each side, stand in profile, looking intently at each other, each grasping a pole. The models were Paul and Donald. A banner unfurls between the tops of their poles. At its center is carved the school motto: "*Aspirando et Perseverando* [To Aspire and Persevere]," Theo's guiding principle. Two cows and a pig peek out from behind one boy. Behind the other are a horse, a dog, and a rooster. The farm motif continues in a scene of animals grazing in front of a country village in the background.

In the center foreground of the bas-relief stands an odd creature staring straight out at those who enter: a winged beaver, the school's symbol. The beaver was not supposed to have wings. There were to be two symbols: a beaver and an eagle—the eagle to represent "aspiring" and the beaver, "persevering." Why the two animals were combined is unknown, but the sculptor Fritz Hammergren's winged beaver provided the townspeople of Farmington with another reason to mock Theo's eccentricity. Unlike a boy who would appreciate Theo's playful imagination, a local resident remarked, "How grotesque to put wings on a rodent!"

The other stone buildings of Pope Quadrangle also have names, epigrams, statues, and figures in bas-relief. The sophomores' building, *Eagle*, symbolizes bravery. *Pelican*, the freshmen's dormitory, features a mother bird, plucking a feather from her breast to put into a nest for two baby pelicans; the image suggests compassion. The building for seniors is *Elephant*, the animal known for its memory and longevity.

Leaving the Pope Quadrangle through the archway of *Eagle*, one comes to the Village Green, which lies in front of the meadows and pastures for the school's sheep and cows. On the left is the large, slope-roofed house for the Provost (Headmaster), and on the right, the Dean's house and the Cottages, which have a general store and post office.

After the Cottages, the boy would arrive at the most fanciful and impressive of the buildings: the Refectory, a grand reproduction of the typical Great Hall of an English university. Upon entering, he would be awed by the high arched ceiling, dark wood, the distinguished portraits on the walls, and the pewter candlesticks adorning the tables. A boy could imagine knights sitting at the long, dark tables dining by candlelight, and the royal family sitting at High Table on the platform at the end of the long, rectangular room.

Attached to the Refectory is the Village Bank, which Theo appropriately built in a classical architectural style, modeling it on the First Bank of the United States in Philadelphia. A boy should learn that there is no fancy or whimsy when it comes to money.

Ignoring criticism and mockery from those who did not recognize the extraordinary feat that she had accomplished, Theo was gratified that people in the field of architecture recognized the originality and brilliance of the school's design. Avon's plot plans and colored perspectives were exhibited in New York, and the following year, *Architecture,* the journal of the American Institute of Architects, featured Avon Old Farms. The American Institute of Architects now considered Theo worthy of membership and elected her a fellow. In 1927, the Architectural Club of New Haven awarded her the Robinson Memorial Medal for her design of the school.

After seeing the article, Florida architect Harry Cunningham wrote Theo that the school was "truly wonderful….It has flavour, romance, sentiment, sturdiness, oh everything that Architecture should have and generally always doesn't." He ended his letter: "Salut! Madame L'Artiste!!!" Addressing Theo as "Mr.," and beginning "Dear Sir:" University of Virginia's Professor Kocher wrote, "What you are doing is exactly what the AIA took such pains to impress upon the profession as desirable."

Theo also received praise from the famous architects Cass Gilbert and Charles Platt and from the noted art critic Roger Fry. In 1940, the Fifth Pan American Congress of Architects recognized the school "for excellence in architecture," and in more recent times, architects and historians, such as Robert Stern and James Lindgren, have agreed with the assessment of architecture critic Judith Paine, who in 1979 pronounced the school "a masterpiece."

Paine described Avon Old Farms as if it were a moving organism. The buildings are "animated forms which sweep and swell toward, around, and through each other. Rooflines intersect, chimneys divide, mottoes speak from the stone walls, and gargoyles watch solemnly from their perches. Narrow slit windows appear here and there merely to emphasize the verticality of a gable, steps rush down to the ground like waves, and in the midst of this medieval exuberance, a Greek Doric Temple rises in all its rational order."

Although most of the buildings were inspired by the architecture that Theo had seen and studied in the Cotswold district in England, critics have pointed out that she was not imitative. There are elements of previous work—"long overhanging roofs, banks of dormer windows and plain surfaces"—but Avon's design goes "beyond these features to include shapes found nowhere in English architecture—mannerist details, curves and sweeps of roofs and walls that exist for pure whimsical effect."

Grace summed up the school: "Everything is sound & honest & forthright as the woman herself." And, struck by the individuality as well as the strange beauty of Avon Old Farms, most people agreed that the buildings somehow embodied Theo's distinctive personality. There were no buildings like these anywhere else in the world because there was only one Theodate Pope Riddle.

As the work progressed and the workers became more familiar with the Cotswold methods of construction, Theo no longer worried about being constantly on-site. She also realized that it was vital that the school receive public support. Thus, she decided that it was important that she mend broken friendships and regain her position in society.

Anna guessed the motivation behind Theo's friendly overtures and sarcastically called these attempts at reconciliation a "re-grande-entrée into the valley." When Theo invited everyone to a large, elegant party, Anna and others declined. Undaunted, Theo sent out invitations for a YMCA meeting at Hill-Stead, with Connecticut's governor as honored guest. Anna said she was "rather amused" because Theo "had always refused a subscription year after year to the YMCA." Few accepted their invitations. "Needless to say," said Anna, "everyone who belongs to me feel that they never wish to speak to her again."

Anna's animosity had another source besides her having been ignored while Theo devoted herself to the school. Anna was angry because Theo was not giving John the financial support he needed in Argentina. He had moved from the expensive home that he and Theo had rented and was living in a hotel room. Not having a house meant that the ambassador could not entertain. "John Riddle I feel very sorry for, as his present quarters must be rather a contrast to last year's," Anna remarked.

In October 1924, John became ill. In November, after a short stay in a hospital in Panama, he sailed to New York. Theo met him with an ambulance, which took him to Miss Makie's Private Sanitarium. Charlie became frantic when he learned about his brother's illness. He was certain that Theo was making light of it. "Theodate is such an ass," he exploded. "No human being with inflammation and rheumatism ever 'convalesced rapidly.'" He expressed dismay that John was probably receiving spiritualist treatments, which he imagined to be "the laying on of hands (possibly feet) and the crooning of Japanese hymns."

John was more optimistic about his condition. His arm and his wrist were still puffed up, but "I am all right now," he wrote his brother, "and

I trust the germ of rheumatism has been exorcised so that there will be no return."

Theo spent Christmas in the sanitarium with John and then remained in New York for another month while he underwent electrical treatments and dental care. They contemplated "a wild orgy of theatre going to make up for lost time" but did not accept dinner invitations because, John wryly remarked, he was "still on a very restricted diet of caviar and champagne."

In late January 1925, John left for Washington, and Theo for Palm Beach with a new friend, Jungian psychiatrist Beatrice Hinkle, who, Theo said, had become "a tremendous refuge" for her. With the loss of other friendships in Farmington, Theo became deeply attached to Beatrice, and the two were constant companions.

Charlie was enraged upon hearing that Theo had gone on vacation with Dr. Hinkle. "Really, after man and wife have been separated for so many many months and, on arriving in New York, the man should have to be taken to a hospital on a stretcher, it strikes me as extremely strange that the wife would hustle down to Palm Beach while her long absent husband was undergoing (as you say) 'electrical treatments.'" Such behavior proved a lack of "affection, devotion—in short, 'love'." But, Charlie continued in this letter to Grace, "to consider love between John & T—well, I shall here have to stop short; I do not wish to become obscene."

Theo also welcomed another member into her family: Dorothea "Dolly" Rutledge, a young woman whom she had met while traveling through Charleston. Theo had stopped at the Villa Marguerita where the girl was working, and, liking her friendly, warm manner, impulsively invited Dolly for a few weeks' visit. Dolly accepted the invitation, arrived in Farmington soon after, and lived at Hill-Stead for the next twelve years. At first Dolly worked at a local bank and then at Theo's school.

On February 13, 1925, claiming health problems, John resigned from the diplomatic service. The following day, he sailed for Argentina to finish his assignment, remaining there until May.

There was much speculation about John's resignation. "Was it because of health," Charlie asked Blair, or "did Theodate fail to 'come across' or what? Only a short time ago I had a cheerful letter from John saying he felt very well and was looking forward with pleasure to sailing for the Argentine in two days." Charlie suspected that the State Department had asked for John's resignation because Theo had not given him enough funds to entertain properly and because his "wife refuses to ambass."

A romantic slant on the story appeared in a South Carolina newspaper. "When the Northern newspapers teem every day with stories of divorces," the writer pointed out, "the resignation of a husband of a post of great honor and importance in order that he may be with his wife is worth recording with emphasis."

There was also a political explanation. In August 1923, President Harding died suddenly. When Vice President Coolidge took over, he concentrated on restoring respect for the presidency after the Teapot Dome and other scandals of Harding's administration. The following year Coolidge was elected. Under a new president, diplomats were expected to hand in their resignations and give him the option of reappointment. In late 1924, John would have handed in his resignation and, if the president were pleased with his service and did not need the post to give to someone with more important political connections, he would not accept it. Although the business community in Buenos Aires wrote in John's support, President Coolidge probably accepted John's resignation for several reasons, including the State Department's displeasure over a wifeless ambassador, John's being unable to entertain lavishly, his lack of political clout, and his illness.

John was probably ready to leave Argentina. What he had liked the most about previous diplomatic positions was the social life, and he had neither the resources nor the good health to live a fast-paced life. Although he did not return immediately to Farmington, he did not seem to harbor any resentment toward Theo.

"John is going home by way of Europe," Charlie announced from *Le Petit St. Paul,* a villa he had bought in Bizy, France. When John arrived in Paris, Charlie joined him, and the brothers attended an Arthur Rubenstein piano recital and dined in places where, Charlie reported to Grace, John could fulfill his "unerring instinct for good food and 'sound' wines."

John remained in France throughout the summer and wrote affectionate letters to Theo. Paris was "charming and really restful," and he was avoiding "the gaieties and people." He claimed to be homesick and sent "Best love and Kisses," signing letters, "Your devoted, loving Totem."

He did not mention the week that he spent with Mrs. Joseph Pulitzer. On John's return, Charlie asked what he had done with the lady. "Oh, we played bridge, rolled-royced all over Normandy, and kept up on champagne," John blithely replied. "When in the country Mrs. Pulitzer believes in living simply—just like the peasants."

Upon John's arrival at Hill-Stead in September, Theo invited Lefty Lewis to dinner. Lefty was one of the few neighbors still friendly to Theo from the old group, and she was delighted that he had expressed an interest in taking part in the management of her school.

Theo stopped trying to reconcile with other former friends. John, however, strengthened his ties to the Farmington valley crowd and, during the fall of 1925 and the following winter, appeared at their homes without his wife. Most afternoons, Marie Bissell sent a car to pick him up, since the Riddles' Crane-Simplex usually remained at the construction site waiting for Theo. "He is not able to have an auto," Anna commented, "& apparently cannot either walk the distance or hire one."

Since the death of her husband, Anna had become more frail and infirm. Sitting in a wheelchair surrounded by admirers and friends, she always gave John an enthusiastic welcome when he arrived to play bridge. Anna's guests enjoyed these afternoon gatherings, where gossip was a more delicious entertainment than card playing. And John joined in, even when the target was his wife. To the others' amusement, John described a recent incident. Theo had insisted that, despite a terrible snowstorm, they drive to New Haven. Why had they risked their lives? Theo had wanted to dine with the president of Yale and talk about Avon Old Farms and progressive educational ideas.

John might have seemed disloyal, but the opposite was true. Always the diplomat, he helped Theo by charming her enemies. They would not do anything against her that would hurt him. John became a buffer between his wife and the gentry of Farmington and Avon who ridiculed Theo's passion and labeled her the valley's eccentric—in Anna's mocking phrase— "the lady on the hill."

Joe Alsop standing in his tobacco field. *(HS)*.

Theo in knickers supervising construction
of Avon Old Farms School. *(AOF)*.

The winged beaver.
William Mercer photograph. *(AOF)*.

Workman using peen hammer at
Avon site. *(AOF)*.

Statue on roof of Elephant dormitory.
William Mercer photograph. *(AOF)*.

CHAPTER FIFTEEN

Avon Old Farms School building, 1927. *(AOF)*.

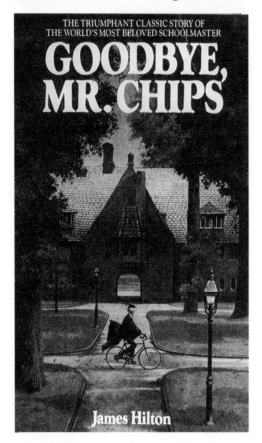

Image of Avon Old Farms's entrance used for novel's cover. *(AOF)*.

SIXTEEN

"Bold and far looking"
1926—1929

DURING THE summer of 1926, expressing no trepidation about an ocean voyage, Theo accompanied John on a two-months' trip to Europe. Brooks Emeny, who was engaged in graduate studies in Vienna, joined them in Germany, where John had made reservations at the Goldener Hirsch Hotel. When they arrived at the large, ostentatious building, however, Theo refused to go in.

Without a word to the men, Theo ran across the street and disappeared into a small, quaint inn. After a few minutes, John and Brooks saw her looking down at them from a second floor window. John shook his head. "Never marry an architect!" he sighed. He went into the inn and shortly reappeared with Theo holding onto his arm. The three entered the grand hotel.

Returning in the fall, Theo met at Hill-Stead with the board of directors she had selected for the school, which included Stephen B. Cabot, Thomas Hewes, William Dorsey Kennedy, Atty. W. Mills Hinkle, and Sheffield Cowles, whom Theo had appointed in another attempt to appease Anna. At the meeting, Atty. Hinkle presented Theo with a certificate of incorporation that he had drawn up.

The certificate established the board of directors as a separate corporation, autonomous from the Pope-Brooks Foundation, and gave it the power to govern the school. According to the document, Theo would be just one member of this Board; thus, the other members could outvote her.

Calmly, Theo explained to the five men that she must have total control of the school for the first four or five years to be certain that it followed her educational policies. The men, however, would not budge from their conviction that the majority of the directors, rather than she, should have authority. Theo offered an amendment to the document. She would choose members of the board for the first ten years and have veto power over any appointment or dismissal of the officers of the school, a veto that the board could override only by a unanimous vote. Cabot and Kennedy expressed their opposition, and the others refused to consider the amendment.

As Theo served tea on that September afternoon, she "pictured herself sitting by the fireside in the years to come as having founded a school which she would have lost control of." She was struck by the absurdity that these men, these outsiders, were presuming to tell her, the founder of Avon Old Farms, what she could or could not do with the school to which she had dedicated her architectural career, energies, and personal fortune.

She announced that she would not allow a separate corporation to run the school. There would be no board of directors. Then, before the startled group could react, she dismissed the men from Hill-Stead.

Avon Old Farms would be run by the Pope-Brooks Foundation, since, as managing director, Theo could outvote the other members of its board. At the same time, she personally, rather than a corporation, would be obligated to assume financial accountability for the school, which meant making up any deficits that occurred.

Theo wrote an unusual brochure to attract students for the fall of 1927. In it appears a remarkable blend of spiritualist ideas and progressive educational philosophy. "Avon Old Farms recognizes the profound importance of imparting to the boys the living truth of a spiritual relationship," she announced. Avon Old Farms would be unlike most elite independent schools of the time, which declared themselves Christian, usually Episcopal: "No instruction will be provided in any given creed, but the Provost will endeavor to develop in the boys a sincere belief in the reality of the life of the spirit and an unfaltering conviction that: 'Though our outward man perish, yet the inward man is renewed day by day, while we look not at the things which are seen, but at the things which are not seen; for the things which are seen are temporal; but the things which are not seen are eternal.'"

Another extraordinary idea appears in the brochure. The school would make "a sincere effort…to determine and develop the particular talent or aptitude of each boy." One of Theo's most deeply felt beliefs was that "the ways in which we are different are more important than the ways in which we are alike."

The requirements for acceptance were not high grades, wealth, or social position: "Character is the first qualification considered in admitting a student." After being admitted, a boy would take achievement and intelligence tests for grade (or form) placement.

Theo's dictum about sports might have discouraged some applicants: "There will be no gymnasium and no indoor inter-school athletics." Later, she explained, "The sense of proportion in sports will be maintained by confining them to intramural games and competitions." Though admitting that sports "form an essential background for health and for certain elements of courage and honor," she deplored "the condition in this country at this time, whereby many individuals regard the colleges less as educational institutions than as pleasant and profitable training grounds for professional athletes."

As far as the academic curriculum was concerned, the traditional subjects were offered, but with a special emphasis on sciences, taught by progressive teachers who trained a student "to seek knowledge and establish facts for himself." Most unconventional in the curriculum were the activities on the farm, in the forest, and in the workshops, which Theo declared "will stress equally the development of mind and body."

The boys would plant gardens, raise poultry, and work in the school's dairy. In addition, they would be required to study the surrounding forest, which Theo poetically described as "in spring, the tender green of new leaves and tasseled buds, birds nesting or in migratory flight, flowers and curled fronds of ferns pushing through wet, black earth; in summer, cool shadows along lazy streams; in autumn, red trees, blue mist, the rustle of fallen leaves; in winter, bare oak branches and murmuring pines, snow delicately patterned with the track of woodland animals."

Readers of the brochure might be surprised by other requirements. Students were expected to work in the machine shop, electrical laboratory, smithy, carpenter shop, and mechanical drafting rooms. If a boy wrote an article for the school newspaper, he would then print it in the school's print shop.

Perhaps most radical was the quasi-democratic organization of the school. Avon Old Farms was modeled after the typical New England town, "organized and governed on the lines of a village political unit, the four upper forms (grades 9-12) being eligible for office as citizens." The village had a court where the students acted as the jury. The classroom was also somewhat democratic because students, chosen by the teacher, would lead each recitation.

The governance of the school was a mix of traditional and less conventional positions. There was a Provost (Headmaster), who hired the faculty and was responsible for the boys' educational and moral training. He also nominated four other officers who were directly responsible to Theo and the board of the Pope-Brooks Foundation. The Bursar managed accounting and business details. The Factor was in charge of non-academic employees and of the boys while they were doing manual labor at the school. The Dame supervised the school nurse and the two housemothers in the dormitories of the younger boys. She also saw to the boys' manners. The Farm Manager directed assistants, including a herdsman and a dairyman, and worked with the boys.

Theo insisted that women run the general store, the post office, and the library. This last position was of great importance. Theo directed that "the use of library books instead of texts will be encouraged in every department....Each boy will not study parrot-like the same book that is being studied by any other boy, but he will seek out information in many different books using what might be called the research method."

In the listing of faculty and staff appeared two unusual positions: the Master of Detail, a military man to coordinate all non-academic activities; and the Psychotherapist, to acquaint himself "with the character and mental capacity of each boy, with the view of helping him develop to the fullest extent his special abilities."

Although the charge for a year was $1,500, which, in 1927, was a substantial amount, income from tuition would never exceed the costs. Theo did not intend to run the school for a profit. She only hoped that she would not have to make up large deficits.

In contrast to the Avon and Farmington residents who ridiculed Theo's ideas and prophesied failure—they wouldn't send their sons to such an outlandish place—leading educators expressed interest and praise when they learned of the new school. In an article in *The New York Times,* Harvard's President Charles W. Elliot called Avon Old Farms a "bold and far looking experiment," and John Dewey praised Theo as a leading progressive educator.

In March, Theo made a final attempt to reconcile with Anna. Sheffield's appointment to the defunct board of directors had not placated his mother. Anna refused to answer Theo's telephone calls, so Theo summoned Hill-Stead's chauffeur and drove the few blocks to Oldgate, where the butler brought her into the parlor. Theo was dressed in "full regalia," Anna later told Sheffield. Anna was having tea with a guest, and, while the other woman was there, Theo behaved agreeably. The three ladies drank tea and chatted. When the guest left, Theo poured out all Anna's "sins of omission and commission" and kept repeating that as much as she hated Anna, she loved her more.

Eventually Theo realized that her words were having little effect. It was impossible to break through Anna's polite, steely composure. Finally resigned to accepting the end of their friendship, which had spanned forty years, Theo changed the subject and spoke matter of factly about plans for the school. Handing Anna the exquisitely printed brochure, she left Oldgate.

During the years when Theo was designing and constructing Avon Old Farms, she had little contact with other old friends. Mary Hillard and Belle Sherwin were both busy with their own careers, and Mary

Cassatt had died in 1926. Grace was also spending less time in Farmington. In the mid-1920s, she traveled about the country and to Africa, writing more articles and books.

Theo's need for a woman friend was met by Dr. Beatrice Hinkle, who, for the past two years, had become a constant presence at Hill-Stead. John expressed no resentment over the prominent part the psychiatrist had in his wife's life, and, in the spring of 1927, Beatrice accompanied Theo and John on a motor trip.

Charlie Flandrau, on the other hand, considered the friendship with Dr. Hinkle the latest manifestation of Theo's ridiculous behavior. Charlie wrote to Grace, describing the kind of conversation he imagined having with the Jungian psychiatrist. "If I happened to sit next to her at dinner and she suddenly exclaimed: 'The sight of mauve, silk stockings in a shop-window excites your lust Mr. Flandrau,' or, 'Mr. Flandrau, you are conducting a passionate affair with a goat,' it might be perfectly true— but what earthly difference could it make?"

Later that spring, John met his brother in New York City. Charlie had just arrived from France to see Max Perkins, his editor at Scribner's. Still angry about what he believed was Theo's sabotaging of John's diplomatic career, Charlie inquired sarcastically about the well-being of the "Ambassadress." John curtly replied that Theo was "well and busy" and refused to discuss her further.

Charlie was not insulted. He adored his older brother and thought him "sweet and kind" and "utterly unlike any other human being who ever lived." The two enjoyed being together. They lunched at the Union Club, drank afternoon tea at the Harvard Club, and then went to see the celebrated actress, Jane Cowl, in *The Road to Rome*. Charlie wrote that Cowl was "a somewhat worn and raddled old bitch who, in this play has a few (a few few) really beautiful moments and, for the most part, is extremely crude mannered and irritating." In contrast, John praised the play and admired the actress. Charlie despaired over his brother's naive, bourgeois taste. "If an actor of either sex is popularly acclaimed, John seems to swallow it in its entirety," Charlie pronounced.

That evening at dinner, John produced from his pocket a small, square bottle that, in mock horror, Charlie described as "terrifyingly" labeled boracic acid. John proceeded to take a sip from the bottle and then handed it to his brother. Tasting it, Charlie congratulated John on the high quality of the whiskey. Procuring good liquor was not easy during Prohibition.

Sharing the bottle, John seemed unaware that Charlie had a serious drinking problem. A few months earlier, Blair had written to Grace that

Charlie was drunk again. "Don't mention it to Theo and John," he warned. Theo and John thought Prohibition foolish, and they regularly drank martinis and champagne, but Theo viewed drunkards as weak and immoral.

Blair's alcoholism actually was worse than Charlie's. When Charlie drank too much, Grace said, he "becomes sprightly at least amusing" but her husband became the opposite. Grace begged Blair to stop drinking. "Sober, you are so delicate, so chic, so dignified, so witty in a very fine and unusual way," she lectured, "but a certain number of drinks does something terrible to you." Alcohol made him "half-stupefied, silly and BORING."

"Your speech is slow, you get a funny sneering look on your mouth," she continued, and "you say things about other people that are both indiscreet and unkind." She reminded him "how painful, how really shocking" it was when twice he became drunk at Hill-Stead. Recently he had humiliated her at the home of a new, very wealthy friend, Alice O'Brien. "I never will sit through another supper like the one at the O'Briens," she declared, "listening to your halting voice, your thick enunciation."

Theo witnessed the two episodes at Hill-Stead, but she never criticized Blair. After the failure of his automobile business in St. Paul, for which she had lent him a substantial sum, Theo even offered him the job of manager of the school's buildings. Grace urged Blair to accept the position, but he refused, embarrassed by Theo's genuine fondness and sympathy for him.

In late spring, while Theo continued to work on plans for the school's September opening, John went to Washington, D.C., where he stayed at the Union Club and saw old friends. He met Charles Lindbergh, who, after his solo flight to Paris in *The Spirit of St. Louis,* had risen from obscurity to become the most famous person in the world. Fond of telling Charlie about celebrities, John wrote that the unassuming, boyishly handsome Lindbergh was the most prominent of all the people he had met in Washington.

During the summer, John again traveled to France alone. Charlie implied that his brother was less than honest about where he was and what he did. "John, I am sure will be in Paris," he pronounced, "and, as usual, having a series of post-cards dated ahead sent to Theodate from some rest cure in the Pyrennes."

At 63, John was still attractive. It was possible that he was seeing another woman in Paris, but he was not dishonest with Theo by pretending to be staying at a health spa. In August, Theo, on a brief motor trip through New England with Beatrice Hinkle, wrote John, "I love to think of your enjoying your beloved Paris!"

Theo's affection for John is obvious. "You adore Paris and I shall encourage you to repeat the pleasure, as often as you like." She planned to go to New York on his return "unless you write me not to meet you. I would most naturally *wish* to meet thee." She ended the letter, "Love my dear one—good night and 'skisses' from Thy Theo."

With the help of Harris, Theo was making final preparations for the school's opening. She established a board of regents to govern the school under the authority and direction of the Pope-Brooks Foundation. She named Stephen Cabot as chancellor of the regents, and, on his recommendation and after a series of interviews, she selected Francis Mitchell Froelicher for the position of provost.

Froelicher was the headmaster of the Oak Lane Country Day School in Baltimore and the president of the Progressive Education Association. A graduate of Haverford College with a master's degree from Johns Hopkins University, he seemed to be an excellent choice. His fine reputation attracted seasoned educators who were interested in working with him at Avon Old Farms, which Froelicher enthusiastically embraced as "a really progressive school."

The seven members of the first faculty had outstanding credentials and experience. They included George Cherry, a graduate of Harvard and Middlebury, whom Froelicher lured from the Loomis Institute to become Avon's first dean. In addition to the faculty members, there was a large staff, including pretty Dolly Rutledge, the girl Theo had invited to live at Hill-Stead, who worked as a secretary.

With the provost, faculty, and staff in place and forty-eight students enrolled, Theo's dream became a reality. According to Brooks Emeny, "due to her state of exhaustion," she was hardly able to attend the opening ceremony in September. To get a much-needed rest, or, as Theo explained, "to give the Provost a chance to prove his mettle," she and John made plans to go abroad.

Theo intended to leave the running of the school entirely to Provost Froelicher. She was seldom seen on campus. Later, the school's historian wrote that "at no time...did she actually interfere in the academic department, with the activities and discipline of the Dean in academic matters nor with individual faculty members."

Two months after the school opened, Theo received devastating news: Harris had suddenly died. There was no one she depended upon and trusted more than Harris. For almost four decades, he had stood by her. Despite her rejection of his marriage proposal and his marriage to another woman, Harris was Theo's truest friend.

Theo grieved for him and also worried about the effect of Harris's death on the school. As treasurer of the Pope-Brooks Foundation, he had been given complete charge of economic matters. Without Harris to negotiate for her, Theo dreaded dealing with the town of Avon. Harris had struck "a gentleman's agreement" with First Selectman Alsop. Now, Theo bitterly noted, Harris was dead, and "Joe Alsop was no gentleman."

After Harris's death, since there was no comptroller at the school, Provost Froelicher asked Theo for authority to sign all requisitions. She agreed to his request. Then, she left with John on a trip to Italy at the end of November 1927.

Returning in the spring of 1928, Theo learned that the *Lusitania* victims' claims against the German government had finally been settled. She received $15,000, one of the largest awards, "for the loss of personal property and for personal injuries."

Theo also discovered that Provost Froelicher had spent a fortune in his eight months of running the school. Referring to herself in the third person, she wrote, "The Founder was appalled, upon looking over financial reports of the Foundation, to see the amount of money which was flowing out of Avon."

Theo met with the school accountant and went over the payroll. The number of laborers was enormous, and she believed that many of these workers were not essential. From the total of eighty-nine, she eliminated thirty-five positions, effecting a yearly savings of almost $90,000.

That summer, Theo and John again sailed for Europe. On their return in the fall, she discovered another unpleasant situation. E. Graeme Smith, a regent who served as secretary-treasurer, had made indiscreet remarks to friends in Hartford about the school's financial situation. Theo was concerned. If people suspected that the school was in a precarious position, they would hesitate to send their sons. Citing Smith's "interference and officiousness," Theo requested his resignation.

There were also other problems. The Farmington River had overflowed and ruined the school's oat crop. In addition, the grounds of the school looked run down. The farm manager, Mr. Worsham, had warned the provost, "With Mrs. Riddle returning from her trip within a short time now, probably one or two extra men may have to be put on to get the grounds in a little better condition." Already in Theo's disfavor because he had spent too much money on the payroll, Froelicher was in a difficult situation. How could he hire more workers? But his financial problems were minor compared to the predicament in which he soon found himself.

For the moment, Theo's attention was diverted from the school because of a lawsuit brought against her by a former draftsman, Leland

Lyon, who wanted more credit and pay for his work on Roosevelt Birthplace several years earlier. Because the case was coming to trial in New York, Theo and John left Farmington and stayed at their apartment in order to meet with lawyers. Theo performed admirably in the courtroom and was triumphant.

While in New York, Theo and John received a visit from Dr. and Mrs. Arthur B. Duel, the parents of an Avon student. Dr. Duel was also on the board of regents. The Duels told Theo distressing news: Provost Froelicher, seemingly a dignified and austere man, was actually a secret and heavy drinker.

For the next three hours, Theo and John listened to the Duels. Mrs. Duel said that Mrs. Froelicher had confided that at night she drove off the school's grounds to bury her husband's empty liquor bottles, and that one morning she had found the provost sick and in a stupor in his library, with a whiskey bottle on the table next to him.

Theo immediately telephoned Stephen Cabot and asked him to meet with Provost Froelicher. Then she contacted Nelson Spencer, a lawyer and a director of the Pope-Brooks Foundation, and informed him of the crisis.

At his meeting with Cabot, Provost Froelicher confessed his intemperate habits. In a letter to Theo, Cabot reported that Froelicher admitted that, after a drinking bout in New York, he would consume a quart of whiskey in the bathroom of the train back to Hartford. The provost conceded that he had been "immoderate in the use of whiskey and was in the habit of taking it regularly at school," but he insisted that he had never been drunk while at Avon. He also swore that he had stopped drinking.

Unconvinced, Stephen Cabot was adamant that Mr. Froelicher should not continue as provost. "I should not want a boy of mine," he declared, "to be under a man as headmaster who was in the slightest degree intemperate in drinking."

After conferring with Dr. Duel, Stephen Cabot, and Nelson Spencer, Theo agreed that she should demand Provost Froelicher's resignation, but she said that "out of consideration," Froelicher would be permitted to ask for a leave of absence, and then to resign because of ill health. In addition, "those who knew the facts" gave their word not to reveal the real reason for his resignation.

Theo did not say whether this arrangement was out of consideration for Froelicher, whom Theo and the others liked as a person and admired as an educator, or for Avon Old Farms, which Theo feared would be hurt by bad publicity. Most likely, she cared more about the school's reputation than about the man.

Provost Froelicher followed instructions. On April 3, 1929, he wrote to Theo, "I have just come back from New York where I have been in consultation with my physician." Because of ill health, the provost said he was "obliged to give up my work at the school at once." He asked for a leave of absence for a period of at least six months. A few weeks later, Theo received the second agreed-upon letter, in which Froelicher resigned.

On June 12, 1929, Theo met with Stephen Cabot at Hill-Stead. Grace and Blair were present, but John was away on another vacation in France. Despite Theo's pledge not to reveal the truth about Froelicher, Cabot assured her that she should feel "free to make public if it should be necessary whatever facts you know in regard to the reasons why Mr. Froelicher left the school."

At their country estate, Dr. and Mrs. Duel hosted a meeting of the Avon faculty to tell them that Froelicher was leaving. Sensing a cover-up, the teachers suspected that illness was not the true reason. The all-male faculty was already uncomfortable with their female founder, whose reputation for being tyrannical had seemed justified after she dissolved the first board of directors and then fired Graeme Smith. Probably unaware of Froelicher's alcoholism, the faculty admired him as an outstanding educator who had successfully run the school. Thus they assumed that Theo had impulsively and unfairly driven him out.

Speaking for the faculty, Dean Cherry addressed Stephen Cabot. Could he swear that "no 'rank injustice' had been done" to the provost? Cabot answered affirmatively but refused to provide further details. Although at least a dozen people knew the real circumstances, no one told the faculty the truth. The result was that they became convinced that Francis Froelicher was the hapless victim of an eccentric virago.

As Theo's cousin and later as a regent of the school, Brooks Emeny must have known that she had not been unfair. He later stated that Froelicher had resigned his post "for the good of the School." His reasons were "personal" and "not related directly to his administration of the School." Emeny praised the provost: "He had succeeded in two years in establishing an excellent faculty, and developing a creditable educational program." His only deficiencies were that "he had not succeeded in increasing sufficiently the enrollment to cut substantially the heavy deficit, and his handling of overall budgetary problems left much to be desired." Emeny was correct about Froelicher's carelessness with money and about the deficit. But he was wrong about the enrollment, which in the fall of 1929 increased to 126 students.

When he became a professor at Yale, Emeny expressed agreement with an undergraduate who had written an essay about Avon Old Farms in which he blamed Froelicher's leaving on Theo's unreasonable demands. Emeny congratulated the student on his "cogent observation": "Her persistent attention and rigid insistence upon details such as dress and sports, while not crucial educational issues, could not help but become frustrating to an ambitious young educator such as Mr. Froelicher." As a youngster, Emeny had been devoted to Theo, but his attitude and actions became ambiguous as he became more involved with the school.

The parents of the students also began to question the mysterious resignation of the popular provost. Dr. George Draper informed Theo that he was dissatisfied with the official explanation of poor health. In an effort to conciliate him, Theo invited him to Hill-Stead, where she told him the true story. Dr. Draper said that he did not blame Theo for firing an alcoholic. He insisted that his major concern was the school's reputation, and he agreed that it was best to keep such information secret. But it was crucial that the next provost be chosen carefully. Draper demanded that Theo immediately appoint an executive committee, on which he would serve, to select Froelicher's successor. In addition, this new committee would have other responsibilities and powers necessary to get the school back on track. Draper threatened to withdraw his son and to effect the withdrawal of twenty other boys whose parents he could influence, if Theo did not go along with his plan.

According to Emeny, the committee was appointed to "procure a permanent successor" and to "supervise the general conduct of the School during Theodate's absence," because, suffering from emotional exhaustion, she needed another vacation. Emeny did not mention Draper's threat. Theo acquiesced to Draper, she maintained, "in order to save Avon Old Farms from the possibility of being wrecked."

In addition to Draper, Theo asked her cousin Herbert Pope, Attorney Champlin Robinson, Dr. Henry S. Canby (the editor of *The Saturday Review*), and Elizabeth Choate to serve on the new executive committee. She then wrote letters of invitation asking the members "to study Avon's existing activities and to organize, correlate and develop" its policies. The members would serve for only two years, at which time the committee would be dissolved.

Although furious over Dr. Draper's threats, Theo controlled her rage. Then, on June 15, 1929, Draper sent Theo an invitation to serve on the committee. Theo saw this as a way of telling her that her authority was no greater than the others' on the committee. That she had purchased the land, founded the school, designed its buildings, built them using her own funds, created its progressive educational program, and paid its bills—"she alone was financing the College!"—were brushed aside. Draper and company ignored the fact that she was the managing director of the Pope-Brooks Foundation, under which Avon Old Farms was established and which legally had ultimate authority over the school.

In addition to being upset over the machinations of Dr. Draper, Theo was shocked when Dr. Duel, the parent and regent who originally had begun proceedings against Froelicher, now insisted that the former provost receive severance pay of a year's salary, $9,000, a sizeable amount in 1929. How could she reward a man who had put the school in jeopardy and endangered her position? The school's attorney, Nelson Spencer, supported Theo's adamant refusal to agree to the doctor's demand.

Furious, Dr. Duel hired a lawyer, George Gordon Battle, to sue Theo if she did not pay Froelicher. In response, Theo called his bluff. Knowing that the doctor valued the reputation of the school that his son attended, she replied that if she were forced to pay the $9,000, she would tell the truth about Froelicher, and the public would learn that the school's provost was a drunkard. The response from Duel's attorney was that he "recognized Mrs. Riddle's constitutional rights in the matter," and the doctor dropped the suit.

In early September, while Theo and John were vacationing in London, the executive committee met without her and without Herbert Pope. The other members proceeded to make decisions. First, they increased their membership to seven, thus further weakening Theo's vote. Then the committee offered the position of provost to John A. Lester, a teacher at the conservative Hill School in Pottstown, Pennsylvania.

Earlier, Theo had interviewed Lester at the Bond Hotel in Hartford. When he arrived, he had forgotten to wear a hat. She could tell immediately that he was "in a complete fog," an "introvert," and "consequently no organizer." In addition, he told her that he disapproved of the position of Master of Detail. Since only Theodate could make this appointment, Lester worried that "a grave undermining of the authority of the Provost was inevitable."

Theo considered the Master of Detail essential to Avon's mission, and in June 1929, she had hired Major Jesse Gaston, a West Point graduate and a veteran of the World War. She hoped that Major Gaston would "jack up" the faculty and students' morale after the Froelicher fiasco and set in motion the extra-academic activities that she thought had never functioned properly. In the fall of 1929, Gaston arrived at the school in full uniform.

The members of the executive committee cabled Theo in London that John Lester would accept their offer of becoming Avon's next provost, but only if the position of Master of Detail were eliminated. Theo responded immediately: "Lester thought that office unnecessary but he must accept it if he wishes to be Provost. That is one of the principles of the Foundation from the beginning."

She sent a second cable to John Lester: "Hear you are willing to accept provostship on basis defined by committee. That has not my approval. Anyone accepting position must sign contract with me to bind himself to policies as outlined in the ordinances and notes. You would however be free in all academic work as long as your attitude is progressive."

And, as to the executive committee's authority: "There is no reason why I should turn over for absolute control a school valued at five million dollars," she told the young man. "This committee is appointed for two years only." At the same time, she was willing to hire him as provost. "I hope you will accept on my condition and you need not worry about interference."

Theo sent copies of the cables to Draper, who was also vacationing in London. Upon receiving them, he walked around St. James Square for two hours to calm himself down. Then he contacted Theo and demanded that she send Lester another cable to tell him to disregard the first one. Docilely, she agreed, since Draper had threatened again to use his influence to "wreck Avon."

Theo's second cable to Lester read: "Have just talked with Draper and understand cable content should have first been taken up with Executive Committee." It was too late. As she probably knew, the initial cable had alarmed the candidate so much that he refused the committee's offer.

The executive committee appointed Dean Cherry as Acting Provost and told him that he had complete authority, subject only to the approval of the executive committee. They then directed Cherry to relegate Major Gaston to sorting mail in the school post office.

The executive committee also made some financial decisions without consulting Theo. They sold the school's flock of 450 Dorset sheep and the Hill-Stead farm's milk route, limiting it to supplying milk only to the school. In addition, they authorized the payment of $9,000 severance pay to Francis Froelicher.

Harris Whittemore.
Courtesy Robert N. Whittemore. *(HS)*.

Provost Francis Mitchell Froelicher.
(AOF).

First faculty, staff, and students, 1927. *(AOF)*.

SEVENTEEN

"The breath of God"
1929—1932

WHILE THEO and the executive committee carried on their battle for control of Avon Old Farms School, larger events were occurring outside of Farmington. On October 29, 1929, the stock market panic that had begun a few days earlier resulted in a crash. Several days later, although John D. Rockefeller announced that he and his son were buying stocks and two big corporations declared extra dividends "as a gesture of stubborn confidence," the prices of stocks continued to fall, reaching bottom on November 13. In a few weeks, the fortunes of millionaires and the savings of the working class—thirty billion dollars—were lost.

Still, many people seemed unconcerned about the drama on Wall Street and the rising numbers of unemployed and homeless. A poll of the members of the National Economic League revealed their opinion that the country's most important problems were (1) Administration of Justice, (2) Prohibition, and (3) Lawlessness. Unemployment was Number 18 on their list. Most Americans thought that the country was in a temporary recession.

In November, when Theo and John returned from abroad, they voiced no apprehension about the worsening economic situation. What disturbed Theo was the present state of turmoil in the microcosm of Avon Old Farms. While in England, Theo wrote an *Instrument of Trust,* which gave her, as director of the Pope-Brooks Foundation, full power of appointment of the members of the executive committee as well as of the trustees of the school, which she planned to merge to become a board of directors in 1931.

On November 14, Theo called a meeting of the executive committee. All were present, except for Dr. Draper. Earlier, the committee had agreed that there was a serious problem at the school because Acting Provost Cherry was proving to be a poor administrator. Cherry had taken too far Theo's ideal of governing the school by the town meeting method. The man appeared unable to make even the most ordinary decisions and was calling on the faculty to discuss and to vote on every detail of the school's management. Even worse was the collapse of student discipline. According to Theo, the students were "running wild" and were "habitually impudent." She said that, on one occasion, a student had actually struck a teacher.

It was crucial that a new provost be appointed quickly. Henry Canby was recommending a Yale English professor, Dr. Robert Dudley French, and had invited the young scholar to meet with the committee that evening. After the interview, the executive committee members, including Theo, were so favorably impressed that they directed Canby to offer a contract to Dr. French.

Then rumors surfaced that French wanted to leave Yale because of problems he had with colleagues in the English department. To squelch the gossip, Canby and Yale's President Angell asked and received permission from French to announce his appointment as provost of Avon, even though he had not yet signed a contract.

Before the announcement was made, *The New York Times* published a story on its front page in December 1929. The headline read: "Yale Men Protest As Professor Quits," followed by "R. D. French's Resignation Laid to Difference With English Department Heads. Sixty-one Prominent Undergraduates Sign Statements." French was quoted: "I have resigned and…accepted the post of Provost at Avon College. Beyond that I do not care to discuss the matter."

In early January 1930, the executive committee sent parents a notice that formally announced French's appointment. Later that month, Professor French, who had not returned his contract, sent word that he wished to decline the offer, citing that "the philosophy of the School, and the agreement under which he would work, were not sufficiently spelled out."

On February 5, 1930, three members of the executive committee—Henry Canby, Elizabeth Choate, and Clement Scott—met with Professor French at Canby's New York City apartment and asked him why he had refused the appointment. French replied that, as a condition of his being hired, Theo had stated that he must accept Major Gaston as the Master of Detail for the school year, 1930-31. French also said he would have to abide by a policy of discipline, a demerit and merit system, which he did not support. Because of these two provisions, the young professor felt that he would not have complete authority as provost.

Canby asked Scott to meet with Theo and confront her with French's statements, and to convey the executive committee's demand that she give them absolute power to run the school. In the meeting with Scott, Theo denied that she had ever asked French to agree to a merit and demerit system, although she admitted that she had "considered its adoption as a possible means of insuring a return of discipline in the school."

Naturally, she told Scott, she would not accept the committee's ultimatum. She would never consider giving control to "a temporary committee, three members of which were openly opposed to the policies for which Avon Old Farms was founded." When told of her refusal, Henry Canby and Elizabeth Choate immediately resigned, followed by Dr. Draper and W. Champlin Robinson.

A few weeks later, on February 19, 1930, *The New York Times* printed another sensational headline: "School Board Quits Over Professor French," erroneously listing Brooks Emeny as having resigned along with the other executive committee members.

Because of the blizzard of adverse publicity, Avon's faculty, students, and parents decided to hold a meeting on February 22 at the school. Theo did not attend. Instead, she asked Clement Scott to represent her. When a student asked Scott why the former provost, Mr. Froelicher, had left, Scott, who had brought along Stephen Cabot's letter attesting to the provost's intemperance, reached into his pocket. There was no point in protecting the man further. At that moment, a faculty member who knew what the letter contained rushed up and implored Scott not to read it.

Later, Theo regretted that she had not attended the meeting. She would have insisted that Scott read the letter. Without knowing that Froelicher was an alcoholic, people could reach only one conclusion: "Mrs. Riddle engaged the best progressive educator in the country and then fires him—that is the way a woman acts."

On that same day, President Angell of Yale announced that Robert Dudley French, who had recently resigned his position at Yale, was returning to the university with a promotion. Theo suspected that Dr. French had cleverly used the Avon offer "as a lever to lift himself into a Professor's chair."

The debacle had damaged the school's reputation and Theo's as well. According to Clement Scott, who attended a meeting of a group of parents, the parents were unanimous in their opinion that Theo turn Avon Old Farms over to a governing board.

In response, Theo declared that she would "nail her flag to the mast." Avon would function according to her policies or not at all. "If there were ten boys at Avon in the autumn," she asserted, "the School would remain open." But "if there were nine, the buildings would be closed and the roofs could fall in," and she would take the multimillion dollar loss.

Theo decided that only a charismatic, highly principled leader could save Avon. Although she did not want to affiliate the school with a Christian sect, she thought that having an Episcopal clergyman as provost would restore dignity and confidence. She had come to the conclusion: "Avon needs the breath of God."

According to an often-repeated account, Theo chose Avon's second provost by going to New York City, opening a telephone directory to "clergymen," and finding a name she liked. "There's my man," she allegedly said when she came to "Percy Gamble Kammerer." Theo admitted that she did consult a directory, but it was a clerical directory. And, from her room at the Barclay Hotel, she telephoned every Episcopal minister listed in New York, a list that did not include Reverend Kammerer. Not one minister was interested in becoming provost of Avon Old Farms School.

The following day, Theo went to the General Theological Seminary to ask for advice. Dean Fosbroke recommended Kammerer, who was the Dean of Trinity Cathedral in Pittsburgh. Besides being a man of God, Percy Kammerer had studied the psychology of adolescents at Harvard, though his Ph.D. dissertation focused not on boys, but on adolescent unwed mothers. The reverend also shared Theo's interest in parapsychology. Kammerer seemed perfect for the position. Theo contacted him, and he agreed to an interview.

When Theo returned to the hotel, she received a telephone call from Clement Scott. He said that the entire Avon faculty had submitted their resignations in protest about what they believed was her unfair treatment of Provost Froelicher. So far, Scott had kept the news from the press.

Theo frantically called Brooks Emeny and asked him to try to persuade the faculty to change their minds. When Emeny reported that he had met with no success, Theo feared that she was truly losing the school. The image of Gordon's death thirteen years earlier rushed into her mind. "I feel as if I am sitting alone," she told Emeny, "at the bedside of a dying child." And she was alone. During this tumultuous time, John was vacationing in Europe.

One might suppose that John would urge Theo to give up and let others manage the school. She was depleting her fortune and wearing down her health. The opposite, however, was true. He once encouraged Theo so strongly to continue holding on to Avon that she responded, "I think you love the school more than I do."

When John returned from Europe, he joined Theo, Clement Scott, and Professor and Mrs. Henry Perkins at Hill-Stead, on March 24, 1930, to interview Reverend Kammerer. Afterward, the group gave their enthusiastic approval, and Theo immediately offered Percy Kammerer the position. Two days later, he wired his acceptance, but he did not sign a contract.

On Friday, March 28, the headline in *The Hartford Courant* was worse than Theo anticipated: "All Members of Faculty at Avon Resign. Refusal of French to Accept Provostship and Attitude of Mrs. Riddle Believed Reasons. Trustees Will Control School."

Shortly after the article appeared, Clement Scott wrote a letter of explanation to the parents of Avon Old Farms' students. Perhaps because Reverend Kammerer had not yet signed a contract, Scott did not mention the new provost. Instead, he described the expanded role of the trustees and implied that Theo would no longer run the school. For the present, Mrs. Riddle would have the power of reappointment of one-third of the board of trustees each year, he said, but "ultimately, and probably within the next two or three years, the Board will be self-perpetuating."

As evident in the newspaper's headline, in which French's refusal to be the school's provost was blamed on Theo's "attitude," Scott was appeasing the many people who believed that, if the school rid itself of its eccentric founder, all would be well. Since most people did not know the real reason for Froelicher's departure and were unaware of the truth concerning Professor French, this seemed a reasonable conclusion. A female architect was odd to begin with, but a woman who designed, built, founded, and demanded control of a boys' school was inappropriate at the very least, even if she were financing it.

Those who hoped to take over the school set about reinforcing this perception of Theo. They told amusing anecdotes, such as the one about her choosing a provost from the telephone directory because she liked his name. Soon, Theodate legends, in which she was painted as overbearing, capricious, colorful, larger-than-life, and not entirely sane, started to make the rounds. Most of the anecdotes overtly stated or subtly implied that, of course, such a person should not be in charge of a school.

For example, in Avon Old Farms' official history, there is a version of an often-repeated story about Theo's hiring a gardener. The writer states that Mrs. Riddle told an applicant that he was to plant six rose bushes upside down "with the leaves of the bushes exactly eighteen inches in the ground, and the roots straight in the air." Concealing his astonishment, the gardener left to do the work. When he finished, he returned to the imposing figure, who was leaning on a silver cane and looking sternly at him through a lorgnette. The man stammered that he had indeed followed instructions.

"Good," Mrs. Riddle pronounced and inspected his work. "You did exactly as I asked you to do, and you are hired." Then, as she walked away, she turned and said, "Now plant them right."

The story is ridiculous, but running a school is serious business. At the end of the tale, the writer attaches its moral: "Bushes could be transplanted more easily than faculty or students…"

Lefty Lewis liked telling entertaining stories about his Farmington neighbor and friend. In his autobiography, Lewis describes a visit to Hill-Stead on a beautiful summer day, during which "thunder clouds gathered on the summer horizon," auguring what was soon to occur.

Lewis was sitting in the ell room with his hostess when Theo rang the bell to summon Earnest. "We'll have Babba," she instructed. Continuing the metaphor of the approaching storm, Lewis described Theo's intonation as one that he had heard on previous occasions, a sound that "prepared the initiated for lightning close at hand."

Theo's reason for summoning Ali Babba the cat was to teach him to stay in the front of the house rather than in the servants' quarters at the back, which the animal seemed to prefer.

Earnest returned holding the cat, followed by another servant, an émigré Russian who carried a wicker basket lined with pink satin and filled with catnip. After Babba "nibbled the catnip and stretched in ecstasy," Theo was certain that she had convinced the cat to stay with her and her guests. After a few minutes, however, Babba started to sneak out of the room. Furious at the pet's disobedience, Theo "turned very red" and announced, "I know what I shall do with Babba. I'll chloroform him."

"And she did," Lewis concludes. His story also has a moral that related to Avon Old Farms School. "She drew up a *Deed of Trust* that contained Thirty-nine Articles, each one of which was to be obeyed without question by the Provost. Disobedience meant going the way of Babba."

If Theo did say she would chloroform Babba, which is improbable, she was joking. She would no more kill a cat than a child. When she was away from Hill-Stead, Theo constantly wrote Earnest expressing concern about the health of her pets. She once asked Foster Kennedy and his wife to stay at a local inn with their dog because their pet, which they had brought with them to Hill-Stead for the weekend, was disturbing hers.

Upon learning that Clement Scott had promised the parents that Avon Old Farms School would soon have a permanent, self-perpetuating board of trustees, Theo angrily insisted that he correct his error, but Scott argued that it would be imprudent because the parents would become upset. Accepting the bitter truth that she was seen as a liability to the school, Theo agreed to remain silent and not refute Scott's letter to the parents.

Theo's reticence did not mean that she would allow the trustees to run the school. As director of the Pope-Brooks Foundation, Theo could legally sign over the school to herself. Engaging three typists and a Yale law student, George Nebolsine, who practically moved into Hill-Stead to assist her, Theo worked at a feverish pace to revise the *Instrument of Trust* into the infamous *Deed of Trust,* which Lefty Lewis alluded to in his Babba story, a document that infuriated her adversaries.

Clement Scott read through the *Deed of Trust* and said that it seemed "a good instrument that protects you." Because Theo still worried that it did not completely guarantee that she would remain in control, Scott asked a colleague, Francis Cole, to read the document. In early April, Theo received Atty. Cole's opinion.

"You will note that I have stated definitely my disapproval of a number of the suggestions without giving any reasons," Cole began. A rather confusing and acrimonious sentence follows: "If present circumstances require the establishment of a trust for the School as such independent of your control, fanciful purposes and requirements defeat the desired end."

Alongside the passage "independent of your control, fanciful purposes and requirements" Theo drew a large, red exclamation mark. Then she sent Atty. Cole the following brief reply:

> Dear Mr. Cole:
>
> I hereby acknowledge receipt of your impudent letter
> of April 1st, 1930.
> I am having it framed to hang in my library.
>
> > Very truly,
> > Theodate Pope Riddle

To placate Theo, Clement Scott met with about eighty Avon Old Farms' parents. Hoping to moderate their perception of the founder, he explained Theo's educational policies and described the new provost she had hired. When he reported that the parents expressed their approval of both Theo's progressive ideas and Percy Kammerer, she felt heartened at what she perceived as their support. To win them over further, Theo announced that she was "now willing to appoint a Board of Directors and turn the affairs of the Foundation over to a trust or corporation." At the same time, she refused to allow the board to be self-perpetuating during her lifetime. Until her death, she would appoint and reappoint the members.

In August 1930, exhausted by the ordeal of the past year, Theo accompanied John to Paris on the *Mauretania,* although it must have been difficult for her to sail on the *Lusitania's* sister ship. Because of a throat problem, John wanted to seek advice and treatment from a French specialist, and both he and Theo looked forward to visiting Grace and Blair at Charlie's villa in Bizy.

At the villa, a fight occurred between Blair and Charlie, concerning Charlie's chauffeur Clark. Grace and Blair hurriedly departed, Blair swearing that he would never again speak to his brother. Theo and John also left, going on to Paris. There they visited the Russian princess Catherine Cantacuzene, a friend of the family of George Nebolsine, the law student who had helped Theo draft the *Deed of Trust*. Nebolsine thought that the princess and John would enjoy conversing because her father and her husband had been prominent in court circles when John was U.S. ambassador to czarist Russia about twenty years earlier.

Princess Cantacuzene arrived at the Café de la Paix accompanied by a fifteen-year-old nephew, Alexander (Sasha) Naryshkine. Like most expatriate Russian aristocrats, the princess lived in greatly reduced circumstances, but she still retained her graceful carriage and fine manners. During lunch, while John and the princess spoke in Russian and reminisced about pre-Communist Russia, Theo talked with Sasha. The boy was living with his aunt because his father had been killed on the Austrian Front in 1916, and his mother had died shortly after, most likely murdered by the communists.

The following day, Theo invited Sasha and the princess to the Crillon Hotel, where she and John were staying. Suddenly she asked the boy, "How would you like to go to school in America?" She told Sasha he could attend Avon Old Farms for no cost and live at Hill-Stead. Sasha accepted the offer. In the fall, he and Princess Cantacuzene's son, Nicholas (Kolya) arrived in Farmington.

Reverend Percy Gamble Kammerer's first year as provost, 1930-31, was highly successful. Reverend Kammerer was a charming, handsome man with regular features, soulful eyes, sensuous mouth, and dimpled chin. His arrival had a calming effect, and he became popular with everyone. He hired a new faculty to replace the previous one that had resigned, including Commander Harold O. D. Hunter to fill the controversial position of Aide to the Provost, formerly known as the Master of Detail.

Brooks Emeny noted that "fortunately" the aide had "integrity and ability." He approved of the dress code Hunter imposed: gray suits and vests for class; and striped gray trousers, black double-breasted jackets, and stiff collars for evening wear.

Theo also applauded these requirements because she believed that good manners and proper clothes went together. At Hill-Stead, one always dressed for dinner. Once when his Aunt Theo and Uncle John were traveling, Donald thought, "Why should I change into my tuxedo? I'll be eating dinner alone, and nobody will know the difference." Earnest served him in the dining room and appeared not to notice the boy's casual attire.

When Theo returned, however, Earnest told her what had occurred, and Donald received a severe reprimand. One always dressed for dinner because one valued gracious living.

During the Depression, other independent schools became less formal, but at Avon Old Farms School, student waiters continued to serve dinner by candlelight, and white tablecloths covered tables set with silver and china. Most of the boys came from homes where they were accustomed to elegance, but many of their families were now finding it difficult to pay Avon's tuition. Theo provided more and more financial aid to boys from families who had fallen on hard times. One such scholarship student was Pete Seeger, who graduated from Avon in the mid-1930s and later became the radical folksinger.

Although she kept making up the school's deficits, Theo remained optimistic. She wrote that "everything seems to be going superbly" because the students were "enthusiastic over the Kammerers, the Aide, and the new faculty in general."

During the summer of 1931, Theo and John went abroad again. While they were away, Anna died at the age of 76, most likely from a series of strokes. On her last day, Oldgate, as usual, was filled with visitors. Anna had been in a coma, but she awakened and appeared in the library beautifully dressed in a white tea gown. Frustrated by an inability to speak, she shut her eyes. Later that evening she died. Throughout the Farmington valley, everyone concurred, "Mrs. Cowles went down like a battleship with all the flags flying."

Theo regretted Anna's death, but at the same time, without her former friend's enmity, it was easier for her to carry on a friendship with Sarah (Sallie) Roosevelt, Anna's cousin and Franklin Delano Roosevelt's strong-willed, domineering mother. Theo got along well with Sallie, perhaps because they had similar traits. At a luncheon at Hill-Stead with the two women, Governor Wilbur Cross commented that he thought there was a remarkable resemblance between Theo and Sallie.

Theo was also fond of Sallie's daughter-in-law, Eleanor, and, despite being a registered Republican, Theo strongly supported the political career of Franklin. FDR had won a smashing victory in the 1930 elections. He was now governor of New York and a likely Democratic candidate for the presidency.

As the country entered the second year of the Depression, President Herbert Hoover realized that people were suffering from hunger and other deprivations, but he felt he must refuse the increasing demands for federal aid. He believed that providing such help was a threat not only to the federal budget but also to the "self-reliance of the American people and the tradition of local self-rule and local responsibility for charitable relief." At the same time, Hoover realized that there was also a threat to his re-election if the present economic distress continued.

The general public still did not seem to be fully aware of the seriousness of the situation. The historian, Frederick Lewis Allen, writes that diversions took people's minds off the economy; for example, there was a boom in miniature golf. The phenomenon of lighthearted Americans across the country hitting golf balls was matched by the popularity of a new radio program, *Amos 'n' Andy*. Millions of people laughed as they followed the breach-of-promise suit that Madam Queen brought against Andy, and in Louisiana, Huey Long was inspired to take on the name "Kingfish" when he ran for the Senate. Backgammon was another craze. At Hill-Stead, John played the game in the evenings with Sasha, speaking to the boy in both English and impeccable Russian.

Americans also focused their attention on handsome Charles Lindbergh, who had just started an air-mail route, and on the remarkable Bobby Jones, who had become a new hero after his golf triumphs. But eventually, the public became afraid. In June 1931, their fears intensified when officers of the Bank of the United States were convicted of mismanaging the bank's funds during the heyday of the stock market in the late 1920s. The trial revealed just the first in a multitude of banking scandals that followed.

Alarmed that a collapse of the European economy would have a disastrous effect on the country, Hoover declared a moratorium on foreign debts, including German reparations from the World War. At first, his efforts seemed to be succeeding, but a panic began in Germany that quickly spread to England. In September, America's banks began failing—305 in one month. In October, another 522 closed. By the end of the year, there were about ten million unemployed workers.

Aware of the disastrous effects of the Depression, Theo sent Dolly Rutledge out into the Farmington community to distribute food, blankets and clothes to poor families. Theo's relatives also were suffering. A cousin, Alfred Borden, had lost almost everything—his house, Arabian horses, speedboat, and Wall Street office. He still had a small plane, which he flew to the school, landing on a field of the farm. The middle-aged Borden climbed down from the plane and walked over to Theo, who stood waiting. Their conversation was brief. He asked for money, and she declined, professing her obligation to Avon Old Farms as the reason. Borden turned from Theo "in a huff," and flew off.

Because the Depression threatened both the school and her fortune, Theo appointed George Nebolsine as her financial advisor, and, acting on his suggestion, ordered an examination of the school's budget as well as of her own income. She hired efficiency experts who recommended a revised budget, which saved the school $57,234, and also reported that the management of the comptroller, Mr. Appleton, was extravagant. Theo then concluded that Appleton was a man of "mediocre ability" who was being paid an "exorbitant salary of $7,500 per year." Ignoring Clement Scott's argument that, since Appleton had not been in full charge of the school's finances, it was unfair to fire him, Theo discharged him in the spring of 1932 and hired Julian C. Howe as his replacement.

Howe proceeded to withdraw Theo's personal funds from the Hartford-Connecticut Trust Company because he felt that the bank had been making excessive charges for its services as treasurer of the Pope-Brooks Foundation. Scott, who was connected to the Hartford bank, was indignant. "Our heart has been in this work," he bristled.

Theo listened to Nebolsine, who next suggested that she transfer a large loan from Scott's Hartford bank to the Chase National Bank in New York in order to get a lower rate of interest. Theo was unpleasantly surprised, however, when, to execute the transfer, Nebolsine requested $1,000 for his services.

Theo had already paid Nebolsine $1,500 for his work with the budget, but she paid him the $1,000. Upon hearing about the transaction, Blair commented, "What in the world has happened to George Nebolsine? He seems to have changed from a nice simple young fellow into a conceited bounder."

Theo did balk at Nebolsine's attempt to transfer her securities to the Chase National Bank. Acting without him, she appointed the Central Hanover Bank and Trust as treasurer of the Pope-Brooks Foundation, with Scott's Hartford bank remaining as only secretary and depository. She was impressed by the fact that the Central Hanover was "the only bank in New York, which, during the 100 years of service, has never sold a security." Theo's switching banks made financial sense, though she alienated not only Clement Scott but other local businessmen, who viewed her actions as disloyal to the community.

Blair denigrated Theo's economies at Avon Old Farms. They amounted to "nothing in the way of cutting down expenses," he observed, "with the exception of the 10% cut in the wages of the teachers." He was convinced that the school was eventually going to "break" Theo, as she used more and more of her own money to meet its deficits. "It's all a terrible mess," he wrote Grace, "and the quicker it busts the better." Blair knew that it was futile to warn Theo. "She will keep on putting in every cent she can lay her hands on till it is impossible to put in any more." Blair did not mention another act that did not make fiscal good sense. The previous year, in April 1931, Theo had forgiven his considerable debt to her.

Blair was traveling about in Europe while Grace remained in Paris. Grace's latest book, *And Then I Saw the Congo,* published in 1929, had been an enormous success. The book was based on a six-months' trek through Africa with her wealthy St. Paul friend, Alice O'Brien; the big-game hunter, Ben Burbridge; the pioneer moviemaker Charles Bell; and Blair. Even though she loved living alone in Paris, Grace could not concentrate on writing because she was not feeling well. This time it was not depression, she wrote Theo. She feared she had stomach cancer.

Theo's response was predictable. Grace must immediately come to Hill-Stead. "Remember your hand is in mine," Theo wrote, "and together we will find the way out." Theo's letter was filled with descriptions of new treatments, in particular one developed by Dr. Abrams, whose method "takes the terror out of that disease if it is taken in time." Abrams's method was being used by about 1,200 physicians across the country, including Dr. Bush in Hartford, who had recently cured a woman of lung cancer.

When Grace arrived in Farmington, she was admitted to Hartford Hospital for tests. They proved negative. Overjoyed that her "darling girl" was not dying, Theo repeated an offer she had made the previous year: she would lend Hill-Stead's cottage to Grace. Grace would have the privacy that she needed in order to write, and it would give Theo the pleasure of having her beloved "sister" nearby. Blair urged Grace to accept. "I can just see Theo saying 'Cottage,'" he mused. "She is so sweet and is so very fond of you and me. I can hardly understand it."

Blair joined Grace for a while after she moved into the O'Rourkery. Sasha described him as a "very elegant gentleman, except for his hat," an old, shabby, wide-brimmed hat Blair liked to wear, though he knew it annoyed Theo. The boy recalled that Theo sent Earnest to tell Blair to bring the disreputable hat to her. Curious, Blair did as instructed. As he handed Theo the hat, she whipped out scissors and, despite his loud protests, proceeded to cut off its brim. When she finished, she gave it back, and Blair jauntily put on the hat-turned-cap and continued to wear it throughout his stay.

Leaving his wife in Theo's care, Blair moved back to St. Paul, where, he wrote Grace, he had an enlightening conversation with a friend about Avon Old Farms School. The friend was trying to decide where to send his son to boarding school. Blair recommended Avon, but the boy said that he had heard that it was the "most snobbish place in the world" and refused to go there. The boy's perception might have related to Avon's dress code or it could have reflected an elitist comment that Theo supposedly had made when the school first opened, expressing horror at the possibility of admitting students from the Midwest. She insisted that "Buffalo was the western limit." It is possible that this was just another Theodate legend or that she was joking. As a student at Miss Porter's exclusive school over forty years earlier, Theo had met girls not only from the Midwest but from the West Coast—even farther away from New England and civilized society.

But recruiting students from anywhere had become increasingly difficult during the Depression. The number of upper-class families who could afford to send their sons to an independent school was diminishing, and anyone with money could now buy acceptances to older, prestigious schools. Why send a child to a school with a short, rocky history, especially one that was run by an eccentric woman? Theo's offering scholarships wasn't much help. Blair reported that the "Yale boys" wouldn't send their sons for any amount and thought the school was "laughable."

Alexander (Sasha) Naryshkine and Nicholas (Kolya) Cantacuzene. *(HS).*

Print shop, Avon Old Farms School, 1930s. Max Stein at far right. *(AOF)*.

Study Hall. *(AOF)*.

Provost Percy Gamble Kammerer.
(AOF).

Theo presenting the Founder's Trophy to W. Rand '32. *(AOF)*.

EIGHTEEN

Dearest of Geniuses
1932—1940

IN ADDITION to Sasha and Kolya, Madame Breshkovsky, and the servant whom Lefty Lewis mentions in his Babba tale, other Russian émigrés appeared at Hill-Stead. John had met the Russian diplomat, Eugene Stein, in Argentina. After the Russian Revolution, support for the Imperial Russian Consulate in Argentina ended. Since Stein was a nobleman of German ancestry, he was warned not to return to Russia if he valued his life. Initially Stein went to Canada and then to New York, where Theo and John discovered him living in poverty. Stein joined the family at Hill-Stead until he was able to support himself.

Theo and John also befriended a young French woman, Louise Desperts. After serving as a nurse during the war, Louise had come to New York and worked at the hospital where Theo had surgery. She told Theo that she wanted to become a doctor, and Theo offered to pay her educational expenses. After graduating from New York University's medical school and finishing a residency at Bellevue Hospital, Louise went on to become a child psychiatrist and the author of several books. Theo also supported the advanced studies of other students, and she made it possible for Sasha and Kolya to attend medical school.

By the early 1930s, Theo's boys, Paul and Donald, had married and left Farmington. Don and Evie lived nearby in Springfield, Massachusetts, where he was employed by an automobile company. Paul and Fern moved to California. The only job Paul could get was at a gas station. He wrote often to Theo, sometimes asking for money for medical expenses and always expressing anger toward the monopoly of the oil industry, which shamelessly exploited its workers.

Like many other Americans during the 1930s, Paul and his wife believed that capitalism was the cause of their financial difficulties, and they turned to political philosophies that seemed more sympathetic to the working class. Theo discouraged Paul from becoming involved with communists. Instead, she suggested, "I am interested in your getting busy with the local branch of the Socialist party." After Paul became a socialist, Theo advised him to join progressive young Democrats since she believed that the socialist party would "wither away."

In the 1932 election, Americans had the choice of Republican Herbert Hoover, Socialist Norman Thomas, Communist William Z. Foster, and

Democrat Franklin D. Roosevelt, who had emerged victorious on the fourth ballot from a three-way deadlock at the party's convention in Chicago. John's niece, Isabella Selmes Ferguson Greenway, made the seconding speech for FDR. To Theo, Roosevelt and his promise of a "new deal" promised the best hope for America, and the voters agreed with her.

Many people were aware that Roosevelt had been stricken by polio, but they assumed that he had completely recovered. Only those in his inner circle knew he was unable to walk. At the inauguration, watching their new president coming up the ramp arm-in-arm with his son, the public thought it a sign of affection. Few realized that this was an extremely difficult performance, especially for James, who was literally carrying his crippled father. No one would suspect any weakness in the confident man who addressed a nation mired in the Depression. "So, first of all," the president boldly proclaimed, "let me assert my firm belief that the only thing we have to fear is fear itself."

Theo was inspired by FDR's courage and determination. She tried to take his advice, but, as the Depression continued, Theo could not stem her fears about the future of the school, even though, now in its fourth year under Provost Kammerer, Avon Old Farms seemed to be doing well. John Dewey, the prominent progressive educator, wrote that he was glad to hear that the school was in "such a flourishing and satisfactory condition." The truth was that Avon was suffering from serious financial problems. If the economy did not improve, there would be even fewer families enrolling their sons, which meant that, to keep the school open, Theo would have to find other revenue sources besides tuition and her personal assets.

On the faint hope that she might earn money from architectural work locally, Theo attempted to secure a license as an architect in Connecticut. She was already licensed in New York but had closed her New York City office. Connecticut granted the license, making Theo one of the state's first registered female architects, but she did not receive any commissions.

Theo then considered selling some of Hill-Stead's paintings. She contacted the new director of Hartford's Wadsworth Atheneum, twenty-six-year-old A. Everett "Chick" Austin, Jr., and asked if he knew anyone who might be interested in buying three Cassatts. "There is no hurry," she told the young man. "It might be well if I waited until business improved, but I am starting the ball rolling."

Like most of those in the Hartford area who supported the arts, Theo had been enchanted by Chick Austin's charm, talent, energy, and extraordinary good looks. Arranging to have Theo lend several of Hill-

Stead's Impressionist paintings for his first exhibit in 1932 was one of Austin's many coups. In April of that year, Chick mounted the Museum of Modern Art's sensational traveling exhibit on modern architecture. Theo's young cousin, the acclaimed and innovative architect, Philip Johnson, organized the show with Henry-Russell Hitchcock. To promote the exhibit they held an open forum and invited eighty architects to participate, including Theo. Always looking for publicity, Chick thought that Theodate might provoke controversy, and he was right.

After listening to the praise that her male colleagues were heaping on modern architecture, Theo suddenly stood up, "like a general," according to an observer. She announced that, in reality, modern architecture was a failure. Why? "Because it was purely intellectual without regard to the emotions." Cold, sterile, modern houses ignored a basic human need. People want to live in "nests," she explained. "Men who worked with machinery during the day might rather not sleep in a machine at night."

The avant-garde architects probably did not take her seriously, but to Chick Austin's delight, *The Hartford Times* reported Theo's remarks. She had added drama and color to the proceedings, and she also had reinforced her public image. Not only was she a rarity, a woman architect, she also was the forceful, "imperious" Mrs. Riddle of Avon Old Farms School, who never hesitated to speak her mind. And most ordinary people would agree with what she said at the forum.

At the beginning of the fall semester, Provost Kammerer paid a visit to Hill-Stead. His handsome face serious, he explained that this was not a social call. Accustomed to Kammerer's easygoing nature, Theo became concerned. But there was nothing wrong. The provost just wanted to discuss a contract.

"Finally," Theo thought. After three years of evading signing a contract, Reverend Kammerer was willing to commit himself to the school. She cheerfully replied, "Certainly!" and directed him to have his lawyer meet with hers.

Not long after, Kammerer returned with a document in hand. As Theo read it, she became outraged. The terms of the contract were preposterous. For the next two years, the provost demanded his present, generous salary of $11,340. After that, she was to give him a raise of at least $1,360 every year. In addition, he wanted the option of retiring in seventeen years with an annual pension of $10,000. If Avon Old Farms were to close before then, Theo must promise to pay him a yearly annuity until his death of $1,000 multiplied by the number of years of his service—though not to exceed $10,000.

Theo left the room and immediately telephoned her lawyer to find out why he had sanctioned the contract. How could she guarantee future raises and a pension for Dr. Kammerer? The attorney responded that he had gone along with the contract because the provost had warned, "If Mrs. Riddle doesn't meet my desires, I will return to the school and at a meeting of the faculty, advise the members to look for other positions, and I myself will pack my little bag and look for another job."

Kammerer's threat was alarming. Theo believed that the school could not survive the publicity of another mass resignation. But she would not sign the contract. If the provost left and the faculty followed him, so be it. She refused to meet with the man.

"Let the damned school close," she told John.

In his customary quiet manner, John again encouraged Theo to hold onto Avon. "That school is a monument to you," he pronounced, "and shall not close."

This time, John acted. He invited the provost to Hill-Stead, greeted him cordially, and, during their talk, applied his considerable diplomatic skills, combining flattery and manipulation. He praised Kammerer's achievements and his stewardship of the school. Kammerer had greatly improved Avon's standing and had exerted a marvelous influence on the students. Many parents had spoken of the wonders he had accomplished with their sons.

The problem, John explained, was that Theo was in a state of exhaustion and could not deal with school business. In fact, Dr. Kennedy had ordered her to take an extended vacation. John urged Kammerer to wait until their return, when Theo would be more able to deal with his contract. In the meantime, John hoped that the provost would not do anything that would hurt the school. "I certainly do not want to kill the thing I love," the provost declared, agreeing to let the matter stand until the Riddles came back from their trip.

Shortly after Christmas, Theo and John sailed to Egypt. Almost immediately, Theo fell on shipboard, suffering a concussion. Upon arriving in Egypt, she came down with influenza. They went on to Paris, where she remained in a hotel room under the care of a private nurse. Charlie drove the short distance from Bizy to visit his brother and sister-in-law, but Theo refused to emerge from the room. When Charlie asked what was wrong, John replied, "Oh nothing—nothing. That is to say, nothing *organic*—just nerves, just nerves." John hoped to stay in Paris throughout the summer, but he told Charlie that at any moment Theo might find that the city didn't agree with her and that they would then go to the Italian lakes or Switzerland.

Soon after, John and Theo left for Switzerland because she desired a consultation with Dr. Carl Jung, the psychiatrist she had met almost twenty years earlier. After several visits, Jung sketched a diagram, a circle split by three diagonals, which he labeled "Mrs. Riddle's functioning." At the right bottom part of the circle, he drew slanted lines to shade in the segment and wrote two words: *Emotions and Unconscious.* He concluded that Theo was an "Intuitive."

Theo asked Louise Desperts about Jung's diagnosis. "The great Intuitives are *sure*," the young doctor informed Theo. "While we falter, hesitate, formulate a thought later to retract it," she explained, "the Intuitives plough ahead because they are sure." Such confidence, however, has a negative side. "Their sureness does not call for justification or explanations," Louise continued, "and it is the rigidity of their attitude and beliefs which makes for so much misunderstanding of their personality. The greatness of their work, in and of itself, masks their personality and even makes it incomprehensible."

Louise urged Theo not to worry about those who misunderstood, mocked, and opposed her. "It seems that anyone who can look back upon such a life of accomplishment as yours," she asserted, "could never fall into a mood of sadness." Theo's claims to greatness were the buildings she had designed, the school she had founded, and the "financial help and moral comfort" she had given to others.

While Theo and John were abroad, they received letters from Commander Harold Hunter, the Aide, who was working diligently to enroll new students. To John, Hunter wrote that he worried that Avon would lose as many as twenty boys. To Theo, he painted an optimistic picture. "At the present time we have thirteen new boys definitely signed on the dotted line," he reported, "and quite a few others showing varying degrees of interest." Commander Hunter also thanked Theo for the salary increase he had recently received.

When Theo and John returned in September 1935, they found a letter from Dr. Kammerer in the stack of mail that awaited them. Almost a year had passed since the provost had presented the contract he desired Theo to sign, and he was becoming anxious. He warned that he had been approached about taking another position. Theo suspected that the provost was trying to force her hand, and she again turned to John for help. His advice was to wait at least a week before responding and let the man worry that he might be out of a job.

Theo finally signed a contract with Kammerer on December 30, 1935. The terms are not known. The following year, *Fortune* magazine listed Avon Old Farms as one of America's twelve best independent schools, and Theo felt that she had made the right decision.

Provost Kammerer had sought economic security at about the same time that President Roosevelt was establishing a major reform of his administration, the Social Security Act. Most of Theo's set were certain that Roosevelt's policies threatened the essence of capitalism and that "that man in the White House" would completely ruin the country. "He's never earned a nickel in his life," they jeered. "What has he ever done but live off his mother's income?"

Theo's neighbor, Corinne Alsop, who was also Roosevelt's cousin, agreed. "Your hero Franklin," she informed her, "is having a whirl and his last pronunciamento will now tax everybody in such a way that capital will hardly exist!!" Corinne was frantic about what was happening in Washington: "the Supreme Court decision on the N.R.S... and last week came the Soak the Rich Tax Message...and stocks tumbling and the business world shaken into a jittery condition again."

Theo believed that her friends' and relatives' animosity toward the president derived merely from their selfish interests. She expressed hearty approval of the president. "Franklin Delano Roosevelt appears to be the miracle man," she claimed, "and to be accomplishing great things for the betterment of our country."

Theo's earlier espousal of the lost cause of socialism had been mocked, but now friends, neighbors, and relatives were furious that she openly supported Roosevelt. Instead of responding angrily to those who attacked her political views, Theo tolerated critics and listened calmly to Grace, who expressed hysterical, reactionary, and bigoted opinions.

Grace had embraced the position of her hero, Charles Lindbergh, although she wasn't quite sure what it was. In a long, breathless letter to Theo, she described having lunch and tea with Lindbergh, who "is such an absolutely enchanting human being that I can't be interested in what he is for or against or anything—just *him*." Grace was aware there were those who believed that Lindbergh was a supporter of Hitler's fascist state. "But how anybody on earth can be DUMB enough—let alone mean enough—to imagine that Lindbergh is anything but utterly sincere and utterly patriotic is simply outside of my comprehension," she lamented. He was "the most absolutely first rate individual, man, human being, we have produced since Lincoln."

After some further gushing, Grace mentioned "a famous Jew chemist," she had met. According to him, Lindbergh "wasn't even a good flyer, nothing but a Nazi spy." She observed, "Gosh, how the Jews fear and loathe him," and pointed to Walter Winchell, "that Jewish paid snooper and professional gossip and scandal monger." Grace resented Jews with positions in Roosevelt's administration and informed Theo that they are "in the saddle in this country more and more." Grace did become confused, however, when she met Michael Gold, author of *Jews Without Money*, at a cocktail party. "He's a jew and a communist," she knew, "but he's an awfully nice person."

In contrast to Grace's anti-Semitism, Theo exhibited not only tolerance but courage when she hired Max Stein as an instructor at Avon Old Farms School in 1935. At the same time, she seemed to share the prejudice of her class and the times, which is apparent in a letter she wrote to Grace inquiring about accommodations in Florida. "What is that hotel where the proprietor won't have jews? at Miami—or near?" she inquired.

Grace had moved back to St. Paul because her mother was dying. After the funeral, she stayed on to care for Blair, who had suffered a stroke. Charlie soon joined them. Most likely because of Blair's poor health, the brothers reconciled.

Charlie said he returned to America because France had become too expensive. The American dollar was worth half as much as it had been barely two years earlier. Meals that were 60 cents were now $1.50, and gas was $1.50 a gallon. "The new government (as you know) is socialist with strong Communist leanings," Charlie told Grace. "I will say for Blum, however, that while he is a sheeny communist, his public utterances have been dignified, sensible and reassuring. He has kept people calm—there has been almost no disorder and no bloodshed."

Then, during the general strike in Paris, Charlie worried about the possibility of a political revolution. A parade of workers on the rue de Rivoli, waving red flags and screaming raucous revolutionary songs, frightened him badly.

Theo's cousin Alden Brooks, who had lived abroad for decades, also returned to America, but he viewed conditions in Europe as only "light clouds" and left his daughter in France. Like many Americans, Alden did not notice, care, or realize the significance of Hitler's armies marching unopposed into the Rhineland, Mussolini's completing his Ethiopian campaign, and civil war in Spain. Indeed, Americans in 1936 were hopeful because there were signs that business was improving. Theo was so encouraged about the apparent upturn in the economy that, after offering to sell Manet's *Woman with a Guitar*, she changed her mind.

To support Roosevelt's 1936 campaign, Theo created a slogan, "Our National Him," with a pun, she explained, on "Hymn." She sent the suggestion to FDR, whose reaction is not known, but he certainly responded graciously. Theo was not only his mother's friend but also a significant contributor to his campaign.

As the election drew near, Theo's cousin Lathem, Betty's son, warned that the continuance of Roosevelt in the White House would have dire consequences for Theo personally. "Hill-Stead is a tradition of quiet dignity in living which we fear may not always endure," he predicted. On Election Day, the Democrats won every state except for Maine and Vermont. Theo was ecstatic, but Lathem was bitter and cynical. "Those of us having a different viewpoint can do little else than follow the mature counsel attributed to Confucius," he wrote, "that when rape is inevitable, one should relax and enjoy it."

The most highly publicized news of the day was not Roosevelt's re-election or reports about the economy. During the summer of 1936, the scandalous romance of King Edward VIII and Wallis Simpson dominated the headlines. American newspapers splashed photos of the two frolicking on a Mediterranean cruise, and in October, readers learned that Mrs. Simpson had divorced her husband. Because of the censorship of the British press, most of the English public did not know about the affair until weeks later when headlines around the world announced, "THE KING QUITS."

On December 11, Theo and John listened to the king in a radio broadcast from London. "I never wanted to withhold anything," Edward said haltingly, "but until now it has not been constitutionally possible for me to speak." Since it was improbable that he could remain as king if he married a divorcée, he had made his choice. "I have found it impossible to carry the heavy burden of responsibility and to discharge my duties as King as I should wish to do," he asserted, "without the help and support of the woman I love."

Theo was flabbergasted. She could not understand "the grotesquerie of Edward's giving up a throne for a woman with two living husbands." And, she dryly remarked, "she is by no means the first and only, simply one of a succession of similar affairs."

Theo felt indifferent about attending the coronation of Edward's brother. After the ceremony, Countess Helena Gleichen asked, "What happened that you were unable to come?" Helena had sat in the King's box behind Queen Mary and had enjoyed the day.

In July 1937, Theo and John again left for Europe to stay for several months. While John remained in Paris, Theo went to England to visit Countess Helena and others, leaving John a loving note. She explained that she wrote it at "one of the times when my heart turns upside down with fear & affection." In reply, he sent adorable, stuffed bears as well as a love letter.

John had become Theo's most trusted confidante and supporter. Now married twenty-one years, they had developed a close, understanding, and affectionate relationship. In a note in Theo's silk box, John addressed Theo as "Dearest of Geniuses" and ended "Best love, Your devoted Old Faithful."

While he vacationed abroad, John became increasingly concerned about Blair. "How is Goo Goo?" he wrote Charlie, using the pet name the two called their youngest brother. "Is it really as serious as we hear?"

Blair was "absolutely weak and practically helpless," Charlie replied.

Grace wrote John that because of Blair's illness, she and he "are terribly hard up, and any extra funds even fifty or a hundred dollars at present will help us a lot."

That winter Grace took her husband to Palm Springs. Charlie planned to visit but became violently ill with stomach pains. On March 28, 1938, Charlie died suddenly. He left $30,000 and the Bizy chalet, *Le Petit Saint Paul*, to his companion Clark. The remainder of the estate, which consisted of the St. Paul house and what turned out to be very valuable shares in the St. Paul Fire and Marine Company, went to Blair. Charlie did not leave anything to John because he assumed that, since Theo was an heiress, John did not need money. Within the year, Blair died. Inheriting both his and Charlie's estates, Grace became wealthier than Theo.

At the same time, the stock market, which had made progress since 1932, began sliding during the fall of 1937. In March 1938, it hit bottom. In nine months, two-thirds of the gains made under Roosevelt's New Deal were lost. Adding to the economic distress, the political situation in Europe was worsening.

At Avon Old Farms School, another storm was threatening. Dean Richard Sears informed Theo that Provost Kammerer was neglecting his duties. He had stopped visiting classes, and his secretary was doing his work. He was also spending a great deal of time off campus, supposedly on admissions trips. Despite Sears's accusations, Theo felt helpless. She worried that if she confronted Kammerer and he resigned, the newspaper headlines would critically damage Avon.

Theo, who was now 71 years old, lacked the strength and energy to fight. More than likely, she was also suffering from fatigue brought on by diabetes. Slipping into depression, she went to London in the summer of 1938, where she consulted several mediums for advice.

A spirit with "very clear skin, almost a white face with blue eyes, and a very fine expression" appeared to Miss Bacon. It was Harris Whittemore.

"I miss him terribly," Theo exclaimed. "He was very wonderful. He was helping me and his going was a calamity to me. Please give him my love, he was one of the truest friends I ever had."

Harris would help her again, the medium declared. But Theo must go on with her life on earth.

"I dread going on," Theo muttered.

The medium responded, "You must live for another four years." Another vision appeared. "I am seeing farms and lovely land, you can go for miles and miles."

"About 3,000 acres," Theo interrupted, certain that the medium was seeing Avon Old Farms School.

"Young men are riding horses—a lovely scene. They get well there, they love it and I should think they hate to go away, they cannot bear to leave and almost weep when they have to go," the medium continued. The school's educational policies were "similar in character to the great training centres in the next plane."

Theo must continue her efforts at Avon. "The highest work on earth is, of course, teaching," the medium pronounced. The boys who attended Avon Old Farms were sent there by the great powers, who planned to use them later on "in a ray of light." The school must carry on its spiritualist mission.

When Theo and John returned to Farmington in the fall of 1938, they saw the effects of a hurricane that had hit New England, flooding Hartford and destroying lives, homes, and businesses. But on September 30, there was good news. At a meeting in Munich, Britain's Prime Minister, Neville Chamberlain; France's Prime Minister, Édouard Daladier; and Germany's Führer, Adolph Hitler, had signed a pact that allowed Germany to take over the Sudetenland.

"I believe it is peace for our time," Chamberlain told a cheering crowd in London. Only a minority of Americans disapproved of Britain and France's appeasement of Germany's fascist dictator. From Switzerland, Princess Cantacuzene wrote Theo, "What a happiness, that for the moment the world troubles are over."

Encouraged by the apparent avoidance of war and inspired by the medium who urged that she continue her life's work, Theo again took charge of Avon Old Farms. Learning that the executive committee had deleted "Old Farms" from the school's name while she was away, she reversed their decision. Then, to stem financial losses, she discontinued the school's farm and eliminated the position of farm instructor, saving his salary of $720, and saving another $1,280 on student board and transportation.

She also decided that, no matter what the consequences, she must take action against Percy Kammerer. At a recent dinner at Hill-Stead, Mrs. Archibald MacLeish, the wife of the poet and mother of an Avon student, had complained that the provost was not providing her son with the proper care. Theo concluded that Kammerer, now in his tenth year at the school, was "lazy," "uncooperative," and "indifferent," as well as "unwilling to make any effort to increase the enrollment."

Theo later said that she also turned against Kammerer because of indiscreet comments he had made. At a dinner dance at his home, he had confided that he could never be faithful to one woman. Another time, in response to Theo's saying that the lovely new alumni secretary looked so much like him that one might think that they were brother and sister, he laughed, "Well, that is scarcely the relationship I am looking for."

Theo had hired Kammerer so that he would restore the school's reputation, but his remarks persuaded her that the flirtatious, handsome, and charming reverend "upheld no principles and had a feeble ethical sense."

"There are certain things that a man cannot do in certain occupations," Clement Scott had earlier pronounced. "In our bank, no one from the president to the least stenographer may gamble on Wall Street without being fired. And no headmaster of a school may be a moral delinquent."

Scott told Theo that there were rumors that Avon's headmaster was carrying on extramarital affairs, but he refused to confront Kammerer. "Men are very loath to approach other men when it is a question of sex immorality," Theo observed. "They move around on padded feet."

In the spring of 1939, at an executive committee meeting, Theo accused the provost of laxity in administrating the school.

Kammerer bluntly asked, "Do you want me to leave?"

"No," she dissembled, "but I wish you would show more interest in the school."

"I am interested in it," Kammerer insisted.

"Oh no, you are not," Theo retorted. "Your libido is in New York with a woman."

Kammerer did not answer. He looked down at the floor.

Having taken the plunge, Theo cited two times when she had tried to reach Kammerer in New York. She had asked his wife how to get in touch with him and had received the reply that she did not know his address. Another time, his daughter Ellie answered, "Why, Mrs. Riddle, I don't think anyone knows Father's address in New York."

Upset at the mention of his daughter, a shy girl who had suffered a disfiguring accident, Kammerer sputtered, "Ellie's just a child. Miss Goodman always has my address."

Theo persevered. Would Miss Goodman be able to find him if there were a serious problem at the school?

Kammerer angrily responded that it was none of Miss Goodman's business.

According to Theo, the conversation "went back and forth over the net like a tennis ball" without accomplishing anything.

During the meeting, Clement Scott sat silently. Afterwards he advised Theo to ease out the provost.

She agreed. Kammerer "is at present as useful as the carved figure on the prow of a ship," she remarked. She told Scott she intended to cut the provost's salary to encourage him to leave.

On a June evening in 1939, alone at Hill-Stead except for the servants, Theo noticed Earnest sitting in his customary chair. For several years, Earnest had been too feeble to attend to his duties, and Theo employed Russian émigrés as butlers to take his place. Because she valued Earnest's loyalty to the family and respected his dignity, the aged man, dressed in a tuxedo, sat in a chair by the door so that he could continue to greet Hill-Stead's guests.

Although they had lived in the same house for over six decades, Theo and Earnest had never stepped out of their roles of mistress and servant and conversed informally at any length. Sometimes their affection for each other emerged, however, for example in Earnest's note of congratulations on Theo's engagement. Another time, when a prominent Farmington family invited Earnest to their daughter's wedding, he cabled Theo, who was vacationing in Europe, asking for advice. She responded that he should accept the invitation and ordered Hill-Stead's chauffeur to drive him to the affair.

Now, in old age, the two sat and chatted. As though she suddenly realized that Earnest might have his own story, Theo asked him about himself and his family. First he spoke about his childhood as a slave on the Patterson plantation near Montgomery, Alabama. His mother was a seamstress in the Patterson house, and his father was Keenan Bollen, a white man who had joined the Confederate army and been killed in his first engagement at Charleston. After the Civil War, Earnest went to Cleveland, where Alfred hired him as a stable boy. He soon became a house boy, and finally the Popes' butler. Theo was surprised to discover that Earnest had kept in touch with his relatives down South even though he had left Hill-Stead only once to visit them. That visit was the single instance of his taking a vacation in sixty-two years. He explained that he preferred staying home at Hill-Stead.

That summer Theo and John left on what would be their last trip to Europe. While they were abroad, Russia signed a non-aggression pact with Germany in late August, and on September 1, Hitler's armies invaded Poland. Two days later, England was at war with Germany.

"If America had shown with firmness that she was for the Allies...Hitler would never have dared," Countess Helena wrote Theo. Unlike the last war when she and Nina drove their ambulance throughout Italy, the two women were "being very sedate this war." Nina had organized a group to knit "woollies," and Helena was vice president of the local chapter of the Red Cross. "What a fantastic war it is," Helena observed, "and how horrible the treatment of Jews and Poles. Those poor people."

In St. Paul, Grace started an isolationist "Defend America Committee," but she told Theo that she was "cutting loose from it." She felt it was futile to try to prevent America from becoming involved in the war now raging in Europe.

During the fall 1939 semester, Dean Sears came to Hill-Stead to give Theo and John additional negative information about the provost. Sears reported that Provost Kammerer and his wife led separate sex lives and that the provost was blatant and open in his lewd behavior. Everyone at the school, including the students, knew about his relations with the school nurse, as well as with a friend of the telephone operator. The provost's admissions trips to New York were actually rendezvous with the woman who had been his secretary in Pittsburgh. In fact, he had taken her with him when he went to Europe in 1936. To make matters even more scandalous, Mrs. Kammerer had conducted an affair with the music teacher at Avon.

Theo believed Dean Sears, though his story seemed outlandish. No longer willing to ease out the provost, she immediately contacted Clement Scott. "Now, by George, we have something," she exclaimed, instructing him to confront Dr. Kammerer.

Scott did so and accused him of immoral conduct. According to Theo, "The Doctor acknowledged the charge" to Scott. Kammerer admitted his affairs with women and agreed that he must retire as the head of the school. At the end of his confession, he became distraught. Soon after, Kammerer suffered a breakdown.

Theo suggested that the Kammerers leave before the students and faculty returned from Christmas vacation. Reverend Kammerer consented and entered a sanitarium in Washington, Connecticut. The headline in *The Hartford Courant* on January 11, 1940, read: "Kammerer Resigns As Avon Provost. Resignation Prompted by Ill Health." The article went on to say that Provost Kammerer had suffered a complete breakdown and was resting at a sanitarium.

The public suspected that once again the school's eccentric founder had dismissed a popular educator. Avon Old Farms's historian explained, "Mrs. Riddle attributed his departure to a nervous break-down. Perhaps she was right, and knew the reason why!"—the implication being that she had driven him to it.

As noted earlier, Lefty Lewis claimed that the reason for Kammerer's resignation was simply the second instance of Theo's "chloroforming" a provost because he would not obey the bizarre *Deed of Trust*. George Nebolsine urged Theo to announce publicly the reason for the provost's forced resignation, but she refused. She cared more about the school's reputation than her own, and she felt sorry for the former provost. "Consciously or unconsciously," she believed, "Dr. Kammerer has a deep feeling of inadequacy."

At the end of January 1940, the newspapers had another juicy story about Avon Old Farms. An article on the front page of *The Hartford Courant* reported that two students had been arrested for placing a bomb that had gone off at the Ensign Bickford Company, a building a few miles from the school. Luckily, no one was injured or dead, though the headline reminded readers that the explosion "Might Have Meant Big Loss of Life." Theo expelled the boys and refused to meet with one of the culprits and his mother, who came to Hill-Stead to plead his case. No matter how critical it was to keep up the school's enrollment, Theo would not allow students of bad character at Avon Old Farms.

Initially, Theo appointed Dean Sears as acting provost, but Commander Hunter became upset that she had chosen Sears instead of him. In order to prevent Hunter from carrying out his threat to leave but unwilling to put him in charge over the dean, Theo asked Sears if he would recommend someone else "under whom he could comfortably serve." Disappointed but understanding her dilemma, Sears suggested Levings Hooker Somers.

With Somers acting as interim provost, Theo started interviewing candidates. The first was a young master at Yale, John Hallowell. When Hallowell and his wife visited Hill-Stead, Theo and John were favorably impressed, although she commented that Mr. Hallowell seemed "exceedingly young." She directed Clement Scott to offer him an $8,000 salary and to give him a copy of the *Deed of Trust* and a draft of another document, *Guiding Principles*. Not much later, Theo received a letter from Hallowell, that criticized the documents because they indicated an "unwillingness on the part of the Executive Committee to allow the provost full exercise of authority." As had other candidates in previous years, Hallowell balked at the position of Aide. Theo telephoned him and rescinded an invitation to luncheon. "I could feel his surprise over the telephone," she recalled. "That was the last of him."

George Nebolsine accompanied Theo and John to New York to meet another candidate, Reverend W. Brooke Stabler, chaplain of the University of Pennsylvania. The Reverend was tall, slender, fair, and thirty-seven years old. Theo thought he looked about seventeen, and later wrote that she "wondered idly what he had done with the other twenty years."

Immediately deciding that Reverend Stabler wouldn't do, Theo pretended that she had come to ask him for recommendations. She was impressed that "without a word in defense of himself or making any claim of his own ability," he suggested Dean Walter H. Gray and Reverend C. Leslie Glenn.

When Theo met Dean Gray, she was taken by his "black eyes shining with excitement." She said to herself, "This man is more important to me than the War." This absurd statement perhaps explains Theo's less-than-successful earlier choices. Always trusting her intuition and acting impulsively, most likely Theo never thoroughly investigated the backgrounds of the first two provosts. Had she done so, she might have uncovered the weaknesses for alcohol and women that she later discovered. She saw only that both men had dynamic personalities, which she valued in educators. Thus she hired them immediately.

John, Grace, Scott, and the others on the Board were also enthusiastic about Dean Gray. Certain that he would accept, Theo had a contract drawn up and planned to announce his appointment on Founder's Day, May 25, 1940. But on May 23, *The Hartford Courant* reported that Dean Walter Gray had been promoted to suffragan bishop of Connecticut. Theo was suspicious. Had Gray used Avon's offer to "lift himself" as Professor French had ten years earlier?

She immediately contacted Stabler's second recommendation: Rev. Leslie Glenn. On July 19, Glenn and his wife arrived on Hill-Stead's grounds in an airplane he had piloted. "He had on a linen suit," Theo recalled, "and his blue eyes looked as though he had indeed come from the skies."

"Georgie and I loved our visit with you," Glenn wrote after the interview. "You and Mr. Riddle were so kind to us and we fell in love with you both at first sight! I should like to work with you. I like your ideas, I like you, and I'd enjoy it."

The feeling was mutual. Theo replied that she and John also "loved and trusted both of you at first sight. I felt that you had 'come home' to us."

Theo offered Glenn the position, but after several weeks, he informed her that he had received another offer at the Church of St. John's in Washington, a small fashionable church that President Roosevelt and his family attended. Glenn advised Theo to take another look at Reverend Brooke Stabler. Glenn had high regard for Stabler, even though "sometimes he makes a poor impression." He added some new information that made Stabler more attractive to Theo and the executive committee: "He is related to the DuPonts and has been extremely successful in raising money."

In the summer of 1940, Theo and the executive committee settled on Brooke Stabler and signed a contract with him. She thought the man had "no charm" and "no imagination," but she believed there was "absolute integrity in his face" and she had been told that he was a "great worker." She also liked Stabler's wife, who was "charming and petite," and his two young children. But she had little faith in her new provost. "By the time he is proven a failure I shall be dead," she wrote Grace. "God help me."

Dean Richard Sears. *(AOF)*.   Rector W. Brooke Stabler. *(AOF)*.

NINETEEN

"No, I don't live for *it—it IS my life"*
1940 – 1946

THEO DID NOT worry about the 1940 presidential election. Clearly, because of the dangerous world situation, the American public would ignore the unwritten rule and re-elect Roosevelt for a third term. The president had written her a note addressed "My dear Theodate," to which she had responded, "My dear Franklin." He considered Theo "an old friend," one "who has done so much in many ways for our generation and for those to come."

In the liberal *Hartford Times,* which competed with *The Hartford Courant,* appeared the announcement: "Mrs. Theodate Pope Riddle of Farmington, the noted architect, contributor to cultural movements and a registered Republican, announces today in a letter to the *Hartford Times* that she will vote for President Roosevelt at the coming election." In her letter, Theo praised Roosevelt's "courage and statesmanship in those dark days of 1933 and 1934, when banks were falling like rows of dominoes," and credited him with saving the country "from widespread and violent disturbances."

A Wilkie supporter, Grace told Theo, "to get him for President instead of the country squire we now have in the White House, I would do *any*thing."

"When you think of all the negroes, all the jews, all the reliefers, all the WPA, PWA, all the bureaucrats which have doubled in number in the past seven years, and the Kelly-Nash machine and the Hague machine, as well as all the legitimate democratic voters and all the radicals who are so much under the thumb of the jewish leaders," Grace ranted, "it seems to me ridiculous to think it [the Democratic Party] can be defeated."

Grace had attended the Republican convention, where she was glad to see "hardly a jew…not *one* in all of our delegates or alternates," unlike the Democratic convention in Chicago, where "they were thick as flies."

Grace could not understand how Theo, a person who fostered the qualities of "initiative, independence, industry, personal effort, and ambition" could be so "bemused by an elegant voice, and a lot of fine words and suave phrases." How could she support "a spoiled Mama's boy and a lot of doctrinaire socialists who are hustling us fast along the road of complete paternalism in government and the turning of a dynamic people into a lot of kept slaves?"

The Flandrau family home was in a ward in St. Paul where there were "mostly jews, Mexicans, shanty Irish, about two thirds of whom are living on relief and boasting they're safe and happy and wouldn't go to work for anything." How could New Dealers like Theo support "degenerate, lazy" people? "If you could spend a week with me, going among the common people, you would just *die*. You'd be *nauseated*."

After years of putting up with Grace's bigotry and mean-spirited, right-wing politics, Theo finally struck back. That her letter was blistering is evident in Grace's reply: "I am, you say, senile, selfish, antisocial; that I live in the dark ages of thought, without good will or kindness, or intellectual enlightenment."

Theo had also attacked Grace's wealthy friend, Alice O'Brien, who had recently built an enormous yacht. Grace argued that Theo's fortune was more reprehensible, since it was based on iron, "a commodity which is irreplaceable," while Alice's was from lumber, which "can be replaced in a few generations."

What hurt Grace most was that Theo had called her "senile." "I'm now going to get my crutches and my wheel chair," she bitterly jested, drawing a smiley face, "and totter to the polls to register a protest vote for a man I know can't win. Then I'm going out to Alice's—who, by the way, built a hospital for crippled children as well as a boat. Who lives with almost austere simplicity and who gives and gives and gives."

Despite their battle over politics, Theo and Grace continued to profess love for each other. Always unhappy in St. Paul, Grace had stayed on after Blair's and Charlie's deaths because of Alice, but she began to spend more time in Farmington, and she served as a member of Avon Old Farms School's executive committee.

In late November, Theo and John celebrated Roosevelt's victory with a luncheon at Hill-Stead, attended by Connecticut Governor Wilbur Cross, Sarah Roosevelt, and Mr. and Mrs. Hewes. Meanwhile, the president rode through the streets of Hartford shaking outstretched hands and kissing babies.

On May 6, 1941, Theo and John quietly celebrated their twenty-fifth wedding anniversary. Life at Hill-Stead had slowed down. Theo, who rarely rose before noon, did little entertaining. On December 7, 1941, a peaceful Sunday afternoon, Theo and John were listening to the radio when the program was interrupted by a startling announcement: the Japanese had attacked Pearl Harbor. The damage and death toll were staggering. Nineteen U.S. ships, including six battleships, were sunk or disabled; 150 planes were destroyed; over 2,400 soldiers and civilians were killed and almost 1,200 wounded. Japanese planes and ships also had attacked U.S. bases in the Philippines, Guam, and Midway.

The following day, President Roosevelt addressed a joint session of Congress. He solemnly declared December 7 as "a day that shall live in infamy" and asked the Senate and House to declare war on Japan.

That evening after dinner, John played solitaire in the living room. He came into the ell room to join Theo, sat down, and drank his night-cap, a Scotch highball. Then he stood up and said he suddenly felt tired. Theo put her arm around him and helped him walk upstairs.

Realizing that he was terribly weak, Theo became frightened and called frantically to the maid. Annie Jacobson scurried up the stairs. Theo later said that the maid's "Swedish lemonjuice face" was contorted with fear. Theo asked Annie to help her undress John. Embarrassed, John shook his head, "No." Then Annie said that she was just an old lady, and John allowed the two women to get him into his pajamas. He lay down on the couch next to the bed. Theo told Annie to fetch a cup of tea. When she returned, John was dead. In a manner similar to Alfred's quick, painless, and shocking death twenty-eight years earlier, John had succumbed to sudden heart failure. He was 77 years old.

On December 10, a funeral service was held at Hill-Stead, with Reverend Brooke Stabler officiating. The seventeen pallbearers included Joe Alsop, Brooks Emeny, Commander Harold Hunter, Lefty Lewis, Paul Martin, and Eugene Stein. Estranged from the family for the past two years because he had left his wife for another woman, Donald Carson did not attend his Uncle John's funeral.

John was buried in Riverside Cemetery in Farmington. A moving tribute written by Eugene Stein appeared in *The Hartford Courant*. Stein recollected that John, as ambassador to Argentina, had included young clerks at receptions and parties—which "one would never see at any other Embassy or Legation." Stein pointed out, "It was this constant delicate thoughtfulness of the little man that made all hearts go out toward Mr. Riddle."

The former Russian diplomat described John's fluency in languages, and he recalled the times when John had asked him to speak Russian at dinner. "In the beginning I would try not to make it too difficult for my host, avoiding intricate terms and colloquialisms. But with the exquisite food and generous wines, I soon forgot my good intentions and rattled away with slang and proverbs, at a terrific speed. Then, toward the end of the meal, when his pet cat had been called in from the coal-bin and had nestled in his lap, Mr. Riddle would suddenly say, 'Well, *cher* colleague, don't you think we better have some English now?'"

The grateful recipient of Theo and John's generosity and hospitality, Stein ended his tribute: "In my now long life, I have had the luck of knowing some thoroughly good men. I have not known a better one."

John's will was neither long nor complicated. In addition to a few other bequests, he left a small sum of money to Ellie Kammerer, the former provost's disfigured daughter.

Unaware that Theo anticipated joining John in the spiritual world the following year as the medium had promised, outsiders might have misinterpreted her outwardly calm acceptance of his death. "You may in the not-too-distant future wish to publish a notice about myself," Theo wrote *The Hartford Courant* to make sure that her obituary would be correct. "I am therefore asking you at this time not to refer to me as the 'daughter of the bicycle man' [the Pope bicycle was manufactured in Connecticut]. My father was Alfred Atmore Pope."

But 1942 passed, and the medium's prophecy that Theo would live only four more years was proved wrong. At 75, she still looked and felt well. Grace observed that Theo became "handsomer as she grew old." She held her short, solid figure straight and wore a "kind of close wrapped wig of blondish hair"; her blue eyes were superb. A cousin's son, who visited Theo while he was a student at Yale, said that in her seventies, Theo was "robust" and "inexhaustible."

Theo continued to read several books simultaneously and to write to friends and relatives, mostly to Grace when she was back in St. Paul. In July 1943, she wrote Wendell Wilkie about improving his image. Theo considered Shakespeare's "For the apparel oft proclaims the man" an important truth, so important that she placed the maxim as the final statement in Avon Old Farms's *Deed of Trust*. Students dressed like gentlemen so that they would act like gentlemen, which, in the true sense of the word, meant being courteous and kind to people of every class and condition. To Wilkie, Theo wrote, "In many of your photographs, you are the only man in a group who shows an expanse of shirt front, with belt and gaudy tie."

After John's death, Theo described her life as being "closed in." "In the evening I go up to bed; in the morning I come down to luncheon and to my chair in the sitting room." Those she was closest to had moved away. Grace divided her time between Farmington and St. Paul. Dolly was now married and living in the South. Paul and his wife remained on the West Coast, and, in 1939, Donald had moved to California.

Early in the morning, on December 11, 1943, about a week before his ninetieth birthday, Earnest died. After his death, Theo was astonished to learn that he had hardly spent any of his earnings. His estate was worth more than John's. In his will, Earnest left $40,000 to Theo, $40,000 to his relatives, and $20,000 to charity. Although Theo's fortune had dwindled so drastically that she finally sold several of Hill-Stead's paintings, she did not feel right about keeping the money and sent her inheritance to Earnest's relatives. Earnest Bohlen was buried in Farmington's cemetery next to John.

After the funeral, Theo came down with grippe. But when Countess Helena's nephew, Roger Machell, telephoned that he had arrived on the *Queen Mary,* she invited him to Hill-Stead. Roger had been badly wounded in France and was now working with the British Ministry of Information. "I was in the midst of my illness," Theo confided to Grace, "but was able to conceal it from Roger and did we have a wonderful time, or, at least, I did."

Roger told her that, because of the Nazis' blitz of London, the directors of the Tate gallery had asked Countess Helena to store portraits in her country home. Three men came along to guard the boxes of paintings and, if Helena's house were in danger of being bombed, to move them. For the past two years, the guards had been a terrible nuisance, getting drunk and chasing girls in the village, but, Roger added, there was "never a murmur from Helena."

In 1944 while World War II raged on, Theo, at seventy-seven, finally engaged in battle with Avon's third provost. Immediately upon his arrival on campus four years earlier, Reverend W. Brooke Stabler had made changes. After informing the faculty and students that he was not to be called "Provost," but instead "Rector" as appropriate for a clergyman, he proceeded to institute communion services, confirmation classes, and other elements of Episcopal Christianity. In addition, reviving the earlier attempt to drop "Old Farms," he changed the school's name to The Avon School. Theo had not protested. She stayed in the background and allowed Stabler to do whatever he wished.

Then she learned that Reverend Stabler was about to eliminate the dress code requirement. Because of the war, Brooks Brothers could no longer supply the material for the school outfits; therefore, following the lead of other prep schools, Stabler decided to allow the students to dress informally. No longer would they attend classes wearing suits, walk about the campus in gray flannel pants and plum blazers with the image of a winged beaver on the breast pocket, or appear for dinner at the Refectory looking elegant in black jackets, black bow ties, and striped gray trousers.

Stabler was subverting Theo's *Deed of Trust,* which mandated uniformity of dress and justified it: "The Founder has observed that when boys are thrown together as in a boarding school, and are permitted at will to wear clothes of varying styles and garish colours, there is a tendency toward exhibitionism which unduly expands the ego and results in self-consciousness and conceit. A boy so dressed has the feeling that he has actually accomplished something, when, as a matter of fact, affectation in dress is a deterrent to accomplishment with head or hands."

According to Dean Sears's wife, in addition to Theo's demand that Avon retain its dress code, she also clashed with Dr. Stabler when he ordered a flimsy, wooden portable chapel to be set up on the campus. "Mrs. Riddle made it clear that she would tolerate changes to her curriculum, to the name of her school, to the format of certain customs," Mrs. Sears commented, "but NEVER to her architecture!"

The issue that caused an impasse between Theo and the rector was the one that had always been troublesome: the position of Aide, which Theo maintained was central to the mission of the school. Like previous provosts and candidates for provost, Stabler wanted complete autonomy. He insisted that he be allowed to run the school without the Aide and without interference from the founder or the board. In May 1943, Reverend Stabler and his lawyer presented an ultimatum: the board of directors must give up its authority for a year, during which time there would be no Aide, or "he and all the members of the faculty would resign and sue for their next year's salary."

Theo later wrote that this threat was "one of the greatest shocks I have ever had." She asked Stabler to meet with her, Attorney Otis T. Bradley, and Grace, who recently had returned to Hill-Stead's cottage. Bradley posed a question to the rector: "If you were asked to accept a position at the head of a Catholic institution, you would have to conform, wouldn't you?" Stabler did not answer. Bradley then repeated the question but substituted "military" for "Catholic." Stabler still did not reply.

Bradley made his point. "Well, Mrs. Riddle is trying to found a school which is entirely different from the usual preparatory school." When Stabler accepted the leadership of the school, he was surely aware that Avon, like a Catholic or a military institution, had a different, distinct mission. Refusal to abide by the *Deed of Trust,* which spelled out that mission, was tantamount to breaking his contract, and central to the *Deed of Trust* were statements that firmly established the position of Aide and the prerogatives of the founder and board of directors.

Stabler's lawyer then asked whether Theo would step down from the board of directors. She laughed and replied, "Certainly not."

Stabler then stated that he and the entire faculty were prepared to protest Theo's interference. On March 12, 1944, having accepted another position at the Cranbrook School, Reverend Stabler handed in his resignation. Two months later, according to a young teacher, Richard Brown, the rector "instructed the entire faculty to come to Hill-Stead and resign in a body."

Since accepting another position invalidated his ultimatum, what Stabler hoped to accomplish by telling the faculty to resign is unclear. Perhaps he thought that Theo and the board would cave in to his demands and not accept his resignation. Then he would rescind his commitment to the Cranbrook School. Obeying Stabler's directive, the faculty went to Hill-Stead and resigned, probably to demonstrate their loyalty to the rector, who, if they lost their jobs at Avon, might hire them at his new school.

Devastated by the incident, Theo sent letters to the faculty, in which she announced that at the end of the spring semester, she would close Avon School. "Mr. Stabler knows that he and all of the members of the faculty have broken Avon," she began. "When the faculty came to Hill-Stead to see me and resigned in a body, I was stunned with surprise. If three or four of you who had been at Avon so happily for so many years, those of you whom my husband and I admired and considered our friends, had stayed by me I would have felt that I must struggle to keep the school alive, and it could have been done." She also let the faculty know "how loyal to the school and to me all of the members of the Technical Staff have been."

Through the years, Theo was often asked the question: "You just live for the school, don't you?" Her answer was always the same. "No, I don't live *for* it—it IS my life." But she saw no reason to continue the life of the school unless it embodied her ideals and perpetuated her vision. In a letter that she sent to every alumnus, each of whom she referred to as "my son," she announced Avon's closing, but she also expressed optimism. She had "high hopes of reopening" the school after the war.

Theo then proposed to Franklin Roosevelt that he use the soon-to-be vacant school as a rehabilitation center for wounded veterans. The president accepted the offer, and in June 1944, Theo turned over the buildings to the army, which converted Avon School into the Old Farms Convalescent Hospital, a facility for soldiers blinded in the war.

The hospital's program brought an enormous amount of attention to the school, which resulted in an increased recognition across the country of the beauty and originality of its architecture. Photographs of the school's buildings appeared in magazines and re-established the reputation of their architect.

Film stars, including Ann Sheriden, visited the campus, and authors wrote about the hospital's innovative training program, which included blind soldiers working in the print shop with Max Stein. The novelist, Bayard Kendrick, stayed at Theo's cottage and wrote *Lights Out,* which, several years later, was made into the film *Bright Victory.* Henry Barry, a blind soldier who went through Old Farms's program, wrote about the hospital in *I'll Be Seeing You.*

Theo was thrilled with the bustling activity at the school and with the excellence of the program. "They are doing perfectly incredible things at Avon," she exclaimed. When the community started a drive to build an indoor pool for the veterans, she was the first to donate, and her gift of $1,000 was among the largest.

In contrast to her fury at Reverend Stabler's erecting a portable chapel among Avon's magnificent, red sandstone buildings, Theo did not protest when the army proposed building two barracks of brick or concrete. "They have selected as the location the end of the Village Green," she wrote Grace, "in which case they would have to cut down all the trees!" The exclamation point was the only indication of horror.

Before the 1944 election, Theo informed Grace, "Of course I shall vote for Roosevelt." But in January 1945, Theo became dismayed over the president's appointment of Henry Wallace, whom she referred to as "that clown Wallace." "Oh Grace," she sighed, "I am really appalled over this because it is clearly an expression of his personal gratitude to Wallace, with no thought whatever to the country." But, after receiving Grace's ecstatic reponse to Theo's finally recognizing the awful truth about the president, Theo replied, "Your note convinces me that Roosevelt is a genius."

When President Roosevelt died in April, Theo thought it "wonderful that he did not suffer and did not linger." The *Hartford Times* quoted Theo's praise of Roosevelt as "the father of our little people for whom he demanded justice and relief." In an article with the headline "Mrs. Riddle Sees Hope of World in 'Four Freedoms'," Theo extolled FDR's great love of humanity and ended, "We shall not look upon his like again."

In the fall of 1945, Theo seemed well and energetic. In letters to Grace, she did not mention any health problems. Instead she expressed concern about the younger woman's latest real or imagined affliction. Theo also lived a fairly active life. In November, she entertained a houseful of guests after the Harvard-Yale football game, and she continued to manage the farm on the hospital's grounds. When it ran up losses, she fired off a note to the overseer, Hans Hess, which showed that age had not softened a formidable temper. "I want you to understand, damn it all, that Old Farms is not a hobby," she sputtered, "and if you do not make the farm pay in this next year, you will find that you have worked yourself out of the position of farmer at Old Farms."

The army still occupied the buildings, but, in anticipation of their being returned at the end of the war, Theo amended her will so that, if she died before that time, Avon Old Farms School could be reopened. Of course, it was to be "maintained and operated in strict conformity with the provisions" of the *Deed of Trust* and "particular care should be taken at all times to see that the students wear either the regulation clothing or the semi-military type of clothing." And the position of Aide would continue.

During 1946, Theo's health began to decline. In June, she had painful cystitis. Arriving from St. Paul to be with her, Grace summoned the doctor to Hill-Stead on August 8. He found that a kidney problem had worsened and that Theo was suffering from uremia. In the early morning hours of August 30, Grace realized that Theo's condition was critical. She again called Doctor Bartner, but nothing could be done. At 3:00 a.m., with Grace sitting next to the bed, Theo quietly died.

Theo's will states that she had spent over $7,000,000 on Avon Old Farms School, which explains why her estate was smaller than most people supposed. Although she wrote that she wished the school to be reopened, Theo did not bequest funds to make that possible. Instead, she left $400,000 in trust to operate Hill-Stead as a museum, and she set up an interlocking trust, which "provided that, should Hill-Stead not succeed as a museum, it was to be closed, and the paintings and furnishings sold to benefit Avon Old Farms School—should the School re-open."

Theo's estate was worth approximately $2,300,000, which, after subtracting $400,000 to run Hill-Stead Museum, she divided among dozens of beneficiaries. The largest personal bequests were $100,000 each to Grace, Dolly, Paul, and Donald. She gave annuities and cash to doctors, friends, protégés, relatives, Russian émigrés and English aristocrats, servants, and servants' children.

She left money to Elizabeth Riddell, who, Theo explained, had "risked her life to join me in England after the *Lusitania* disaster," and to Mrs. Theodore Naish, the woman who noticed Theo's eyelash flickering when she lay among the dead bodies pulled from the Irish Sea. Theo explained that she had omitted some Pope and Brooks cousins "not in forgetfulness or for lack of affection but because their families were unusually well remembered in my father's will and in my mother's will."

Theo also directed that she be buried on Hill-Stead's grounds and provided a sketch of the site between the two greenhouses and under a pine tree. She ordered that the bodies of John, Gordon, and Earnest be moved and buried there as well—John on her left and Gordon on her right. Next to Gordon, she reserved a plot for Annie Jacobson, and Earnest was to be placed beyond Annie.

After the funeral, however, Theo's body was brought to Cedar Hill Cemetery in Hartford because Farmington officials refused to permit the establishment of a private cemetery at Hill-Stead. The town won the ensuing legal battle, and Theo joined her family at Farmington's Riverside Cemetery. Of the many lawsuits she had engaged in, this was the only one she lost.

The obituaries in the local papers told how Theo had barely escaped death when the *Lusitania* was torpedoed. They lauded her as an architect: the designer of Westover School, private residences, and Avon Old Farms School—neglecting to mention Hill-Stead, the Hop Brook School, and the reconstruction of Roosevelt Birthplace. They did not refer to her psychical research activities or to her contributions to progressive education. And, following Theo's instructions after John's death, they did not confuse her with the bicycle-manufacturing Pope family.

EPILOGUE

IN 1947, Old Farms Convalescent Hospital closed, the army and the blind veterans left, and the government paid $100,000 to cover damages to the campus. Henry Perkins, who was in charge of the Pope-Brooks Foundation, contacted alumni who supported his efforts to reopen the school. Donald W. Pierpont, an instructor at Columbia University, was appointed provost. Pierpont spent a year raising money. He then hired a faculty, recruited students, and, in 1948, Avon Old Farms School resumed operations.

Newsweek and *Time* greeted the event. Under the headline "For Little Gentlemen," *Time* described the school as "an $18 million imitation English Village" built by an "eccentric old woman." The article also contained an oblique reference to the infamous *Deed of Trust:* "Pierpont was willing to comply with the minor provisions of Avon's code, such as fly-casting and a school uniform, so long as he didn't have to be too literal about the major ones." Pierpont "doesn't believe, as Mrs. Riddle did, that there is one class privileged to produce gentlemen."

Theo would have approved of Provost Pierpont, who devoted the rest of his life to the school. He generally followed her philosophy of education while broadening her dictates. For example, Avon's outstanding music program more than conforms to the *Deed of Trust's* requirement: "Instruction shall be given in choral singing, emphasizing hymns, ballads, and spirituals."

Provost Pierpont also adhered to "the extensive use of the print shop, forge, farm, forest, stable, art studio, ceramic shop, and woodworking shop." Students were able to study surveying and navigation as well as drafting and design. Because of her own difficulties trying to learn mathematics and languages when she was a girl, Theo would have applauded Pierpont's expanding the program in remedial reading.

After Pierpont's death in 1969, his successor, George Trautman, said that the "breathtaking" campus attracted him to Avon. "It is, in a certain way," he stated, "the most singularly beautiful place in the world." According to the official history of the school, Trautman spent the next twenty-nine years upholding Theo's "highest ideals, while facing, head-on the challenges of changing times." The headmaster "embraced the *Deed of Trust,* and said he 'found very little I disagree with in its philosophy.'"

Trautman not only maintained "the coat and tie rule" but also insisted during the turbulent Vietnam era that "no student would be permitted to register unless his haircut was short enough to satisfy the Headmaster personally." Like Pierpont, Trautman devoted himself completely to the school, increasing its financial stability and academic reputation. On his retirement, a booklet commemorating "The Trautman Years" notes: "Embracing Mrs. Riddle's original philosophy, Trautman sought to break the stereotype of the 'elitist' private boys' school by seeking out an ethnically and culturally diverse student body. In 1998, 14 nations are represented; 16 percent of the student body are members of a minority group." Financial aid had increased to approximately $1,700,000. During Trautman's tenure, following the petition of a student who discovered that the founder's name did not appear on any of Avon's buildings, the school named the Refectory after Theo in 1992.

Today, Avon Old Farms still enforces a dress code: students wear jackets, ties, "appropriate" pants, and shoes to class; for Sunday evening vespers and special occasions, they are required to wear white shirts, ties, polished tie-shoes, and the official navy-blue Avon blazer with the winged beaver crest.

Vestiges of Theo's progressive program continue. In addition to community service, every boy has a job at the school. There is no longer a requirement to work on the farm because the farm no longer exists. There is a student council but not the town meeting and court system.

Theo would commend the school's policy of allowing no second chances to students who are caught stealing or taking drugs. She probably would not approve, however, of the change in the athletic program. Like most independent schools, Avon now participates in interscholastic sports.

Thirty years after Theo's death, *The Hartford Courant* published an article with the headline: "Rich Woman's Will Still Poses a Riddle." As is apparent from the pun, the writer of the article found it humorous that Theodate Pope Riddle left "the most complicated estate in the town's history."

The controversial issue in Theo's will concerns the interlocking trusts of Hill-Stead Museum and Avon Old Farms School. After the school reopened, it engaged in several court battles with the museum because the will stipulates that if Hill-Stead were to fail as a museum, its paintings and furniture were to be sold to benefit the school. The school lost in court, and for years the relationship between the two institutions was strained.

Theo's architectural achievements have had the greatest impact on the students of Westover School, the Hop Brook School, and Avon Old Farms School, and on the general public who visit Roosevelt Birthplace and Hill-Stead Museum. In 1979, the National Park Service hosted an exhibition of Theo's work at the Birthplace, which, as a National Historic Site and the nation's first Victorian period restoration, has hosted hundreds of thousands of visitors. In October 1998, the Arts & Entertainment channel featured Hill-Stead on *America's Castles*. Hill-Stead Museum is also a National Historic Site; every year, 30,000 visitors tour the house and view its magnificent collection of Impressionist paintings, extraordinary clocks, rare Italian and Chinese porcelain, and elegant furnishings. They also attend a summer poetry-reading series in Hill-Stead's sunken garden and other functions that the museum sponsors. On a sunny afternoon, one sees joggers running along the winding private drive and, on the crest of the knoll, artists seated at their easels painting the idyllic scene of the stately house and its gardens, the fields beyond, and the blue mountains in the distance.

"Yes, I think you'll find the place pretty well just as you left it when we took it over."

Cartoon from *Punch.(AOF).*

NOTES

IN GENERAL, I do not repeat citations that are apparent in the text. My apologies for any oversights. Pope Family memorabilia, documents, correspondence, photographs, and interviews; JWR's *Memoirs*, notebooks, correspondence and other documents; TPR's diaries, journals, notes, most correspondence, transcripts of sittings with mediums, dictation to E. McCarthy, drawings, and *Documents and Comments* are housed in the Archives of the Hill-Stead Museum, Farmington, Connecticut. TPR's *Memoirs*, some correspondence, other documents, photographs, and drawings are at Avon Old Farms School. Most correspondence and other documents of the Flandrau Family are at the Arizona Historical Society/Tucson; other Flandrau correspondence and materials are at the Minnesota Historical Society in St. Paul; copies of many of these documents are available at the Archives of the Hill-Stead Museum. Elizabeth Failing Connor's diary is at Miss Porter's School in Farmington, CT. The Archives of Westover School house photographs and other documents relating to TPR and Mary Hillard.

ABBREVIATIONS

AHS	Arizona Historical Society/Tucson—Flandrau Family Collection, #1018.
AOF	Avon Old Farms School
HS	Hill-Stead Museum
MHS	Minnesota Historical Society
MPS	Miss Porter's School
WS	Westover School
MC	Mary Cassatt
EFC	Emily Failing Connor
ARC	Anna Roosevelt Cowles
BE	Brooks Emeny
BF	(Wm) Blair Flandrau
CMF	Charles M. Flandrau
GHF	Grace H. Flandrau
EF	Edwin Friend
HG	Helena Gleichen
MH	Mary Hillard
AJ	Augustus (Gus) Jaccaci
HJ	Henry James
AAP	Alfred Atmore Pope

ABP	Ada Brooks Pope
JWR	John Wallace Riddle
TPR	Theodate Pope Riddle. I have used this abbreviation throughout, although Theodate was Effie Brooks Pope until she was 19, then Theodate Pope, and finally Theodate Pope Riddle when, at 49 she married John Riddle.
BS	Belle Sherwin
LTT	Leonard T. Troland
HW	Harris Whittemore

BOOK JACKET

most distinguished American —Gill, Brendan. "What Climbs the Stairs?" *Sarah Lawrence Alumnae Bulletin* (Summer 1975), p. 8.

intuitive —TPR, *Memoirs*, April 27, 1937, Number 4113-25. AOF and HS Archives.

ONE: "She will probably end up in jail." 1867 – 1886

1. *Nugent Publishing Company* —TPR to ABP, March 11, 1915. HS Archives.

1. *"a gentleman's profession"* —Judith Paine, *Theodate Pope Riddle: Her Life and Work* (New York: The National Park Service, 1979), p. 1.

1. *Eton Roundabouts* [and other details of Theodate's parents' courtship] —TPR, *Memoirs*, April 27, 1937, Number 4113-21. AOF and HS Archives. TPR writes: "When father was sixteen, he gave mother a ring. Neither of them ever had any love except for each other."

2. *"atmosphere of gaiety"* —Frances E. Pope, "Notes of a Quiet Life: 1840-1937," 1917, p. 29. HS Archives.

2. *married on a Tuesday evening, May 3, 1866* —Marriage invitation. HS Archives.

2. *souvenirs of Maine* —Louise Pope Johnson, "The Passing of an Elderly Quaker," 1949, p. 1. HS Archives.

2. *born at midnight, on February 2, 1867* —Date recorded in Pope family Bible. Other dates, usually one or ten years later, appear, e.g., on TPR's death certificate and gravestone (1868) and her AIA membership (1877).

2. *a "love child"* —Interview: D. Carson with Polly Huntington and Sandra Wheeler, May 3, 1994. HS Archives.

3. *would not bear a child* —TPR, *Memoirs*, Number 4113-24. April 28, 1937. AOF and HS Archives. TPR writes that her mother "deliberately brought on two miscarriages" during the two years after TPR's birth.

3. *light, crispy donuts* —Louise Pope Johnson, "The Passing of an Elderly Quaker," 1949, p. 3. HS Archives

3. *net Quaker bonnet* —Ibid., p. 1.

3. *"body isn't me"* —TPR, *Memoirs*, Number 4113-25. April 28, 1937. AOF and HS Archives. TPR writes that the experience caused her to avoid looking into mirrors.

3. *Ada never held* —Ibid.

3. *Mark Hanna* —Gordon Ramsey, *Aspiration and Perseverance: The History of Avon Old Farms School* (Avon, Conn.: privately printed, 1984), p. 2.

4. *"they smelt of business"* —TPR, *Memoirs*, Number 4113-20. April 27, 1937. AOF and HS Archives.

4. *settle strikes* —TPR, Diary of 1886. HS Archives

4. *unhappy in the family's new home* —Ibid.

4. *"I am seldom myself"* —Ibid.

7. *listen to advice* —TPR, *Memoirs*, Number 4113-25, April 28, 1937. AOF and HS Archives.

8. *singing old songs* —Ibid.

9. *"end up in jail"* —This quotation and the chapter title are taken from TPR, Notes, transcribed by E. McCarthy, 1941. Number 935. HS Archives.

10. *afraid she will stop* —TPR to AAP, May 22, 1886.

11. *a college degree* —TPR, *Memoirs*, Number 4113-20, April 27, 1937. AOF and HS Archives.

12. *colonial days* —"Proof of Eligibility." The Colonial Dames of the State of Connecticut trace TPR's descent from Kenelm Winslow of Massachusetts, who was the representative for Marshfield, Mass., at the Plymouth General Court from 1642-1644. HS Archives.

TWO: "This, what I want...is making me miserable." 1886 – 1888

14. *"I would prefer to guide"* —John T. Dallas, *Mary Robbins Hillard* (Concord, N.H.: Rumford Press, 1944), p. 41.

15. *bitter aversion to marriage* —EFC, Diary. February 16, 1888. MPS.

15. *"an indestructible school"* —TPR, *Memoirs*, Number 4113-28, April 28, 1937. AOF and HS Archives.

15. *"fond of argument"* —TPR, Diary, November 16, 1886-July 10, 1887. HS Archives.

15. *"opium eating"* —Pencil note written on an essay titled "Marks of True Womanhood," Number 716A and B. HS Archives.

16. *Miss Mary Hillard* —John T. Dallas, *Mary Robbins Hillard* (Concord, N.H.: Rumford Press, 1944), p. 82

16. *"to educate and elevate"* —Ibid., p.27.

16. *writhed in jealousy* —EFC, Diary, February 29, 1888. MPS.

17. *"this, what I want"* —This quotation and the chapter title are from TPR, Diary, 1888. HS Archives.

18. *job on a farm* —TPR, Diary, spring 1887. Another version appears in TPR, *Memoirs*, 4113-29,30,31, which she wrote fifty years later. AOF and HS Archives.

20. *"how natural"* –Letter from Elizabeth Brooks Emeny to TPR, 1888. HS Archives.

20. *put a strain* —EFC, Diary, April 12, 1888. MPS.

21. *Snowed in* —TPR, Diary, HS Archives; and EFC, Diary, March 20, 1888. MPS.

21. *"a bright woman"*–EFC, Diary, March 16, 1888

22. *"had run after Theo"*—Ibid., July 6, 1888.

22. *"the Rest Cure"*—Mrs. Dow to TPR, March 26, [1888]. HS Archives.

THREE: "Of all the unlovely things." 1888 – 1890

The title, quotations and incidents concerning Harris, the trip, Theo's debut, and moving to Farmington are from TPR's Diaries, August 28, 1888-May 21, 1890. HS Archives.

35. *embroidering or crocheting*—M. Carpentier to TPR, [October 1889]. HS Archives.

35. *"heart and hands"*—S. Porter to TPR, November 6, 1889. HS Archives.

36. *"Four dollars a week"*—G. Brooks to TPR, [June 1890], Number 509A. HS Archives.

FOUR: "It will be a Pope House." 1890 – 1901

Except where otherwise noted, quotations about and descriptions concerning TPR's arriving in Farmington and renovating and living in the O'Rourkery are from TPR's Diaries June 11, 1890–March 3, 1891, and from TPR, *Memoirs*, Numbers 4113-32,33,34,35, April 28, 1937. AOF and HS Archives.

39. *"Clean and fresh-airy"*—Alice Hamilton to TPR, January 1891, Number 235. HS Archives.

40. *"the kind of man"*—TPR, Diaries, August 26, 1890–September 19, 1890. HS Archives.

40. *a fine theme*—Ibid.

40. *"stepped over a frame"*—TPR, Diaries, August 29, 1890-March 3, 1891. HS Archives.

40. *very dearest friend*—Ibid.

40. *"study of the Bible"*—Ibid.

40. *"danced, played whist"*—Ibid.

41. *chickens belonging*—TPR, *Memoirs*, Numbers 4113-35,36. AOF and HS Archives.

41. *"unfortunate neighbors for me"*—TPR to Mrs. Keith, February 20, 1940. HS Archives.

41. *train trip west*—TPR, Diaries, July 10, 1892–August 17, 1892.

42. *ancient wooden gates*—TPR, *Memoirs*, Number 4113-33. AOF and HS Archives.

42. *"you do run around"*—Ibid.

42. *"really repellent"*—TPR to AAP and ABP, May 8,[1889]. HS Archives.

42. *controversial "new religion"*—James W. Lett, "The Persistent Popularity of the Paranormal," *Skeptical Inquirer,* Summer 1992, p. 1.

42. *a large following*—Alex Owen, *The Darkened Room: Women, Power and Spiritualism in Late Victorian England* (Philadelphia: University of Pennsylvania Press, 1990), p. 18.

43. *"white crow"*—W. James, *Science,* Vol. VII, No. 172, April 15, 1898.

43. *engaging a detective*—R.L. Moore, qtd. in Deborah J. Coon, "Testing the Limits of Sense and Science: American Experimental Psychologists Combat Spiritualism, 1880-1920," *American Psychologist,* Vol. 47, No. 2, February 1992, p. 147.

43. *"eyes and ears and wits"*—W. James, *Science,* Vol. VII, No. 172, April 15, 1898.

43. *distinguished people*—Sandra Wheeler, "Spiritualism in Nineteenth Century America: A Case Study in the Emergence of a Democratic Epistemology," December 1989, p. 23. Privately owned. Also see James Webb, *The Occult Underground.* (LaSalle, Ill.: Open Court Publishing Co., 1974), pp. 37ff, and R.W.B. Lewis, *The Jameses: A Family Narrative* (New York: Farrar, Straus and Giroux, 1991), p. 493.

43. *Sigmund Freud and Carl Jung*—William H. Salter, *The Society for Psychical Research: An Outline of its History.* 1948. Reprint, London: [Society for Psychical Research], 1970), p. 31.

43. *Quakers in particular*—Ann Braude, *Radical Spirits: Spiritualism and Women's Rights in Nineteenth-Century America* (Boston: Beacon Press, 1989), pp. 58, 66.

44. *Lily Dale*—Ibid., p. 96.

44. *loose clothing*—Ibid., p. 154.

44. *parsley, and lettuce*—TPR to ABP, September 29, 1893. HS Archives.

44. *Alice mentioned that Agnes*—A. Hamilton to TPR, January 1891. HS Archives.

44. *a female architect*—Susana Torre, *Women in American Architecture: A Historic and Contemporary Perspective* (New York: Whitney Library of Design, 1977), p. 65.

45. *partial commission*—Memo to the Board of Governors from Director, January 19, 1987. HS Archives. *The Dictionary of Art,* ed. by Jane S. Turner (New York: Grove, 1996), Vol. 15, p. 237, states that TPR designed Hill-Stead "in cooperation with the architect Stanford White." Eugene R. Gaddis, in *Magician of the Modern: Chick Austin and the Transformation of the Arts in America* (New York: Knopf, 2000), p. 83, also states that Stanford White designed Hill-Stead "in part." This seems to be a common error. Katharine Warwick states, in *The Hill-Stead Museum: A Guidebook* (August 1988, p. 61): "There is no documentary evidence to confirm that Stanford White…was personally responsible for the design…most of Theodate's communications were with Egerton Swartwout, one of White's principal assistant designers, as well as with William R. Mead, the partner most concerned with the business affairs of the firm." I did not find any letters in the Hill-Stead Museum archives to or from Stanford White concerning the design and construction of Hill-Stead.

46. *"it will be a Pope house"*—This quotation and the chapter title are from TPR to W. Mead, September 17, 1898. TPR's letter to W. Mead is at the Columbia University Archives, Documents Numbers 8 and 9. TPR's other letters to McKim, Mead, and White are at the New York Historical Society; copies are at the HS Archives. Other directions concerning construction to McKim, Mead, & White and to Swartwout are at HS Archives: Numbers 977, 984, 985, 986, 993; Fall 1898; Spring 1899. AAP paid $50,000 to M,M,& W, who reduced their fee by 5 percent because of TPR's work. The contractor, Richard F. Jones of Unionville, Conn., submitted a bill for $18,316.

47. *In Whistler's correspondence*—James Whistler to AAP, September 1894. HS Archives.

48. *"a dreadful fire"*—ABP to AAP, [August 10, 1899]. Photograph in newspaper, Number 651. HS Archives.

49. *camping trip*—TPR, Diaries, September 9, 1899-December 26, 1902.

50. *her "sickness" descended*—Ibid.

50. *Dr. Charles Loomis Dana*—Ibid. When Theo met him, Charles Loomis Dana, M.D., L.L.D. (1852-1935), was a widower with a teenage daughter. He was a professor of neurology at Cornell University Medical College and a consulting neurologist at Manhattan State Hospital for the Insane.

51. *name the estate "Hill-Stead"*—originally there was no hyphen; it was later inserted by TPR.

FIVE: "Split the canopy and peep through." 1901 – 1907

54. *"momentary effect"*—Henry James, "The American Scene," *North American Review.* 1907, p. 650.

54. *"finest Colonial Revival house"*—Mark Hewitt and Richard Cheek, *The Architect and the Country House: 1890–1940* (New Haven: Yale University Press, 1990), p. 157.

54. *the hearth as a symbol*—H.-R. Hitchcock, qtd. in Meryle Secrest, *Frank Lloyd Wright: A Biography* (Chicago: The University of Chicago Press, 1992), p. 130.

54. *Mr. Steinway*—Georgia Sheron, "Theo Pope's House," *Yankee Magazine.* Spring 1979, p. 2. The article also appears in *Westover Alumnae Magazine,* Spring 1979.

54. *"apt to sleep together"*—This and quotations and descriptions in several of the following paragraphs are from TPR's diaries from May 30, 1901-October 1, 1902.

56. *Anna Roosevelt Cowles*—Lillian Rixey, *Bamie: Theodore Roosevelt's Remarkable Sister* (New York: David McKay Co., Inc.), 1963.

59. *"Dow Row"*—The Hartford Diaries of Mary Vaill Dudley Talcott (Mrs. Charles Hooker Talcott), 1896-1919 [4 vols.], by Mary Dudley Vaill Talcott and Alice Dudley Talcott Enders. Privately published, 1990: Vol. II, June 23, 1903, pp. 335-36. Also, Vol. IV, Notes, pp. 547-548.

60. *"telling the truth"*—George McLean to TPR, August 13, 1902. HS Archives.

60. *"seek its interpretation"*—Ibid., August 19, 1902.

61. *"if you have seen Hodgson"*—MC to TPR, November 30, [1903]. HS Archives.

61. *investigate the Theosophical Society*—*Proceedings of the Society for Psychical Research,* Vol. III, Part IX, 1885, 201ff., qtd. in James Webb, *The Occult Underground* (LaSalle, Ill.: Open Court Publishing Co., 1974), p. 89.

62. *sparsely furnished room*—transcripts and synopses of sittings are in HS Archives.

64. *"split the canopy"*—This quotation and the chapter title are from the Piper sitting, March 22, 1904. HS Archives.

66. *"dreadful Mrs. Piper"*—Alice James, qtd. in R.W.B. Lewis, *The Jameses: A Family Narrative* (New York: Farrar, Straus and Giroux, 1991), p. 494.

66. *said he was "alien"*—Ibid., HJ qtd., pp. 485, 491.

66. *start a fire*—TPR to AAP, September 6, 1910. HS Archives. TPR writes this after William James's death.

66. *"not a good girl"* —William James to TPR, May 8, 1908. HS Archives.

67. *"thought I was a Frenchman"* —Richard Hodgson to TPR, December 30, 1904. HS Archives.

68. *"most readily with you"* —George Dorr to TPR, January 10, 1906. HS Archives.

68. *a back-stabber* —Lucy Edmunds to TPR, January 12, 1906. HS Archives.

68. *"too much time"* —TPR to George Dorr, January 8, 1906. HS Archives.

68. *"less of an exception"* —James H. Hyslop to TPR, January 6, 1908. HS Archives.

69. *"old English methods"* —Ibid., February 3, 1906.

69. *Clark University* —Deborah J. Coon, "Testing the Limits of Sense and Science," *American Psychologist*, Vol. 47, No. 2, February 1992, p. 146.

69. *check for $25,000* —James H. Hyslop to TPR, June 26, 1906. Number 2089. HS Archives.

69. *"incorrigible idiot"* —James H. Hyslop to TPR, July 11, 1906. HS Archives.

SIX: "The fear feels good." 1907 – 1910

73. *"always open"* —ABP to TPR, February 25, 1904. HS Archives.

73. *apple orchards* —Printed notice. Number 742. HS Archives.

73. *"tired farmers' wives"* —TPR to ABP, August 10, 1907. HS Archives.

74. *"not allow him to butt in"* —TPR to AAP and ABP, June 30, 1907. HS Archives.

74. *"Be quiet"* —Elizabeth Choate Spykman, *Westover: 1909–1959* (New Haven: Yale University Press, 1959) p. 116.

74. *sea sand, goats' hair* —Ibid., pp. 114-15.

75. *"beautifully designed"* –Cass Gilbert, qtd. in Susana Torre, *Women in American Architecture*, p. 65.

75. "the best *that I know of*" —AJ to TPR, May 22, 1913. HS Archives.

75. *"Dear, dear, dear, dear"* —Lucy Pratt to TPR, April 30, 1909. HS Archives.

75. *"freedom to become themselves"* —BS to TPR, March 20, 1910. HS Archives.

75. *"mentally fagged"* —TPR to AAP and ABP, August 18, 1910. HS Archives.

75. *"put her up to it"* —Elizabeth Choate Spykman. *Westover*, pp. 53, 55.

75. *the demands made* —James Hyslop to TPR, January 6, 1908. HS Archives.

77. *to Canada on a camping trip* —quotations and descriptions about the trip are from TPR's Journal beginning August 1909, Numbers 743–762. HS Archives.

77. *a companion, Mrs. Spagge* —TPR to ABP, August 1, 1909. HS Archives.

78. *"lean toward socialism"* —MC to TPR, December 23, [1909]. HS Archives.

78. *"right of ownership here"* —Lillian Wald to TPR, January 9, 1911. Number 1808. HS Archives.

78. *"nothing wrong"* —MC to TPR, [September 1905], Number 63. HS Archives.

79. *"appearance and wretchedness"* —TPR to AAP, September 6, 1910. HS Archives.

79. *Eusapio Palladino* —TPR, *Memoirs*, Numbers 4113-6,7,8, April 20, 1937. AOF and HS Archives.

80. *Henry James* —TPR, *Memoirs*, Numbers 4113-9,10,11, April 22, 1937. AOF and HS Archives.

81. *"lived incognito"* —TPR to ABP, July 22, 1910. HS Archives.

81. *"Jim Jam"* —TPR to AAP, September 6, 1910. HS Archives.

81. *Countess Helena Gleichen* —TPR to ABP, July 19, 1910. HS Archives.

81. *"the very devil"* —TPR to AAP and ABP, August 10, 1910. HS Archives.

81. *"doubly lovely"* —Ibid.

81. *visited the Fergusons* —Blanche Wiesen Cook, *Eleanor Roosevelt, Vol. I: 1884-1933* (New York: Viking Penguin, 1992), p.173.

82. *Eleanor to endure* —Ibid.

83. *"a dreadful loss"* —TPR to AAP, September 6, 1910. HS Archives.

83. *"a single design"* —W. Andrews, qtd. in Judith Paine, *Theodate Pope Riddle: Her Life and Work* (New York: The National Park Service, 1979), p. 11.

83. *"calmly on the hill"* —Ibid., p. 10.

SEVEN: "A grievous shock and strain." 1911 – 1913

86. *"must talk to her"* —MC to TPR, December 23, 1910. HS Archives.

86. *"majority of women"* —ARC to TPR, October 20, 1912. HS Archives.

86. *"women and the parsons"* —M. van Rensselaer to TPR, September 13,[1912]. HS Archives.

86. *Ida Tarbell* —Kathleen Brady, *Ida Tarbell: Portrait of a Muckraker* (University of Pittsburgh Press, 1989), pp. 116, 120.

87. *Mrs. Hepburn* —*The Hartford Diaries of Mary Vaill Dudley Talcott*, Vol. IV., pp. 591-2, 595.

87. *an anti-suffrage petition* —*The Hartford Daily Courant*, June 1, 1911, p. 6. Number 242. HS Archives.

87. *"laughed, even my father"* —TPR's Notes, June 10, 1942. HS Archives.

87. *"forceful ladies"* —HJ, in Henry James, Leon Edel, and Lyall Powers, *The Complete Notebooks of Henry James* (New York: Oxford University Press, 1987), p. 207.

88. *"little attendant"* —HJ to TPR, May 14, 1911. HS Archives.

88. *Augustus "Gus" Jaccaci* —Kathleen Brady, *Ida Tarbell*, p. 116.

88. *"much motoring"* —HJ, in Leon Edel and Lyall Powers. *The Complete Notebooks of Henry James*, p. 329.

88. *"to visit Westover School"* —Elizabeth Choate Spykman, *Westover*, pp. 43-44.

89. *"a page of Keats"* —HJ to TPR, June 6, 1911. HS Archives.

89. *"take your maid"* —ARC to TPR, July 21, 1911. HS Archives.

90. *"any part of oneself"* —ARC to TPR, July 26, 1911. HS Archives.

90. *was a hysterectomy* —MH to TPR, August 19, 1911. HS Archives.

90. *"abhorrent to William"* —Alice James to TPR, January 6, 1912. HS Archives.

91. *"a tissue of trash"* —HJ to TPR, January 12, 1912. AOF Collection. Number 20, HS Archives.

91. *"my mind put tidy"*—HG to TPR, no date. Number 4015. HS Archives.

92. *"dignified at the same time"*—Judith Paine, *Theodate Pope Riddle*, p. 13.

92. *"approach to Dormer house"*—"Lockjaw Ridge" brochure, 1984. HS Archives.

92. *"texture of the materials"*—Judith Paine, *Theodate Pope Riddle*, p. 13.

92. *"ingeniously shaped"*—quoted from "Dormer House," *Country Life*, Vol. XXXV (February 1919), p. 56; in Judith Paine, *Theodate Pope Riddle*, p. 13.

92. *decoration of the rooms*—TPR to ABP, January 20, 1914; March 24, 1914; March 26, 1914. HS Archives.

93. *Gatsby-like parties*—Monica Randall, qtd. in *Designers' Showcase*, 1992. HS Archives.

94. *"that mezzotint"*–TPR's Notes, 1941. HS Archives.

95. *"story that Isabella Selmes Ferguson told"*—Sympathy letters date from August and September 1913; these include one from Isabella Ferguson, January 5, 1914, HS Archives. Isabella Selmes Ferguson (later Greenway) (1886–1953) was John Riddle's niece, daughter of his stepsister, Martha (Patty) Flandrau Selmes. Isabella was a U.S. Representative (Democrat) from Arizona from October 3, 1933–January 3, 1937.

95. *"in a minor key"*—HJ to TPR, February 23, 1913. HS Archives.

95. *"a grievous shock and strain"*—This quotation and the chapter title are from HJ to TPR, August 22, 1913. HS Archives.

EIGHT: "My architectural work, psychical research…" 1914 – 1915

97. *$5.5 million*—Memo to Board of Governors from Director, January 19, 1987. HS Archives.

97. *300 pages*—Georgia Sheron, "Theo Pope's House," p. 2.

97. *gigantic mastodon*—Frederick Cook, "The Finding of the Farmington," p. 8. Privately owned. WS Archives.

97. *a rarity*—Phyllis Fenn Cunningham, *My Godmother: Theodate Pope Riddle: A Reminiscence of Creativity* (Canaan, N.H.: Phoenix Publishing Co., 1983), pp. 44-45.

98. *new architectural office*—*National Cyclopedia of American Biography*. Vol. XXX (New York: James T. White and Co., 1943), p. 288ff. TPR lists two offices on her stationery, January 14, 1914: her Farmington office and the New York office at Fifteen East Fortieth Street.

99. *Gordon Brockway*—Watrous & Day correspondence: Numbers 1832, 1822, 1834. HS Archives. Gordon's surname is the same as Harris Whittemore's wife Justine's maiden name, but there does not seem to be a connection.

100. *Miss Guy*—TPR to ABP, April 7, 1914. Number 840. HS Archives.

100. *give us a holiday*—A. Wood to TPR, May 20, 1914. HS Archives.

101. *because of gambling*—GHF, undated document, Box 13. AHS.

102. *"beyond recognition"*—TPR to S. Brown, August 12, 1914. HS Archives.

102. *"you lose the money"*—G. Ruffier to TPR, August 4, 1914. HS Archives.

103. *"Under no circumstances"*—Marjorie Friend to President Wilson, October 5, 1914. HS Archives.

103. *the Austrian border*—From script of Marjorie R. Friend, August 20, 1914. Number 2603. HS Archives.

103. *"Darwin played a bassoon"*—James Hyslop to EF, August 5, 1914. HS Archives.

103. *"prove a nightmare"*—Ibid.

105. *"This is a sop"*—TPR to C. Neave, March 11, 1915. HS Archives.

105. *"Bully; bully; bully!"*—TPR to ABP, March 11, 1915. HS Archives.

106. *"She can do it"*—TPR's *Memoirs*, unnumbered page. AOF and HS Archives.

106. *"my architectural work"*—Quotation and the chapter title are from TPR to HW, July 8, 1914. WS Archives; copy: Number 845. HS Archives.

106. *"Whose little boy"*—ABP to TPR, January 9, 1915. HS Archives.

107. *"I call a sport"*—BE to TPR, April 2, 1915. HS Archives.

NINE: "A damned dirty business." 1915

109. *A damned dirty business*—Lord Mersey, qtd. in Colin Simpson, *The Lusitania* (Boston: Little, Brown and Co., 1973), p. 241.

109. *Lusitania was palatial*—Colin Simpson, *The Lusitania*, p. 2.

109. *129 children*—*New York Times*, June 8, 1915, qtd. in Diana Preston, *Lusitania: An Epic Tragedy* (New York: Walker and Co., 2002) p. 132.

109. *"Information for Passengers"*—brochure. HS Archives.

110. *"not to travel"*—Colin Simpson, *The Lusitania*, p. 97.

110. *munitions*—Robert D. Ballard, "The Riddle of the *Lusitania*," *National Geographic*, April 1994, p. 80. Also see cargo list in Diana Preston, *Lusitania*, p. 134.

110. *gun cotton*—Colin Simpson, *The Lusitania*, p. 95.

110. *"Swarming about were reporters"*—Colin Simpson, *The Lusitania*, p. 112.

110. *Charles Sumner*—Diana Preston, *Lusitania*, p. 93.

111. *"intend to get us"*—TPR to ABP, May 1915. HS Archives. This quotation and subsequent quotations and descriptions of TPR's experience are from this letter, which was privately published.

111. *the Candidate's crew*—Colin Simpson, *The Lusitania*, p. 139.

111. *the Centurion*—Ibid., p. 140.

111. *"only 3"*—Ibid., p. 142.

112. *"Submarines active"*—Ibid., p. 144.

112. *"no need for alarm"*—Diana Preston, *Lusitania*, p. 172.

112. *120 miles away*—Colin Simpson, *The Lusitania*, p. 146.

112. *"The Blue Danube"*—Diana Preston, *Lusitania*, p. 191.

112. *Schwieger spotted it*—Colin Simpson, *The Lusitania*, p. 151.

113. *geyser of water*—Robert D. Ballard, "The Riddle of the *Lusitania*," p. 73.

113. *ship's heavy list*—Diana Preston, *Lusitania,* p. 132. Although there were enough lifeboats, "Cunard had not followed the *Titanic* inquiry's recommendation that high-sided liners should use a type of davit that would allow lifeboats to be swung out effectively, even if the ship was listing."

113. *Lost children*—Ibid., pp. 212-213.

113. *elegant grilles*—Ibid., p. 210.

114. *sliding down the deck*—Diana Preston, *Lusitania,* pp. 232-233.

114. *fifty-two degrees*—Ibid., p. 249.

114. *"the wreakage"*—Ibid., p. 244.

114. *including corpses*—Ibid., p. 246.

115. *"Why fear death?"*—Ibid., p. 237. Preston quotes actress Rita Jolivet, a survivor who was traveling with Frohman. Also see Colin Simpson, *The Lusitania,* p. 163.

116. *eyelids flicker*—Notes for D. Pratt, August 31, 1965. HS Archives.

117. *figure was 1,195 dead*—Ballard, Robert. "The Riddle of the *Lusitania,*" pp. 72-74.

118. *Alfred Vanderbilt*—Colin Simpson, *The Lusitania,* p. 61.

118. *mass graves*—Ibid.

TEN: "Unthinkable, unthinkable." 1915 – 1916

120. *"Had we heard"*—Alice Hamilton to family, May 15, 1915. HS Archives.

120. *no remorse*—Ibid., May 31, 1915. HS Archives.

120. *cablegram with the one word "Saved"*—MH to TPR, May 13, 1915. AOF Collection. HS Archives.

120. *the Haughtons and the Newsoms*—TPR, *Memoirs,* October 10, 1939. Numbers 4113-12,13,14,15. AOF and HS Archives.

121. *"need money"*—Ibid.

121. *"cried my heart out"*—Ibid.

121. *"infinite care"*—HJ to TPR, May 12, 1915.

122. *"Unthinkable, unthinkable"*—This quotation and the chapter title are from HJ to TPR, May 20, 1915. HS Archives.

122. *Dr. Foster Kennedy*—Foster Kennedy, M.D., F.R.S.E., was an assistant professor of neurology at Cornell University and a neurologist at Bellevue Hospital, New York City.

122. *"like a mezzotint"*—TPR, *Memoirs,* April 23, 1937. Number 4113-16. AOF and HS Archives.

123. *"takes me to a play"*—TPR to ABP, June 2, 1915. HS Archives.

123. *"trying to work"*—TPR to ABP, June 7, 1915. HS Archives.

124. *"Theodora, Theodora"*—transcript, May 10, 1915. Number 2503. HS Archives.

125. *life and death*—TPR to ABP, June 7, 1915. HS Archives.

125. *"for the suffrage"*—G. Pankhurst to TPR, May 15, 1915. HS Archives.

125. *"all wish for painting"*—HG to TPR, May 3, 1915. HS Archives.

126. *"splitting headaches"*—Ibid.

127. *kissed Theo's picture*—Mrs. W. A. Rutherford to ABP, [1915]. AOF Collection. HS Archives.

127. *"your little son"*—TPR to E. Frothington, September 10, 1915. HS Archives.

128. *"utter discouragement"*—TPR to Mr. Carrington, August 18, 1915. HS Archives.

128. *"Your life"*—E. Worcester to TPR, August 15, 1915. HS Archives.

128. *"the state called 'trance'"*—TPR to C. Neave, April 10, 1916. HS Archives.

128. *"Alfred Atmore Pope Chair"*—Ibid. Also see TPR's will, in which she bequeaths money for the study of trance. HS Archives.

129. *"peculiar condition"*—J. Woods to LTT, December 13, 1915. HS Archives.

129. *"for three years"*—TPR, note on Woods's letter, May 9, 1916. HS Archives.

129. *Electric Stimulus Shuffler*—TPR to LTT, [1916]. HS Archives.

ELEVEN: "The voice of Little Blue Feather" 1916

131. *"a dull moment"*—Preface to *Memoirs* of JWR, Number 1038. HS Archives.

131. *Rebecca Blair McClure Riddle*–D.P. Skrief, "Viva Flandrau!" *Twin Cities,* February 1986, p. 32.

131. *"claimed was manipulative"*—Sandra Wheeler, Report on visit to AHS, April 1993. HS Archives.

132. *pretty women*—JWR to CMF, April 19, 1891. B68. AHS.

132. *"a patrician"*—Ibid., May 5, 1891.

132. *"while one of the weaker sex is uncomfortable"*—JWR, Journal, October 13, 1886. Number 1051. HS Archives.

133. *"a big jolly man"*—D.P. Skrief, "Viva Flandrau!" p. 32.

133. *$56 debt*—Eller and How to Charles Eugene Flandrau, August 7, 1894. B1. AHS.

133. *"hotbed of intrigue"*—JWR, *Memoirs.* Number 1039. HS Archives.

133. *"brained with clubs"*—JWR to CMF, October 13, 1895. B68. AHS.

133. *"some wretched victim"*—JWR, *Notebooks,* 1905. HS Archives.

134. *an open boat*—CMF to Rebecca Flandrau, November 11, 1896. B3. AHS.

134. *"Roosevelt's sister"*—JWR to CMF, March 20, 1901. B70. AHS.

134. *"another planet"*—JWR, *Notebooks:* "Russia." HS Archives.

134. *nine languages*—S.F. Cutchen to TPR, March 2, 1916. HS Archives. JWR's stepsister Sarah (Sally) might have been exaggerating. JWR's friend, the Russian diplomat, Eugene Stein, said that John spoke six languages. *The Hartford Courant,* [December 9, 1941], undated clipping. HS Archives.

134. *"general prosperity"*—JWR, *Notebooks.* "Egypt." HS Archives.

134. *"a most interesting letter"*—Theodore Roosevelt to ARC, June 28, 1906. B71. AHS.

135. *"beg your pardon"*—Preface to *Memoirs* of JWR. HS Archives.

135. *"he wouldn't have resigned"* —CMF to P.F. Selmes, June 2, 1909, MHS.

135. *"like a lunatic"* —GHF to BF, undated. B12. AHS.

135. *kill Papee* —GHF to "Carl," [1950s]. B27. AHS.

135. *drama critic* —Obituary, CMF, 1938. B2. AHS.

135. *"witty, urbane"* –D.P. Skrief, "Viva Flandrau!", p. 31.

135. *"smelling books"* —CMF to P.F. Selmes, March 12, 1910. MHS.

136. *"an appalling number"* —Ibid., January 1, 1911.

136. *"How peaceful"* —Ibid., July 12, 1913.

136. *"rest from travel"* —"Ulysses," Alfred, Lord Tennyson.

136. *"two Mrs. Vanderbilts"* –JWR, qtd. by CMF to P.F. Selmes, March 24, 1915. MHS.

136. *"the flesh-pots"* —CMF to P.F. Selmes, December 18, 1914. MHS.

137. *"pathetic about Googoo"* —CMF to P.F. Selmes, November 16, 1909. MHS.

137. *"remarkably intelligent girl"* —CMF to P.F. Selmes, September 4, 1912, MHS.

137. *Grace also had* —Georgia Ray, "In Search of the Real Grace Flandrau," *Minnesota History,* Vol. 56, Number 6, Summer 1999. Copy in HS Archives.

138. *"voice of Little Blue Feather"* —This quotation and the chapter title are from GHF to BF [1916], Box 27. AHS.

138. *"could not be printed"* –CF, qtd. by GHF to BF, n.d. B27. AHS.

138. *Brooks Brothers* —CMF to P.F. Selmes, February 18, 1915. MHS.

138. *"survivor of the* Titanic" —Number 4518. HS Archives.

138. *in love* —CMF to P.F. Selmes, March 14, 1916. MHS.

138. *was a lesbian* –B. Gill, "What Climbs the Stairs?" *Sarah Lawrence Alumnae Magazine,* Summer 1975, p. 8. Also, several years ago, the author asked Mr. Gill why he assumed that TPR was a lesbian, and he answered, "Everyone knew she was."

139. *"a 'companion'"* —C.H. Baslington to TPR, March 3, 1916. HS Archives.

140. *"loving thoughts"* —TPR to HW, April 16, 1916. HS Archives.

140. *wedding took place* —The description of the wedding was probably written by BE, May 8, 1916. Number 466. HS Archives.

141. *"Charlie Flandrau my brother"* —TPR to Mrs. D. Robinson [Corinne Roosevelt], June 19, 1916. HS Archives.

141. *"perpetual visiting"* —CMF to P.F. Selmes, July 14, 1918. MHS.

142. *"Theodate, I prezume"* —CMF to GHF, August 13, 1918. B2. AHS.

142. *tragic marriage"* —CMF to P.F. Selmes, August 4, 1916. MHS.

TWELVE: "Through the eyes of boys." 1916 – 1918

144. *looked pale* —TPR to ABP, August 22, 1916. HS Archives.

144. *a health measure* —Ibid., July 31, 1916.

144. *away from crowds* —Ibid., August 22, 1916.

145. *Grace was called* —GHF, MS., n.d. B13. AHS.

146. *secretary to type* —TPR to LTT, January 31, 1917. HS Archives.

146. *never lose interest* —Ibid.

147. *"superb motives"* —TPR to ABP, February 7, 1917. HS Archives.

148. *"doomed to failure"* —TPR to LTT, October 12, 1917. HS Archives.

148. *"points in democracy"* —Ibid., January 1918.

148. *Madame Catherine Breshkovsky* —Georgia Sheron, "Theo Pope's House," p. 3; and Elizabeth Choate Spykman, *Westover*, p. 64.

148. *Paul Martin* —Lee Martin (Paul's son) to Sandra Wheeler and Polly Huntington, October 8, 1998. HS Archives.

149. *"shock and sorrow"* —TPR to ABP, July 7, 1917. HS Archives.

149. *"through the eyes of boys"* —This quotation and the chapter title are from TPR to ABP, April 13, 1917. HS Archives.

149. *tried to enlist* —CMF to P.F. Selmes, August 16, 1917. MHS.

150. *Patience Worth* —TPR to LTT, December 3, 1917. HS Archives.

150. *"48 hours"* —JWR to CMF, November 7, 1917. B68. AHS.

151. *"electric storm"* —GHF, qtd. in Georgia Ray DeCoster, "Chronology of the Relationship between John and Theodate Riddle and Grace H. Flandrau." n.d. MHS and HS Archives. Account of TPR's bringing GHF to Hill-Stead: Number 2655. HS Archives.

151. *"Most Unforgettable Character"* —GHF to "Carl" [1950s]. Carl was probably an editor at *Readers' Digest*. GHF's essays on TPR and ARC were not published. B27. AHS.

151. *slap his face* —Henry Flanagan, *Aspirando et Perseverando: The Evolution of the Avon Old Farms School as Influenced by its Founder* (Ph.D. diss., University of Michigan, 1978), p. 66.

152. *"quite the rage"* —GHF to BF, n.d. B12. AHS.

152. *"Lefty" Lewis* —Wilmarth Sheldon Lewis. *One Man's Education* (New York: Alfred A. Knopf, 1967). Lewis writes this autobiography in the third person, referring to himself as "Lefty."

152. *a domineering mother* —Ibid., pp. 138, 160.

153. *beggars description* —GHF to BF, undated [1918]. B12. AHS.

153. *marries him* —Ibid.

153. *his existence* —Ibid.

153. *"God awful fools"* —BF to GHF, June 2, 1918. B58. AHS.

153. *"swell lunch"* —GHF to CMF, undated [1918]. B13. AHS.

153. *"I.W.W's"* —CMF to GHF, February 8, 1918. B2. AHS.

THIRTEEN: "This plan means peace to my soul." 1919

156. *"gang agley"* —TPR to ABP, February 18, 1918. HS Archives.

156. *IV. Provide in will* —TPR to E. McCarthy. Number 2199B. HS Archives.

156. *Ada to change her will* —Ibid. & Number 2200. TPR's Notes. HS Archives.

156. *"peace to my soul"* —This quotation and the chapter title are from TPR to ABP, February 7, 1918.

157. *"Dear heaven!"*—CMF to GHF, July 4, 1918. AHS.

157. *"guts amputated"* —Ibid.

157. *"in good spirits"* —CMF to GHF, August 16, 1918. B2. AHS.

157. *all the buildings* —TPR's Notes. Number 2201A. HS Archives.

157. *possessed, dedicated* —GHF, qtd. in Henry Flanagan, *Aspirando et Perseverando*, p. 66.

157. *one of her theories* —BF to GHF, July 25, 1918. B58. AHS.

157. *"devote herself to work"* —DeCoster, Georgia Ray. "Chronology of the Relationship between JWR and TPR and GHF," p. 2. MHS and HS Archives.

158. *Donald Carson's* —Interview: Donald Carson with Polly Huntington and Sandra Wheeler, 1994. HS Archives.

159. *"in a terrible state"* —GHF to BF, undated [1919]. B12. AHS.

160. *"No more separations"* —GHF to BF, January 18 [1919]. B12. AHS.

160. *"Keekface"* —BF to GHF, March 8, 1919. B58. AHS.

160. *"fond of Theo"* —BF to GHF, March 15, 1919. B58. AHS.

161. *"fifty-fifty basis"* —TPR to GHF [1919]. B76. AHS.

161. *tour of the Orient* —Quotations and descriptions are from TPR to ABP, beginning April 14, 1919, and from JWR to ABP, beginning August 14, 1919. HS Archives.

161. *"I don't blame her"* —BF to GHF, March 27, 1919. B58. AHS.

164. *"slunk away"* —BE, *Theodate Pope and the Founding of Avon Old Farms* (Avon, CT: privately printed, 1973), p. 11.

165. *"a living soul"* —William Wordsworth. "Lines…Tintern Abbey."

166. *"graves graves"* —GHF to BF, April 5, [1919]. B12. AHS.

166. *want to go home* —Ibid., May 1 [1919].

166. *"Use my maiden name"* —TPR to W.S. Parker, June 10, 1918. HS Archives.

FOURTEEN: "The Ambassadress" 1919 – 1923

168. *"the great American"* —F. Kennedy to TPR, January 2, 1920. HS Archives.

168. *"Illness Fails"* —*The Hartford Courant*. February 11, 1920. Number 1034. HS Archives.

168. *19th-century appearance* —Tara F. Callahan, "To Help the Cause of Good Architecture": *Theodate Pope Riddle and the Colonial Revival* (Dartmouth College Senior Fellowship Project, June 1996), p. 172. In *Theodate Pope Riddle*, Judith Paine notes (p. 14) that Roosevelt Birthplace is a "National Historic Site, and is the nation's first Victorian period restoration."

168. *"In her quest"* —David M. Kahn, in Judith Paine, *Theodate Pope Riddle*, "Foreword."

169. *colonial-block print* —Tara Callahan, *To Help the Cause of Good Architecture*, p. 171.

169. *"I do not think"*—Marcus Holcomb to TPR, February 13, 1919. HS Archives.

170. *"dear Aunt Ada"*—J. Brooks to TPR, May 9, 1920. HS Archives.

170. *"dear little mother"*—"Blakie" to TPR, May 24, 1920. HS Archives.

170. *"Ada Bo Peep"*—GHF. B13. AHS.

170. *"Earnest's last name"*—K.B. Knight to E. McCarthy, May 9, 1920. HS Archives.

170. *"boys were quite different"*—TPR to BF, April 14, 1920. B76. AHS.

171. *Will Power*—TPR to GHF, April 19, 1921. B76. AHS.

171. *"little automobile"*—Ibid.

171. *"didn't quite fall"*—Interview: Donald Carson with Polly Huntington and Sandra Wheeler, May 3, 1994. HS Archives.

171. *moving trolley*—Transcription: Richard Bissell, April 18, 1984. HS Archives.

173. *coast of Norway*—This incident is described by TPR to E. McCarthy, 1937. Numbers 4113-43,44. HS Archives.

174. *the competing demands*—Georgia Ray Decoster. Grant Proposal. MHS and HS Archives.

174. *"a sickening thing"*—TPR to GHF, [1921]. B76. AHS.

175. *"devil of a time"*—GHF to BF, [December 1921, January 1922]. B12. AHS.

175. *"Mr & Mrs Trafford"*—Ibid.

175. *"all is rosy"*—Ibid.

176. *motorcade approached*—Ibid.

176. *"makes me nervous"*—TPR to GHF, [January 1922]. B76. AHS.

176. *"favorite black & white"*—TPR to GHF, March 18, 1922. B76. AHS.

177. *"The Ambassadress"*—This quotation and the chapter title are from TPR to GHF, March 18, 1922. B76. AHS.

177. *"We go no place"*—TPR to GHF, [April 1922]. TPR repeats *"I have practically nothing to do"* in a letter to ARC and her husband, April 20, 1922. B76. AHS.

178. *turning in slow circles*—TPR to GHF, July 10, 1922. B76. AHS. Also, TPR to E. McCarthy, 1937. Numbers 4113-45,46. HS Archives.

178. *"nor more attractive"*—ARC to GHF, [1922]. B71. AHS.

178. *paraded up and down*—GHF to BF, [1922]. Number 6108. HS Archives.

179. *center of attention*—GHF to JWR, [December 1922]. B12. AHS.

179. *"any American novel"*—GHF to CMF, [1923]. B13. AHS.

179. *"copper ringlets"*—CMF to GHF, January 6, 1923. B2. AHS.

179. *flaccid udders*—Ibid., May 23, 1923.

180. *"much talk"*—ARC to GHF, [1923]. B13. AHS.

180. *"an alley cat"*—TPR to GHF, [1923]. B13. AHS.

180. *"a violent pitch"*—GHF to BF, [1923]. B12. AHS.

180. *"very popular"*—ARC to GHF, October 17, 1922. B12. AHS.

181. *"she was so mad"*—GHF to BF, [1925]. B12. AHS.

FIFTEEN: "The lady on the hill" 1923 – 1926

183. *"pleasant little gentlemen"*—TPR, Memoirs, unnumbered. AOF and HS Archives. Also see BE, *Theodate Pope and the Founding of Avon Old Farms*, p. 10.

183. *oak saplings* —BE, *Theodate Pope and the Founding of Avon Old Farms*, p. 18.

184. *dispense with all mechanical methods* —Ibid., p. 14. BE quotes TPR's memo of December 7, 1923.

184. *"the purest mess"*—P. Johnson, qtd. in Nadia M. Niggli, "Theodate Pope Riddle and Avon Old Farms School for Boys: The 'Gendering' of Architecture." Senior essay (Department of Architecture, Yale University, May 1995), p. 7. Also see B. Gill, "Philip the Bold," *The New Yorker*, November 14, 1994: Philip Johnson "poked fun" at his cousin, TPR.

184. *"hired in the morning"*—Interview: Verna Deming with Polly Huntington and Sandra Wheeler, August 11, 1992.

184. *"pleasant woman"*—Ibid.

184. *"when he gets home"*—Ibid.

185. *Theodate ever divulge* —ARC to GHF, July 12, 1924. B71. AHS.

186. *property at $107,000* —"The Tax Suit." TPR's Notes, Number 2210. HS Archives.

186. *"avoid human contacts"*—TPR to GHF, October 18, 1923. B76. AHS.

186. *"because they interfered"*—Ibid.

186. *"No messages"*—ARC to GHF, November 9, 1923. B71. AHS.

186. *"the lady on the hill"*—This quotation and the chapter title are also from ARC to GHF, November 9, 1923.

187. *"my pelvic bones"*—TPR, *Memoirs*, May 7, 1937. Number 4113-37. AOF and HS Archives.

187. *"a secondary school"*—TPR to GHF, December 6 [1923]. B76. AHS.

187. *"medieval Castle Keep"*—Daniel Davis, "The Architecture of Theodate Pope Riddle," presentation at HS, February 2, 1997.

188. *"grotesque to put wings on a rodent"*—Gordon Ramsey, *Aspiration and Perseverance*, pp. 13-14.

189. *elected her a fellow* —BE, *Theodate Pope and the Founding of Avon Old Farms*, p. 14.

189. *Robinson Memorial Medal*—Callahan, Tara. *To Help the Cause of Good Architecture*, p. 151.

189. *"a masterpiece"*—Judith Paine, *Theodate Pope Riddle*, p. 15.

189. *"animated forms"*—Ibid.

190. *"pure whimsical effect"*—Ibid.

190. *"sound & honest"*—GHF to "Carl," [1950s]. B27. AHS.

190. a *"re-grande-entrée"*—ARC to GHF, February 19, 1924. B71. AHS.

190. *"feel very sorry for"*—ARC to GHF, May 20, 1924. B71. AHS.

190. *"such an ass"*—CMF to GHF, December 22, 1924. MHS.

191. *"germ of rheumatism"*—JWR to CMF and BF, January 7, 1927. B6. AHS.

191. *"a tremendous refuge"*—TPR to GHF, March 29, 1925. B76. AHS.

191. *"become obscene"*—CMF to GHF, March 21, 1925. B2. AHS.

191. *"to 'come across'"*—CMF to GHF, March 30, 1925. B2. AHS.

191. *Northern newspapers*—*The State*, Columbia, S.C., March 16, 1925. B68. AHS.

192. *"by way of Europe"*—CMF to GHF, May 15, 1925. B2. AHS.

192. *"just like the peasants"*—CMF to GHF, July 30, 1925. B2. AHS.

193. *"not able to have an auto"*—ARC to GHF, February 24, 1926. B71. AHS.

SIXTEEN: "Bold and far looking." 1926 – 1929

196. *"Never marry an architect!"*—BE, *Theodate Pope and the Founding of Avon Old Farms*, p. 20.

197. *Theo could outvote*—TPR's battle to maintain control of Avon Old Farms School is documented in materials that she tied up in a package and labeled *"Documents and Comments* arranged and translated by TPR," and placed in the HS Vault. The letters, documents, and comments are numbered 2199–2321. HS Archives.

197. *any given creed*—AOF 1928 catalog, pp. 13-14.

197. *"we are different"*—Gordon Ramsey, *Aspiration and Perseverance*, p. 28.

198. *"grounds for professional athletes"*—Ibid., pp. 13, 17.

198. *acted as the jury*—Ibid., p. 15.

199. *"use of library books"*—Ibid., p.17.

199. *the Psychotherapist*—Ibid., p. 10.

199. *"bold and far looking"*—This quotation and the chapter title are from C.W. Eliot, *The New York Times*, November 17, 1924. Number 2203. HS Archives.

199. *John Dewey praised*—J. Dewey to TPR, March 29, 1935. HS Archives.

199. *"full regalia"*—ARC to W. S. Cowles, March 11, 1927. Number 2445.1. HS Archives. The other guest was Jean Chase.

200. *Dr. Beatrice Hinkle*—Dr. Hinkle (1874-1953) was associated in practice with Dr. Charles Dana. She translated Dr. C.C. Jung's *The Psychology of the Unconscious*.

200. *"mauve silk stockings"*—CMF to GHF, January 6, 1926. B2. AHS.

200. *"well and busy"*—CMF to BF, April 2, 1927. B5. AHS.

200. *"terrifyingly" labeled boracic acid*—Ibid.

201. *"Don't mention it"*—BF to GHF, December 31, 1926. B59. AHS.

201. *"you are so delicate"*—GHF to BF, n.d. B13. AHS.

201. *Charles Lindbergh*—JWR to CMF, June 23, 1927. B68. AHS.

201. *"series of post-cards"*—CMF to GHF, July 15, 1927. B5. AHS.

202. *Stephen Cabot*—BE, *Theodate Pope and the Founding of Avon Old Farms*, p. 21.

202. *"Francis Mitchell Froelicher"*—Ibid., p. 24.

202. *"prove his mettle"*—Ibid.

202. *"at no time"*—Gordon Ramsey, *Aspiration and Perseverance*, p. 18.

203. *"Alsop was no gentleman"* —*Documents and Comments,* TPR's Notes. HS Archives.

203. *received $15,000* —BE, *Theodate Pope and the Founding of Avon Old Farms,* p. 24.

203. *"Founder was appalled"* —*Documents and Comments.* TPR's Notes. TPR refers to herself, in the third person, as The Founder. Number 2215. HS Archives.

203. *almost $90,000 [The actual figure was $89,776.]* —Ibid.

203. *"interference and officiousness"* —*Documents and Comments.* Autumn 1928. Number 2217. HS Archives.

204. *Dr. Duel was also* —*Documents and Comments,* Number 2218. HS Archives.

204. *"a boy of mine"* —S. Cabot to TPR, June 14, 1929. *Documents and Comments.* HS Archives.

205. *"in consultation with my physician"* —F. Froelicher to TPR, April 13, 1929. *Documents and Comments.* HS Archives.

205. *second agreed-upon letter* —Ibid., April 30, 1929. HS Archives.

205. *"no 'rank injustice'"* —S. Cabot to TPR, June 14, 1929. *Documents and Comments.* HS Archives.

205. *"the good of the School"* —BE, *Theodate Pope and the Founding of Avon Old Farms,* p. 25.

206. *"Her persistent attention"* —Ibid. BE quotes Douglas Redefer, whose 1966 Yale undergraduate thesis was entitled "An Interpretive Early History of Avon Old Farms School."

206. *Dr. George Draper* —*Documents and Comments,* Number 2223ff. HS Archives.

207. *dropped the suit* —*Documents and Comments,* Number 2218. HS Archives.

207. *"a grave undermining"* —BE, *Theodate Pope and the Founding of Avon Old Farms,* p. 25.

207. *Major Jesse Gaston* —*Documents and Comments,* Number 2225. HS Archives.

208. *sorting mail* —*Documents and Comments,* Number 2227A and B. HS Archives.

208. *$9,000 severance pay* —Ibid.

SEVENTEEN: "The breath of God." 1929 – 1932

210. *thirty billion dollars* —Frederick Lewis Allen, *Since Yesterday: The 1930s in America, September 3, 1929-September 3, 1939* (New York: Harper and Row, 1972), p.20.

210. *(2) Prohibition, and (3) Lawlessness* —Ibid., p. 24.

210. *full power* —BE, *Theodate Pope and the Founding of Avon Old Farms,* p. 26.

211. *"discuss the matter"* —*Documents and Comments.* Number 2229. HS Archives.

211. *"not sufficiently spelled out"* —Gordon Ramsey, *Aspiration and Perseverance,* p. 27.

212. *"School Board Quits"* —*The New York Times,* February 19, 1930. *Documents and Comments.* Number 2240. HS Archives.

212. *"the breath of God"* —This quotation and the chapter title are from TPR's Notes, "The Boston Meeting," *Documents and Comments.* Number 2241. HS Archives.

213. *telephone directory* —Gordon Ramsey, *Aspiration and Perseverance,* p. 27.

213. *"All Members of Faculty at Avon Resign"* —*The Hartford Courant,* March 28, 1930. *Documents and Comments.* Number 2241B. HS Archives.

214. *"will be self-perpetuating"* —TPR, "Chicanery and 'Self-Perpetuating Board.'" *Documents and Comments.* Number 2256. HS Archives. Also, BE, *Theodate Pope and the Founding of Avon Old Farms,* p.27.

214. *"leaves of the bushes"* —Gordon Ramsey, *Aspiration and Perseverance,* p. 13.

215. *"thunder clouds"* —Wilmarth Sheldon Lewis, *One Man's Education,* pp. 179-81.

216. *"a good instrument"* —C. Scott to TPR, March 27, 1930. *Documents and Comments.* HS Archives.

217. *Sasha* —Interview: N. Naryshkine with Polly Huntington and Sandra Wheeler, May 5, 1994. HS Archives.

217. *"integrity and ability"* —BE, *Theodate Pope and the Founding of Avon Old Farms,* p. 27.

217. *"my tuxedo"* —Interview: Donald Carson with Polly Huntington and Sandra Wheeler, May 3, 1994. HS Archives.

218. *"like a battleship"* —Lilian Rixey, *Bamie,* p. 290.

218. *remarkable resemblance* —W. Cross to TPR, October 14, 1936. HS Archives.

218. *President Herbert Hoover* —Frederick Lewis Allen, *Since Yesterday,* pp. 26-40.

219. *ten million unemployed* —Ibid.

219. *distribute food, blankets* —*Avonian,* Vol. 22, Number 2, Fall 1991, p. 17.

219. *"in a huff"* —Interview: Donald Carson with Polly Huntington, March 8, 1991. HS Archives.

220. *"Our heart"* —C. Scott to TPR, February 16, 1933. *Documents and Comments.* HS Archives.

220. *"a conceited bounder"* —BF to GHF, April 30, 1932. B59. AHS.

220. *"a terrible mess"* —BF to GHF, April 30, 1932. B59. AHS.

221. *his considerable debt* —Official document stating that Blair paid Theo $1.00. B76. AHS.

221. *"Theo saying 'Cottage'"* —BF to GHF, May 13, 1932. B59. AHS.

221. *"most snobbish place"* —BF to GHF, July 22, 1933. B59. AHS.

222. *"laughable"* –Ibid.

EIGHTEEN: "Dearest of Geniuses" 1932 — 1940

224. *Eugene Stein* —Interview: Joseph Gordon with W. Shep Holcombe, May 25, 1995. HS Archives.

225. *John's niece, Isabella* —After the death of Robert Munroe Ferguson, John's niece, Isabella Selmes, married Jack Greenway of Arizona.

225. *"the only thing we have to fear"* —Quotation is from F. D. Roosevelt's speech, March 4, 1933.

225. *"flourishing and satisfactory"* —J. Dewey to TPR, March 29, 1935. HS Archives.

225. *first registered female architects* —the pronoun "He" appears on TPR's license, which is dated 1933. Number 247. HS Archives. Women architects were not granted licenses in Connecticut until 1933, when TPR was one of six female architects "grandfathered" in. Gordon Ramsey, *Aspiration and Perseverance,* p. 12.

225. *"starting the ball rolling"*—TPR to A. E. Austin, Jr., October 10, 1934. HS Archives.

226. *Impressionist paintings*—Eugene R. Gaddis, *Magician of the Modern: Chick Austin and the Transformation of the Arts in America* (New York: Knopf, 2000), p. 83.

226. *like a general*—Ibid., Notes, Chapter Nine, Number 34, p. 449. Gaddis cites *The Hartford Times*, May 12, 1932, and quotes Florence Berkman, September 11, 1997.

226. *forceful 'imperious' Mrs. Riddle*—Ibid., p. 83

226. *discuss a contract*—*Documents and Comments.* Number 2269A. HS Archives.

227. *"just nerves"*—CMF to GHF, June 4, 1935. B2. AHS.

228. *an "Intuitive"*—C. C. Jung sketch, Number 1153. HS Archives.

229. *"that man in the White House"*—Frederick Lewis Allen, *Since Yesterday*, pp. 186-7.

229. *her hero, Charles Lindbergh*—GHF to TPR, undated [1936]. B13. AHS.

230. *"nice person"*—Ibid.

230. *that hotel*—TPR to GHF, undated [1936]. B76. AHS.

230. *$1.50 a gallon*—CMF to GHF, May 1935. B2. AHS.

230. *waving red flags*—Ibid.

230. *"light clouds"*—A. Brooks to TPR, August 1936. HS Archives.

230. *significant contributor*—Henry Flanagan, *Aspirando et Perseverando*, p. 113.

231. *"KING QUITS"*—Frederick Lewis Allen, *Since Yesterday*, pp. 198-199.

231. *"one of a succession"*—TPR to GHF, [1937]. B76. AHS.

231. *"my heart turns"*—TPR to JWR, September 18, 1937. B76. AHS.

232. *"Dearest of Geniuses"*—Quotation and chapter title are from a note written by JWR to TPR, 1937. HS Archives.

232. *"Goo Goo"*—JWR to CMF, December 10, 1937. B68. AHS.

232. *"practically helpless"*—CMF to JWR, December 14, 1937 and December 29, 1937. B5. AHS.

232. *"terribly hard up"*—GHF to JWR, November 23, 1937. B13. AHS.

232. *left $30,000*—*Twin Cities*, February 1986, p. 37. Ridgedale Library, Minnetonka, Minn.

232. *stock market*—Frederick Lewis Allen, *Since Yesterday*, pp. 244-5; 266.

232. *admissions trips*—Gordon Ramsey, *Aspiration and Perseverance*, p. 30.

233. *"peace for our time"*—Arthur M. Schlesinger, Jr. *The Almanac of American History* (New York: Barnes & Noble, 1993), p. 475.

234. *"lazy"*—TPR's Notes, Number 2273. HS Archives.

234. *"upheld no principles"*—Ibid.

234. *"sex immorality"*—TPR to GHF, January 14, 1940. Number 2274A. HS Archives.

235. *"the prow of a ship"*—TPR to C. Scott, October 18, 1939. *Documents and Comments.* HS Archives.

235. *Earnest sitting*—TPR, *Memoirs,* June 5, 1939. AOF and HS Archives.

236. *"Defend America Committee"*—GHF to TPR, [1939]. B13. AHS.

236. *Sears reported* —TPR to C. Scott, November 15, 1939. *Documents and Comments.* HS Archives.

236. *Kammerer admitted* —C. Scott to TPR, April 8, 1940. *Documents and Comments.* HS Archives.

237. *Mrs. Riddle attributed* —Gordon Ramsey, *Aspiration and Perseverance*, p. 30.

237. *"chloroforming" a provost* —Wilmarth Sheldon Lewis, *One Man's Education*, p. 181.

237. *Theo expelled the boys* —*Documents and Comments*, Number 2283A, HS Archives.

237. *"he could comfortably serve"* —Gordon Ramsey, *Aspiration and Perseverance*, p. 31.

238. *"the other twenty years"* —TPR to GHF, August 12, 1940. B76. AHS.

238. *suffragan bishop* —*Documents and Comments*, Number 2284A. HS Archives.

239. *"God help me"* —TPR to GHF, August 12, 1940. B76. AHS.

NINETEEN: "It IS my life." 1940 – 1946

240. *"vote for President Roosevelt"* —Number 1758. HS Archives.

240. *him for President* —GHF to TPR, [1940]. B13. AHS.

241. *"you'd be nauseated"* —Ibid.

241. *"senile, selfish"* —Ibid.

241. *Pearl Harbor* —Arthur M. Schlesinger, Jr., *The Almanac of American History*, p. 484ff.

242. *John was dead* —Interview: Donald Carson with Polly Huntington, March 6, 1991. HS Archives.

242. *A moving tribute* —E. Stein, *The Hartford Courant*, undated [December 9, 1941]. HS Archives.

243. *"not-too-distant future"* —TPR to *The Hartford Courant*, August 1942. HS Archives.

243. *"handsomer as she grew old"* —GHF to "Carl," [1950s]. B27. AHS.

243. *"robust"* —Interview: Brooks Shephard with M. Roberts, September 10, 1983. HS Archives.

243. *she wrote Wendell Wilkie* —TPR to W. Wilkie, July 26, 1943, qtd. in Henry Flanagan, *Aspirando et Perseverando*, p. 111.

243. *"closed in"* —TPR to GHF, [January 1943]. B76. AHS.

244. *"midst of my illness"* —TPR to GHF, December 30, 1943. B76. AHS.

244. *Stabler had made changes* —Gordon Ramsey, *Aspiration and Perseverance*, pp. 31-32.

244. *Brooks Brothers* —Ibid.

245. *Mrs. Sears commented* —Ibid.

245. *position of Aide* —Ibid.

245. *presented an ultimatum* —*Documents and Comments*. Number 2308A. HS Archives.

246. *"it IS my life"* —This quotation and the chapter title are from TPR, qtd. by GHF in letter to "Carl" [1950s]. B27. AHS.

246. *announced Avon's closing* —*Documents and Comments*, Number 2308A. HS Archives.

246. *Convalescent Hospital* —Gordon Ramsey, *Aspiration and Perseverance*, pp. 41ff.

247. *"incredible things"* —TPR to GHF, June 8, 1945. B76. AHS.

247. *"cut down all the trees!"* —Ibid.

247. *"vote for Roosevelt"* —TPR to GHF, October 1944. B76. AHS.

247. *"really appalled"* —TPR to GHF, January 1945. B76. AHS.

247. *"is a genius"* —TPR to GHF, February 5, 1945. B76. AHS.

247. *"did not suffer"* —TPR to GHF, April 18, 1945. B76. AHS.

248. *"an interlocking trust"* —Gordon Ramsey, *Aspiration and Perseverance,* p. 60.

249. *reserved a plot* —At Riverside Cemetery in Farmington, the graves of John and Theo are in the middle, with Earnest to John's right and Gordon to Theo's left.

EPILOGUE

250. *government paid $100,000* —Gordon Ramsey, *Aspiration and Perseverance,* p. 60.

250. *Henry Perkins* —Ibid., p. 58.

250. *Donald W. Pierpont* —Ibid., pp. 58-59.

250. *Newsweek and Time* —Ibid., p. 61.

250. *"forge, farm, forest"* —Ibid., p. 63.

250. *"singularly beautiful place"* —G. Trautman in *Avonian,* Spring 1998, p. 8.

250. *"embraced the* Deed of Trust*"* —AOF Commemorative booklet, May 1998, p. 46.

250. *"haircut was short enough"* —Gordon Ramsey, *Aspiration and Perseverance,* p. 90.

251. *petition of a student* —Interview: F. Leavitt with Sandra Katz, 1996. The student was Ronald Stevenson.

251. *"Poses a Riddle"* –The Hartford Courant, October 3, 1973. WS Archives.

252. *hundreds of thousands of visitors* —D. Kahn, qtd. in Judith Paine, *Theodate Pope Riddle,* "Foreword."

252. *30,000 visitors* —Interview: Ruth Apeldorf with Sandra Katz, 1998.

SELECTED BIBLIOGRAPHY

Archival Sources

Arizona Historical Society, Tucson: Flandrau Family Collection.

Avon Old Farms School, Avon, Conn.: correspondence, alumni magazines, photographs, Theodate Pope Riddle's *Memoirs*, architectural drawings.

Columbia University, New York, NY: Lillian Wald papers; Walker Cain Collection: two letters—Theodate Pope Riddle to W.R.Mead of McKim, Mead & White.

Archives, Hill-Stead Museum, Farmington, Conn.: Pope family memorabilia, photographs, correspondence; Theodate Pope Riddle's diaries, journals, notes, architectural drawings, correspondence; interviews; transcripts of sittings; John Wallace Riddle's journals, photographs, books, notebooks, memoirs; copies of documents from other archives.

Minnesota Historical Society, St. Paul: Flandrau family manuscripts and correspondence; Georgia Ray DeCoster's biographical work on Grace Flandrau.

Miss Porter's School, Farmington, Conn.: school records, correspondence, diaries (diary of Emily F. Connor), photographs.

New York Historical Society, New York, NY: McKim, Mead & White correspondence.

Theodore Roosevelt Birthplace, New York, NY: memorabilia, correspondence, photographs.

Schlesinger Library, Radcliffe Institute, Harvard University, Cambridge, Mass.: Leland T. Troland papers, Hamilton family papers.

Wellesley College, Wellesley, Mass: Belle Sherwin papers.

Westover School, Middlebury, Conn.: school records, correspondence, diaries, photographs, alumnae magazines.

Books, Periodicals, Newspaper articles

[Anonymous]. "The Home of Mrs. Chas. O. Gates, Theodate Pope, Architect," *Country Life in America*, Vol. XXXV, Feb. 1919, pp. 56-57.

Allen, Frederick Lewis. *Since Yesterday: The 1930's in America, September 3, 1929-September 3, 1939.* New York: Harper and Row, 1972.

Andrews, Kenneth R. *Nook Farm: Mark Twain's Hartford Circle.* Cambridge: Harvard University Press, 1950.

Andrews, Wayne. *Architecture, Ambition and Americans; A Social History of American Architecture.* New York: Free Press, 1964.

Aron, Peter, et al. *George Trautman.* Privately printed, 1998.

Avonian, Avon Old Farms School. Fall 1995: Vol. 26, No. 1; Winter 1996: Vol. 26, No. 2; Summer 1996: Vol. 26, No.3; Fall 1996: Vol. 27, No. 1; Spring 1998.

Baedeker's Guide to the Continental United States. 1893.

Ballard, Robert D. *"The Riddle of the* Lusitania,*" National Geographic*, April 1994.

Brady, Kathleen. *Ida Tarbell: Portrait of a Muckraker.* Pittsburgh: University of Pittsburgh Press, 1989.

Bragdon, George. "Noted Woman Architect Left Mark in Guernsey Herd Progress," *Hartford Times,* Nov. 15, 1958.

Braude, Ann. *Radical Spirits: Spiritualism and Women's Rights in Nineteenth-Century America.* Boston: Beacon Press, 1989.

Bull, Titus. *The Imperative Conquest.* New York: James H. Hyslop Foundation, Inc., 1936.

Callahan, Tara. *Theodate Pope Riddle: A Pioneer Woman Architect.* Eastern National, 1998.

Cassatt, Mary, and Nancy M. Matthews. *Cassatt and Her Circle: Selected Letters.* New York: Abbeville Press, 1984.

Cigliano, Jan. Showplace of America: *Cleveland's Euclid Avenue, 1850 – 1910.* Kent, Ohio: Kent State University Press, 1991.

Cook, Blanche Wiesen. *Eleanor Roosevelt, Vol. I: 1884-1933.* New York: Viking Penguin, 1992.

Coon, Deborah J. "Testing the Limits of Sense and Science: American Experimental Psychologists Combat Spiritualism, 1880 – 1920," *American Psychologist,* Vol. 47, No. 2, Feb. 1992, pp. 143 ff.

Coss, Clare. *Lillian D. Wald: Progressive Activist.* New York: Feminist Press at the City University of New York, 1989.

Cunningham, Phyllis Fenn. *Hill-Stead Yesterdays: Theodate Pope Riddle, My Godmother.* Privately printed, 1973.

_____. *My Godmother: Theodate Pope Riddle: A Reminiscence of Creativity.* Canaan, New Hampshire: Phoenix Publishing, 1983.

Dallas, John T. *Mary Robbins Hillard.* Concord, New Hampshire: Rumford Press, 1944.

Edel, Leon. *Henry James: The Master: 1901 – 1916.* New York: Lippincott, 1972.

Emeny, Brooks. *Theodate Pope Riddle and the Founding of Avon Old Farms.* Avon, CT: Privately printed, 1973 and 1977.

Flandrau, Grace. *Being Respectable.* New York: Harcourt, Brace and Co., 1923.

_____. *Cousin Julia.* New York: D. Appleton and Co.,1917.

_____. *Entranced.* New York: Harcourt, Brace and Co., 1924.

_____. *Indeed This Flesh.* New York: H. Smith and R. Haas, 1934.

_____. *Then I Saw the Congo.* New York: Harcourt, Brace and Co., 1929.

George M. Trautman of Avon Old Farms School: Commemorating Three Decades of Service. Privately printed: 1998.

Gill, Brendan. "What Climbs the Stairs?" *Sarah Lawrence Alumnae Magazine.* Summer 1975.

_____. "Philip the Bold," *The New Yorker,* Nov. 14, 1994, pp. 132-40.

Gleichen, Helena. *Contacts and Contrasts.* London: John Murray, 1940.

Goldsmith, Barbara. *Other Powers: The Age of Suffrage, Spiritualism, and the Scandalous Victoria Woodhull.* New York: Alfred A. Knopf, 1998.

Hall, Helen. *Hill-Stead Museum.* Windsor, CT: The Fox Press, 1988.

Hartman, Mary and Lois Banner, eds. *Clio's Consciousness Raised: New Perspectives on the History of Women.* New York: Harper Colophon Books, 1974.

Hedrick, Joan D., *Harriet Beecher Stowe: A Life.* New York: Oxford University Press, 1994.

Heilbrun, Carolyn G. *Writing a Woman's Life.* New York: W.W. Norton, 1988.

Hewitt, Mark, and Richard Cheek. *The Architect and the American Country House: 1890—1940.* New Haven: Yale University Press, 1990.

"Hill-Stead Museum," *Colonial Homes,* April 1992, 77 ff.

Howe, Helen. *The Gentle Americans, 1864-1960; Biography of a Breed.* New York: Harper & Row, 1965.

James, Henry. "The American Scene," *North American Review,* 1907.

_____. *The Bostonians.* 1886. Reprint, New York: Dial, 1945.

James, Henry, Leon Edel, and Lyall H. Powers. *The Complete Notebooks of Henry James.* New York: Oxford University Press, 1987.

James, William. *Science,* Vol. VII, No. 172, April 15, 1898.

_____. *The Varieties of Religious Experience: A Study in Human Nature.* 1902. Reprint, Cambridge: Harvard University Press, 1985.

Kahn, David M. "The Theodore Roosevelt Birthplace in New York City," *Antiques,* July 1979, 173 ff.

Kerber, Linda and Jane De Hart, eds. *Women's America: Refocusing the Past.* 3rd ed. New York: Oxford University Press, 1990.

Lett, James W. "The Persistent Popularity of the Paranormal," *Skeptical Inquirer,* Summer 1992.

Lewis, R.W.B. *The Jameses: A Family Narrative.* New York: Farrar, Straus and Giroux, 1991.

Lewis, Wilmarth Sheldon. *One Man's Education.* New York: Alfred A. Knopf, 1967.

McCormick, Kathleen. "Hidden Jewel," *Historic Preservations.* Nov./Dec. 1995, p. 22 ff.

McCullough, David. *Mornings on Horseback.* New York: Simon & Schuster, 1981.

Moore, R.L. *In Search of White Crows: Spiritualism, Parapsychology and American Culture.* New York: Oxford University Press, 1977.

Osborn, Norris G. *Men of Mark in Connecticut; Ideals of American Life Told in Biographies and Autobiographies of Eminent Living Americans.* 5 vols. Hartford, CT: William R. Goodspeed, 1906-1910.

Owen, Alex. *The Darkened Room: Women, Power and Spiritualism in Late Victorian England.* Philadephia: University of Pennsylvania Press, 1990.

Paine, Judith. *Theodate Pope Riddle: Her Life and Work.* New York: The National Park Service, [1979].

Preston, Diana. *Lusitania: An Epic Tragedy.* New York: Walker and Co., 2002.

Proceedings of the Society for Psychical Research, Vol. III, Part IX, 1885.

Ramsey, Gordon. *Aspiration and Perseverance: The History of Avon Old Farms School.* Avon, CT: Privately printed, 1984.

Ray, Georgia, "In Search of the Real Grace Flandrau," *Minnesota History,* Vol. 56, No. 6. Summer 1999, 306 ff.

Rixey, Lilian. *Bamie: Theodore Roosevelt's Remarkable Sister.* New York: David McKay Co., Inc., 1963.

Salter, William H. *The Society for Psychical Research: An Outline of its History.* 1948. Reprint, London: [Society for Psychical Research], 1970.

Schlesinger, Arthur M., Jr. ed. *The Almanac of American History.* New York: Barnes & Noble, 1993.

Schulze, Franz. *Philip Johnson: Life and Work.* New York: Alfred A. Knopf, 1994.

Secrest, Meryle. *Frank Lloyd Wright: A Biography.* Chicago: The University of Chicago Press, 1992.

Sheron, Georgia. "Theo Pope's House," *Yankee Magazine.* Spring 1979. Also in *Westover Alumnae Magazine,* Spring 1979.

Sicherman, Barbara. *Alice Hamilton, A Life in Letters.* Cambridge: Harvard University Press, 1980.

_____. and Carol H. Green. *Notable American Women: The Modern Period: A Biographical Dictionary.* Cambridge: Harvard University Press, 1980.

Simpson, Colin. *The Lusitania.* Boston: Little, Brown and Co., 1973.

Skrief, D. P. "Viva Flandrau!" *Twin Cities,* Feb. 1986, 31 ff.

Sommer, Mimi, "Renaissance Woman," *Colonial Homes,* April 1992, 22 ff.

Spykman, Elizabeth Choate. *Westover: 1909-1959.* New Haven: Yale University Press, 1959.

Talcott, Mary Dudley Vaill, and Alice Dudley Talcott Enders. *The Hartford Diaries of Mary Dudley Vaill Talcott (Mrs. Charles Hooker Talcott), from 1896-1919* [4 vols.] Privately published, 1990.

Terry, Mrs. Alfred H. "Hill Stead: A Museum in Farmington," *CT Antiquarian,* Vol. VI, No. 1. June 1954.

Torre, Susana, *Women in American Architecture: A Historic and Contemporary Perspective.* New York: Whitney Library of Design, 1977.

Upton, Dell. *Architecture in the United States.* New York: Oxford University Press, 1998.

Webb, James. *The Occult Underground.* LaSalle, Illinois: Open Court Publishing Co., 1974.

Wolff, Cynthia Griffin. *A Feast of Words: The Triumph of Edith Wharton.* New York: Oxford University Press, 1977.

Yates, Richard. *A Good School: A Novel.* New York: Delacorte Press, 1978.

Zinn, Howard. *A People's History of the United States: 1492 – Present.* Rev. and updated. New York: HarperPerennial, 1995.

Unpublished Manuscripts:

Callahan, Tara K. *"To Help the Cause of Good Architecture": Theodate Pope Riddle and the Colonial Revival.* Dartmouth College Senior Fellowship Project, June 1996. Hill-Stead Museum.

Connor, Elizabeth Faling. *Diary,* n.d. Miss Porter's School

Cook, Frederick B. "The Finding of the Farmington," Westover School, 1978.

Davis, Daniel. "The Architecture of Theodate Pope Riddle." Abstract, n.d.

DeCoster, Georgia R. "Chronology of the Relationship between John and Theodate Riddle and Grace H. Flandrau." n.d. Hill-Stead Museum.

_____. Grant proposal. Oct. 1, 1991-1992. Minnesota Historical Society.

Flanagan, Henry E. *Aspirando et Perseverando: The Evolution of the Avon Old Farms School as Influenced by its Founder.* Ph.D. diss., University of Michigan, 1978.

Flandrau, Grace. "The Most Unforgettable Character: Theodate Pope Riddle," in a letter to Carl. n.d. Arizona Historical Society, Tucson, Ariz.

_____. "The Most Unforgettable Character: Anna Roosevelt Cowles," in a letter to Carl. n.d. Arizona Historical Society, Tucson, Ariz.

Goodrich, Betty Price. "Theodate: Gift of God." Privately owned. 1968.

Johnson, Louise Pope. "The Passing of an Elderly Quaker." 1949. Hill-Stead Museum.

Kaplan, Rosalind. "Lillian D. Wald, A Woman of Valor," November 1990. Privately owned.

Mooney, Barbara. Author to Architect: Letters from Henry James to Theodate Pope." Westover School, 1981.

Niggli, Nadia M. *Theodate Pope Riddle and Avon Old Farms School for Boys: The "Gendering" of Architecture.* Thesis. Yale University, May 1995.

Pope, Frances E. "Notes of a Quiet Life: [1840 – 1937]," 1917. Hill-Stead Museum.

Powers, Barbara. Master's thesis in Architectural History, Westover School, 1980.

Smith, Sharon Dunlap. *Theodate Pope Riddle: Her Life and Architecture,* 2002. <http://www.valinet.com/~smithash/>

Wheeler, Sandra. "Spiritualism in Nineteenth Century America: A Case Study in the Emergence of a Democratic Epistemology." December 1989. Privately owned.

Whittemore, Robert. "J.H. Whittemore and Tranquility Farm." Mattatuck Historical Society, Waterbury, Conn., n.d.

ACKNOWLEDGMENTS

FIRST, I want to thank my daughter Melissa. On a summer day several years ago, we visited Hill-Stead Museum, and after taking a tour, we looked for a biography of Theodate in the museum's bookstore. Upon discovering that one had never been written, Melissa said, "Why don't you write it?" I took her suggestion and from that time until now, I have depended upon Melissa's and her sister Stacey's encouragement and willingness to read and edit multiple drafts. I also wish to thank my husband Bill and my son Jim for their insights and support.

The project has been enjoyable from the start, in large part because I have had the good fortune of working with Hill-Stead Museum's archivists, Polly Pasternak Huntington and Sandra Wheeler. My research was greatly facilitated because the archives are so well organized. Polly and Sandy were generous with their time and knowledge: they read and commented on much of the manuscript, offered insights about Theo and her world, and searched the archives for answers to my questions. Without their help and friendship, I could not have written this biography. I also wish to thank the entire Hill-Stead staff for making me feel welcome, especially Denise Bowen, Cindy Cormier, Sarah Lytle, Alison Meyers, and Linda Steigleder. The people and archives of Avon Old Farms School were another major resource. I have been most fortunate to have the support and friendship of Peter Aron, the dynamic chairman of the school's Board of Directors, and one of its most dedicated alumni. I greatly appreciate his kind words, encouragement, and advice. I also wish to thank Margaret DeGraaf, Carol Ketcham, Kenneth H. LaRocque, F. Reed Estabrook, Jr., and Frank G. Leavitt for their interest and assistance. I particularly enjoyed hearing about the school's past from Mr. Estabrook and touring the campus with Mr. Leavitt.

At Westover School, Maria Allen was very helpful. I also appreciate the enthusiastic comments of Ann Pollina, Head of School, after she read the manuscript. In addition, I am indebted to Shirley Langhauser and Susan Tracy of Miss Porter's School for their willingness to help me find material in the school's archives. Other archivists who provided information include Jean N. Berry, Archives, Wellesley College; Bernard R. Crystal, Columbia University Rare Book and Manuscript Library; Adelaide B. Elm, formerly of the Arizona Historical Society in Tucson; Joseph T. Gregory, formerly of Yale University's Peabody Museum; and James McCarthy, Harvard University Archives.

I appreciate having had the opportunity to interview Theodate's ward, Donald Carson, and the architectural critic, Brendan Gill. Ms. Katharine

Hepburn was kind enough to respond to my questions about an incident that took place at Hill-Stead when she was a girl.

I wish to thank the University of Hartford for awarding me a Coffin Grant and a sabbatical leave so that I might pursue this project. I appreciate the help of my colleagues at the university, in particular Professor Daniel Davis, who shared with me his architectural expertise and his own work on Theodate's buildings. Thanks also to Professor Marilyn Smith, an alumna of Westover School, who took me on a tour of the school. Gordon Clark Ramsay, a colleague and the author of the history of Avon Old Farms School, helped me in countless ways. Members of the university's Hillyer College English department, Professors Mary Fister, Jill Ghnassia, Howard Mayer, the late Edward McKenney, John Roderick, and Marcia Seabury, always expressed interest and encouragement.

Without the support and inspiration of my friends and fellow biographers, Stephen B. Oates, Linda H. Davis, Elizabeth Lloyd-Kimbrel, William Kimbrel, Ann Meeropol, Helen Sheehy, Harriet Sigerman, and Leslie Stainton, I would not have attempted to write this book. Stephen B. Oates, Paul Murray Kendall Professor of Biography at the University of Massachusetts, introduced me to the art of biography and welcomed me into the Amherst Biography Group, which, through the years, has listened to and commented on my manuscript. Even though Linda Davis and Helen Sheehy were immersed in their own research and writing, they always found time to read and discuss my work. I am especially grateful to Helen for her help in getting the biography published.

I also appreciate the interest and support I have received from family and friends: Ginnie and Bill Crabtree, Roxie Davis, Liz and Dave DiLalla, Leila and David Fisher, Ron and Joey Fisher, Andrew Hoffer, Julie Hoffer, Sally and Stu Hoffer, Andy Hudson, Charlotte Kassab, Marcia Kaufman, Judy Maddox, Mileta Roe, Esther Rosenbaum, Phyllis and Sheldon Rosenbaum, Temma Schaller, Gigi and Michael Stein, and Robin Swett. I want especially to thank Marshall Fisher for his excellent suggestions.

I am indebted to my agent, Philip Spitzer, for his continued efforts and encouragement. I also appreciate my publisher Scott Kaeser's commitment to the book. I have great admiration for Carolyn Wilcox not only because of her meticulous editing of the manuscript but also because of her good-natured patience with me.

For permission to quote from archival material and reproduce images, I wish to thank the Arizona Historical Society, Tucson; Avon Old Farms School; Archives, Hill-Stead Museum, Farmington, Connecticut; the Minnesota Historical Society; Miss Porter's School; Westover School; and Mr. Robert N. Whittemore.

INDEX

Cassatt, Mary, 27, 47, 54, 60-61, 66, 69, 78, 81, 86, 95, 126, 200
  paintings, 225
Cedar Hill Cemetery, 249
Central Hanover Bank and Trust, 220
Centurion (ship), 111
Chamberlain House, *83*, 92
Chamberlain, Joseph, 83
Chamberlain, Neville, 233
channeling, *see* writing, automatic
Charpentier, Mme., 35
Charpentier, Pauline, 35
Chase, Jean, 270n
Chase National Bank, 220
Chenoweth, Mrs., 124
Cherry, George, 202, 205, 210
  appointment as acting provost, 208
chicken war, 41
China, *see* Riddle, John Wallace: trip to Orient; Riddle, Theodate Pope: trip to Orient
Choate, Elizabeth, 206, 211-12
Churchill, Winston, 112
City of New York (ship), 33
Clark University, 69, 146
Clark, William Dundee, 142, 160, 217, 232
Cleaveland, Rev., 110
Cleveland (Ohio), *see* residences (Pope family)
Cleveland Malleable Iron Company, *see* National Malleable & Steel Castings Company
Coke, Henry, Sir, 115
Cole, Francis, Atty., 216
Colonial Dames Society, 55
Columbia Law School, 133
Columbia University, 250
Comstock, Professor, 169
Connecticut, governor of, *see* Cross, Wilbur, Gov.; *see* Holcomb, Marcus, Gov.; *see* McLean, George, Gov.
Connecticut Pomological Society, 73, 84
cooking school (Farmington, Conn.), 55
Coolidge, Vice President, 192
Cornell University, architectural program, 44
Corot, Jean-Baptiste-Camille, 28
Cotswolds (England), construction methods, 82-83, 172, 183, 189
Cousin Julia (Flandrau), 149
Couture, Thomas, portrait by, 9

Cowl, Jane, 200
Cowles, Anna Roosevelt, 56, *72*, 76, 78, 81-82, 86, 88-89, 93-94, 99, 123, 134, 138, 140, 145, 161, 168-69, 173, 180-81, 185-86, 190, 193, 199, 218
Cowles, Sheffield, 56, *72*, 94, 149, 196, 199
Cowles, William, Admiral, 56, 82, 88, 94, 140, 151, 173
Craig, William, Jr., 127
Cranbrook School, 246
Cromwell Hall, 157
Cross, Wilbur, Gov., 218, 241
Crown Princess of Sweden, 82
Cunard Steamship Company, 109, 111, 118, 120
Cunningham, Harry, 189
Curran, John, 150
Curran, Mrs. John, *see* Worth, Patience
Curtis, Dr., 89
Cutcheon, Frank, 149
Cutcheon, Sally, 139

Dairymen's Association, 73, *84*
Daladier, Edouard, 233
Dana, Charles Loomis, Dr., 50-52, 55-59, 66-67, 69, 88, 103, 127, 258n, 270n
Daubigny, Charles-François, landscape by, 9
de Castex, Madame, 177
Degas, Edgar, 47, 54, 99
Deming, Verna, 184
Desperts, Louise, Dr., 224, 228
Dewey, John, 199, 225
Doll's House, A (Ibsen), 33
Dormer House, 92-93, *96*, 105
Dorr, George B., 68-69
Dow, Mary, 14, 22, 58
Dow Row, 59-60
Doyle, Arthur Conan, 43
Dr. Pagensteacher's Eye Hospital (Germany), 136
Draper, George, Dr., 206-8, 210, 212
Duckworth, Mrs., 117
Duel, Arthur B., Dr., 204-5, 207
Duel, Mrs. Arthur, 204-05
Duke of Sutherland, 82
Dunning, Miss (housemother), 15, 19-20
Dunning's, Miss (boarding house), 15-16, 18-19, 21, 74
DuPont family, 239

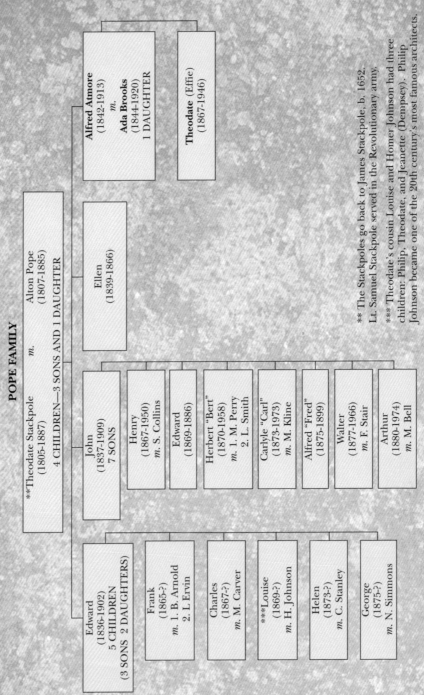

POPE FAMILY

Theodate Stackpole (1805-1887) **m.** **Alton Pope** (1807-1885)

4 CHILDREN—3 SONS AND 1 DAUGHTER

Alfred Atmore (1842-1913)
m.
Ada Brooks (1844-1920)
1 DAUGHTER

Theodate (Effie) (1867-1946)

Ellen (1839-1866)

John (1837-1909)
7 SONS

Henry (1867-1950)
m. S. Collins

Edward (1869-1886)

Herbert "Bert" (1870-1958)
m. 1. M. Perry
2. L. Smith

Carlyle "Carl" (1873-1973)
m. M. Kline

Alfred "Fred" (1875-1899)

Walter (1877-1966)
m. F. Stair

Arthur (1880-1974)
m. M. Bell

Edward (1836-1902)
5 CHILDREN
(3 SONS 2 DAUGHTERS)

Frank (1865-?)
m. 1. B. Arnold
2. L Ervin

Charles (1867-?)
m. M. Carver

***Louise** (1869-?)
m. H. Johnson

Helen (1873-?)
m. C. Stanley

George (1875-?)
m. N. Simmons

** The Stackpoles go back to James Stackpole, b. 1652. Lt. Samuel Stackpole served in the Revolutionary army.

*** Theodate's cousin Louise and Homer Johnson had three children: Philip, Theodate, and Jeanette (Dempsey). Philip Johnson became one of the 20th century's most famous architects.